The Definitive Guide to Firebase

Build Android Apps on Google's Mobile Platform

Laurence Moroney

Apress®

The Definitive Guide to Firebase: Build Android Apps on Google's Mobile Platform

Laurence Moroney
Seattle, Washington, USA

ISBN-13 (pbk): 978-1-4842-2942-2   ISBN-13 (electronic): 978-1-4842-2943-9
https://doi.org/10.1007/978-1-4842-2943-9

Library of Congress Control Number: 2017959876

Cover image by Freepik (`www.freepik.com`)

Managing Director: Welmoed Spahr
Editorial Director: Todd Green
Acquisitions Editor: Steve Anglin
Development Editor: Matthew Moodie
Technical Reviewer: Val Okafor
Coordinating Editor: Mark Powers
Copy Editor: Karen Jameson

Distributed to the book trade worldwide by Springer Science+Business Media New York, 233 Spring Street, 6th Floor, New York, NY 10013. Phone 1-800-SPRINGER, fax (201) 348-4505, e-mail `orders-ny@springer-sbm.com`, or visit `www.springeronline.com`. Apress Media, LLC is a California LLC and the sole member (owner) is Springer Science + Business Media Finance Inc (SSBM Finance Inc). SSBM Finance Inc is a **Delaware** corporation.

For information on translations, please e-mail `rights@apress.com`, or visit `http://www.apress.com/rights-permissions`.

Apress titles may be purchased in bulk for academic, corporate, or promotional use. eBook versions and licenses are also available for most titles. For more information, reference our Print and eBook Bulk Sales web page at `http://www.apress.com/bulk-sales`.

Any source code or other supplementary material referenced by the author in this book is available to readers on GitHub via the book's product page, located at `www.apress.com/9781484229422`. For more detailed information, please visit `http://www.apress.com/source-code`.

Printed on acid-free paper

Contents at a Glance

Contents

About the Author

Laurence Moroney is Firebase Developer Advocate at Google. He is also a top-selling author. He is host of "Coffee with a Googler" on YouTube! He has over 10 years in software development and architecture, specializing in interoperability, security, and performance in such diverse industries as casinos, jails, the U.S. Border Patrol, airports, professional soccer teams, and financial services. He has written several books on computing, including some on Web Services Security, ASP.NET, and Java/.NET interoperability, as well as dozens of articles on various technology issues. He lives in Sammamish, Washington, with his wife, Rebecca; and children, Claudia and Christopher.

About the Technical Reviewer

Val Okafor is a software architect with expertise in Android development and resides in sunny San Diego of California, USA. He has over 12 years of industry experience and has worked for corporations such as Sony Electronics, The Home Depot, San Diego County, and American Council on Exercise. Val earned his BSc in IT from National University, San Diego; and Masters in Software Engineering from Regis University, Colorado. He is the creator and principal engineer of Pronto line of mobile apps including Pronto Diary, Pronto Invoice, and Pronto Quotes.

His passion for software development goes beyond his skill and training; he also enjoys sharing his knowledge with other developers. He has taught Android development to over 5,000 students through Udemy, and his blog valokafor.com is considered an essential reading for Android developers. Val was also recently named among the first cohort of Realm MVP program because of his active participation in the Realm database community.

Chapter 1

An Introduction to Firebase

In a survey conducted in 2016,[1] it was found that 52% of developers fall below what is called the *poverty* line, $500 or less per month, in mobile revenue. Only 18% of developers were in the high earning category – $25k or more per month. Of those in the high earners bracket, 88% targeted three platforms: Android, iOS, and the Web. Thus, it would be logical that in order to emulate the most successful developers, you would want to target these platforms. However, doing so can be difficult when it comes to skillsets – managing separate code bases for complex tasks such as database management, identity, messaging, and other common attributes of apps will greatly increase the time and effort you need to invest to build and launch your app.

Additionally, marketing and growing an app can be an onerous task. One cannot simply put an app into the Play Store or App Store and expect the downloads to keep coming. In an increasingly crowded marketplace, continued investment and continued effort to grow the app are necessary to prevent your app from being lost in the crowd.

Finally, earning from your hard work is also important. Otherwise you wouldn't be spending the time and effort in creating the app to begin with! There are a number of ways that you can earn from an app – first, of course, is to charge for it. But increasingly, developers are going with a no-cost option, where users can get your app without paying for it, and are then monetized by in-app content, advertising, or both.

With these three needs in mind, Google released Firebase in the summer of 2016. Its goal is to provide the tools and infrastructure that you need to build great apps, grow a successful business, and earn from your hard work.

It's not a *replacement* for your existing APIs for building Android, iOS, or Web apps. It's an *enhancement*, giving you common services that you might need – such as a database back end, secure authentication, messaging, and more. This saves you the need to build them yourself, allowing you to focus on what makes your app distinct. Additionally, it has technologies that you can put into your app and site that will help you grow your business through referrals, linking, and more. It has an easy-to-use Advertising API that you can drop into your app to start earning, and importantly, the whole platform is tied together by analytics.

© Laurence Moroney 2017
L. Moroney, *The Definitive Guide to Firebase*, https://doi.org/10.1007/978-1-4842-2943-9_1

Let's take a look at the full Firebase stack. In this chapter we'll take a brief look at each of the technologies, and later we'll do a deeper dive into each one. In this book you'll be learning how to use each of these in an Android app. The principles for iOS are very similar, but all the code here will be for Android.

Firebase: An Overview

Firebase is built on three pillars: Develop, Grow, and Earn, and represented in Figure 1-1:

Figure 1-1. The Firebase Pillars

Each of these technologies is tied together using Analytics. It's important to note that you can choose which of these technologies that you want to use in your app or site. You aren't required to use them all.

Many of the technologies are available at no cost. These include Analytics, App Indexing, Authentication (with the exception of Phone Auth), Cloud Messaging, Crash Reporting, Dynamic Links, Invites, Notifications, and Remote config.

For all the others, there is a free tier that will work for testing and with reasonable limits for smaller apps. For example, for the Realtime Database, the free tier will allow you to store 1Gb of Data and have 100 simultaneous connections. Similarly for Cloud Functions for Firebase, the free tier allows you 125,000 invocations per month. Full details on pricing are available at https://firebase.google.com/pricing/.

Let's look at the columns in turn.

The Develop Technologies

Firebase has eight technologies that are designed to enhance your app development experience. These are listed on the left of the diagram above.

Firebase Authentication

When your app needs to know the identity of the user in order to provide distinctive data to that user, a form of secure sign-in is necessary. Building and maintaining sign-in infrastructure is a difficult and expensive proposition. From a user perspective, giving credentials and personal data to an app can also be a user experience bump – potentially causing them to reject using it. Thus, apps that allow users to sign in with known credentials, such as those provided by Google, Facebook, and Twitter, are becoming more popular. With these issues and trends in mind, Firebase Authentication has been built to give you an easy API that will allow you to use sign-in from federated providers, a simple email/password scheme, or integrate with any existing authentication back ends you own. It integrates with Firebase services such as the Realtime database so you can control who accesses what data. You'll learn how to build for Firebase Authentication in Chapter 2.

The Realtime Database

This is a cloud-hosted NoSQL-based database. It provides syncing across connected devices and is available when there is no network connectivity through a local cache. It is an event-driven database that works very differently from traditional SQL databases. There's no server-side code and database access tiers; all coding is done in the client. Whenever data changes in the database, events are fired in the client code, and you can then handle and update the state of your user interface in response. It contains an expression-based rules language, called the Firebase Realtime Database Security Rules, which define how data is structured and which users have rights to that data. Its ultimate design is to be *responsive*, allowing you to build a realtime experience that can serve users at high scale. As such it is a little different to program against than a traditional database. It's also very simple – and we'll cover it in Chapter 3.

Cloud Storage for Firebase

In addition to storing data, it's a common requirement that apps store files such as photos or videos. Building and managing an infrastructure to handle this – particularly one that deals with large files such as videos – can be a difficult and expensive proposition. Cloud Storage for Firebase makes this easier by providing a simple API that is backed up by Google Cloud Storage. In Chapter 4, you'll look at this API, and see how you can easily handle uploading and downloading of files, including what to do to handle communications failures and resume where you left off.

Firebase Hosting

All apps need an associated web site for their Play Store or App Store listing. If you're using Firebase, you'll get hosting space that you can use to host static assets such as HTML, CSS, JavaScript, or images. Using JavaScript frameworks you can build some pretty sophisticated sites. In Chapter 5 you'll learn about Firebase Hosting, and you'll step through building a site with it.

Firebase Test Lab

A common complaint for App Developers, particularly those that use Android, is that it is very difficult to get access to all types of devices that your end users might need. In many cases, the device isn't even available in your country. With Firebase Test Lab, you can take advantage of devices that are hosted by Google in a Test Center for you! In Chapter 6 you'll learn about tests that have already been written for you by Google (aka Robo Tests) as well as how to build your own tests. You'll see the results in the form of screenshots and crash reports.

Firebase Crash Reporting

The number 1 reason for bad reviews in the App Store and Play Store is unexpected crashes. Figuring out why an app crashed, and fixing it quickly is paramount, but a very difficult process if the app is run on a device that you don't know, in a country or city that's far away! Crash Reporting helps with this by providing a Stack Trace of all crashes in the Firebase Console. You can use these to figure out the cause of the crash, and roll out a fix quickly. You might even be able to use Firebase Cloud Messaging to let your users know of the update, so they can avoid the crash in the Future! You'll take a look at this technology in Chapter 7.

Cloud Functions for Firebase

While the Firebase architecture is primarily geared toward code running in your mobile app or web site front end, there are often circumstances where you need logic to execute on the back end. Cloud Functions for Firebase gives you the facility to write code that responds to events on Firebase elements. For example, changes in the Realtime Database, Authentication, or other elements can be used to trigger a function. You'll see more about Cloud Functions and learn how to use them in Chapter 8.

The Grow Technologies

In addition to providing services that help you build apps, Firebase has a number of technologies that can be used to help you systematically grow your app.

Firebase Cloud Messaging

In Chapter 9 you'll learn about Firebase Cloud Messaging and Firebase Notifications. These allow you to reliably deliver messages at no cost. Over 98% of connected devices receive these messages in less than 500ms. Messages can be delivered in a variety of ways – driven by analytics to pick audiences, or using topics or other methods.

Firebase Remote Config

Remote Config is a cloud service that provides server-side variables that can be driven by analytics, allowing you to change the behavior and/or appearance of your app without requiring an app update. For example, if you are building an e-commerce app, and you want to periodically provide discounts to your users, you could have a remote config variable that contains the value of the discount. Traditionally it could be 0%, but at certain times of the year you could set it to 10%. But then you could go further – what if you want to give a bigger discount to people in a country that you want to grow in – you can set the value based on analytics to give them, say 20%. In Chapter 10, you'll learn how to do this.

App Indexing

A common scenario is that a user installs your app, but then it gets lost in their universe of applications. But an everyday scenario is that they search on their phone. Logically, if they are searching for content that's already in your app, and they previously made the decision to install that app, then the app should be surfaced, and the content should be opened in that app directly from search. App Indexing allows you to do this, and in Chapter 11, you'll see how to link your site and app so that Google Search knows to make the connection!

App Invites and Dynamic Links

Friends help friends discover great apps. App Invites is a technology that, should you implement it in your app, will make the process a lot simpler. It allows your user to choose who to send the invite to from an intelligently sorted list. You'll learn how to do this in Chapter 12, including how to use Dynamic Links technology that underpins it.

Earning with AdMob

Chapter 13 will introduce you to how you can use AdMob in your app. You'll learn about how to use banner ads, interstitial ads, video, or native ads within your app. This will require an AdMob account, and you'll be stepped through this.

Google Analytics for Firebase

At the heart of Firebase is analytics, a solution that's free to use and very comprehensive. It has a number of common analytics that it will gather for you without writing any code, as well as the ability to define custom analytics that will be gathered for you. It helps you understand your audience well, which can be used to continually grow your app, as well as driving technologies such as Firebase Remote Config, and Cloud Messaging!

Getting Started with Firebase on Android

For this book, the main development tool you will use is Android Studio. This is available at developer.android.com/studio. For the purposes of writing this book, I used version 2.3.1 for Mac, so if you're using a later version, some of the screenshots may differ, but the principles should be the same.

Install Android Studio

You can download Android Studio from https://developer.android.com/studio. When you visit the page, you'll see something like Figure 1-2:

Figure 1-2. Android Studio Download Site

Click the button to download and install Android Studio. Depending on your platform, the experience may differ.

Once you've gone through the install process, launch Android Studio for the first time. You'll likely see a welcome screen like that in Figure 1-3.

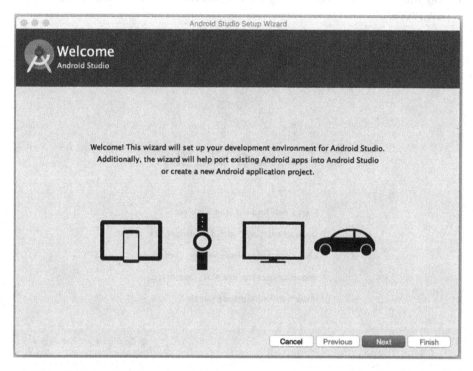

Figure 1-3. Welcome to Android Studio

Press 'Next' and you'll be asked for the Install Type. You can choose 'Standard' or 'Custom'. Choose 'Standard' and press 'Next'.

You'll then be given a number of settings that Android Studio needs to download and install. Click 'Finish' to let it do them. Once they're done, press 'Finish' and you'll be taken to the next step. Note that you may be asked for your password on some stages – such as installing HAXM (which speeds up the emulator). It's perfectly okay to do so.

Upon finishing you'll see the screen in Figure 1-4, letting you know that you're ready to go in building a new project.

Figure 1-4. Starting Android Studio

You'll still need to install the Firebase tools, and you'll see that in the next section.

Create Your First Firebase Application

From the screen in Figure 1-4, select 'Start a new Android Studio project'. You'll be asked to give the project a name and a domain. Give it the name FirebaseCh1, but choose a company domain name that's unique to yourself. In mine I called it laurencemoroney.com, but you should choose something else! This will determine the package name for your app. See Figure 1-5.

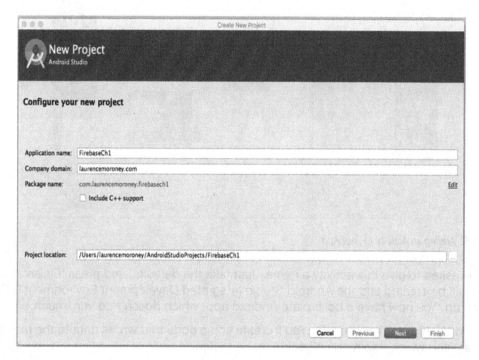

Figure 1-5. Creating a new Project

Click Next and you'll be asked about the form factors to run on. Just accept the defaults, and click Next. The app will be created, and once you see 'Done', click Next. You'll be asked to add an activity to your app. For simplicity, pick the 'Empty Activity'. See Figure 1-6.

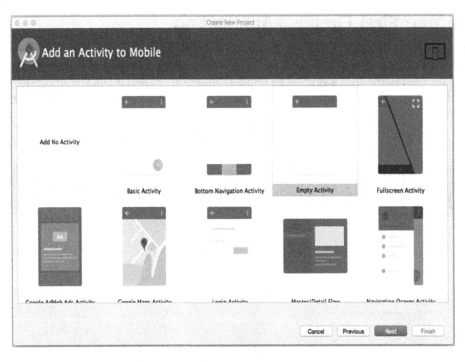

Figure 1-6. *Adding an Activity to your App*

You'll be asked to give this activity a name. Just take the defaults, and press 'Finish'. The project will be created and the Android Studio Integrated Development Environment (IDE) will start up. You now have a boilerplate Android app, which doesn't do very much.

Let's start by adding Firebase to it. You'll create some code that writes data to the realtime database, and which also reads it back!

In Android Studio's Tools menu, you should see a 'Firebase' option. See Figure 1-7.

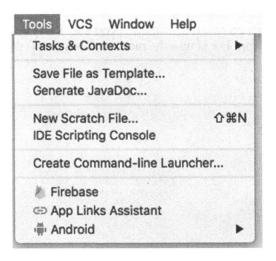

Figure 1-7. *Android Studio Tools Menu*

Select 'Firebase' and the Firebase Assistant will open on the right-hand side of Android Studio. See Figure 1-8. This gives you a number of handy shortcuts to creating Firebase projects, handling dependencies, and even some boilerplate code!

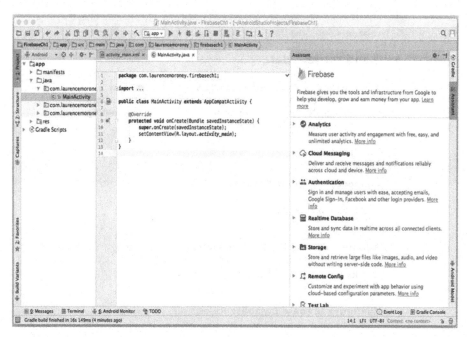

Figure 1-8. Android Studio with the Firebase Assistant

You'll be using this assistant extensively as you work through this book, so let's look at a simple example to get started. You aren't limited to using the assistant, of course, and can add a Firebase project manually to your Android application by downloading the Google-Services.json file from the Firebase Console, and setting up the required libraries in your build.gradle. For simplicity, I'll use the assistant throughout this book.

Find the section that says 'Realtime Database' and expand it. Your screen should look something like Figure 1-9.

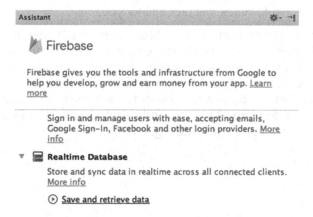

Figure 1-9. Using the Realtime Database in Firebase

Click the 'Save and Retrieve data' link. The assistant will change to give you a step-by-step process to follow to connect to the Realtime database. See Figure 1-10.

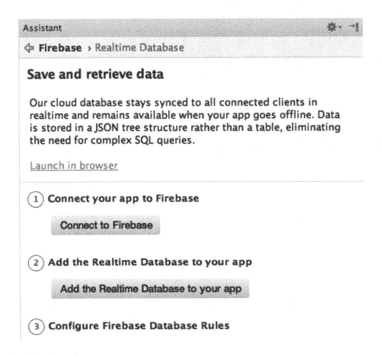

Figure 1-10. Realtime Database Steps

Let's go through these steps.

Step 1. Connect to Firebase

Step 1 connects your Android app to Firebase. As Firebase is a back end as a service, it needs to run in the cloud, and be administered through a cloud-based console. You create projects in this console and associate them with apps built in Android Studio, XCode, or elsewhere. The assistant automates this process for you.

Press the 'Connect to Firebase' button, and a browser page will open asking you to sign in. This will be your sign-in to the Firebase Console, so it asks for all the relevant permissions. When you're done, you'll see a success message in the browser. Close this, and Android Studio will give you the dialog in Figure 1-11 that you'll use to connect to Firebase. Here, you can create a new Firebase project to connect to, or if you have existing ones, you can connect this Android app to them. Go ahead and select 'Create New Firebase project', and you'll see it defaults to your app name. See Figure 1-11.

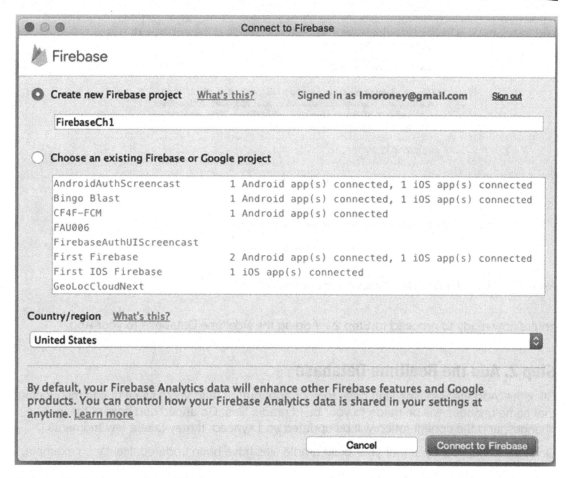

Figure 1-11. Connect your App to Firebase

When you click the 'Connect to Firebase' button, Android Studio will create the project on the Firebase Console, as well as add all the required dependencies to your Android app. This will take a few moments, but when you're done, you'll see that the status in the assistant has changed to 'Connected'. See Figure 1-12.

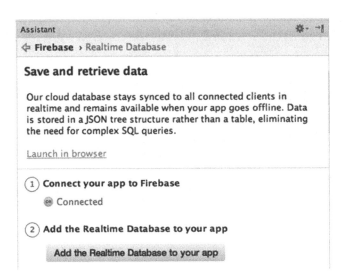

Figure 1-12. Updated assistant to show app is connected to Firebase

You're now ready to proceed to Step 2 – Adding the Realtime Database to your App.

Step 2. Add the Realtime Database

Click the 'Add the Realtime Database to your app' button, and you'll see a dialog mentioning that some changes will be made to your build.gradle files. Go ahead and accept these changes, and the configuration will be updated and synced. It may take a few moments.

Once it's done, you'll see that your build.gradle files have been updated. Here's an example:

```
apply plugin: 'com.android.application'

android {
    compileSdkVersion 25
    buildToolsVersion "25.0.3"
    defaultConfig {
        applicationId "com.laurencemoroney.firebasech1"
        minSdkVersion 15
        targetSdkVersion 25
        versionCode 1
        versionName "1.0"
        testInstrumentationRunner "android.support.test.runner.AndroidJUnitRunner"
    }
    buildTypes {
        release {
            minifyEnabled false
            proguardFiles getDefaultProguardFile('proguard-android.txt'), 'proguard-rules.pro'
        }
    }
}
```

```
dependencies {
    compile fileTree(dir: 'libs', include: ['*.jar'])
    androidTestCompile('com.android.support.test.espresso:espresso-core:2.2.2', {
        exclude group: 'com.android.support', module: 'support-annotations'
    })
    compile 'com.android.support:appcompat-v7:25.3.1'
    compile 'com.android.support.constraint:constraint-layout:1.0.2'
    compile 'com.google.firebase:firebase-database:10.0.1'
    testCompile 'junit:junit:4.12'
}

apply plugin: 'com.google.gms.google-services'
```

Note the dependency for 'com.google.firebase:firebase-database:10.0.1' that is the libraries for the Firebase database and the 'com.google.gms.google-services' plug-in also being applied.

You'll also see that the assistant has updated Step 2 to be complete. See Figure 1-13.

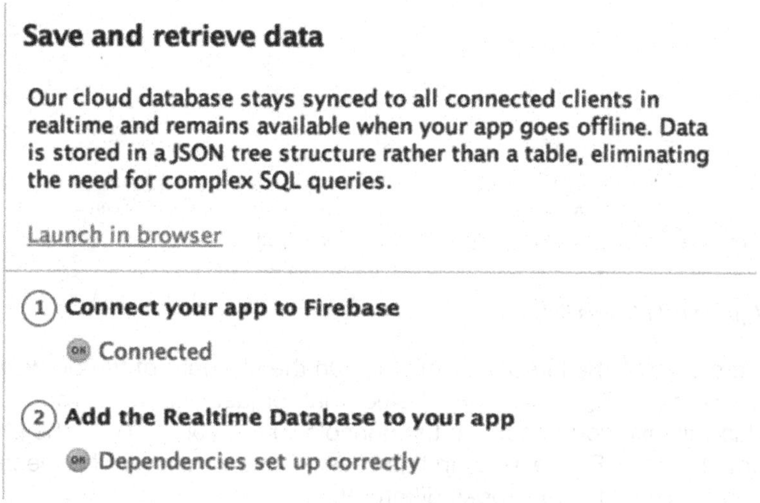

Save and retrieve data

Our cloud database stays synced to all connected clients in realtime and remains available when your app goes offline. Data is stored in a JSON tree structure rather than a table, eliminating the need for complex SQL queries.

Launch in browser

(1) **Connect your app to Firebase**

    (OK) Connected

(2) **Add the Realtime Database to your app**

    (OK) Dependencies set up correctly

Figure 1-13. Step 2 is complete

This also gives you the google-services.json file that is autogenerated by the Firebase Console. This file is used to define a number of parameters that Firebase and the underlying Google Services need to operate on Android. You can learn more about the file and its structure here: https://developers.google.com/android/guides/google-services-plugin.

Next up you'll configure the data access rules using the Firebase Console.

Step 3. Configure Data Access Rules

The next step in the assistant asks you to set up your data access rules. You'll go into these in more detail in Chapter 2, but for now you'll just set up your data for public access by following the link in the text. This will take you to the documentation web site showing you how to do this. Note that there are several tabs on the rules section. Be sure to pick the 'Public' tab so you can see what public rules look like. They simply allow anybody to read and write data on your app. See Figure 1-14.

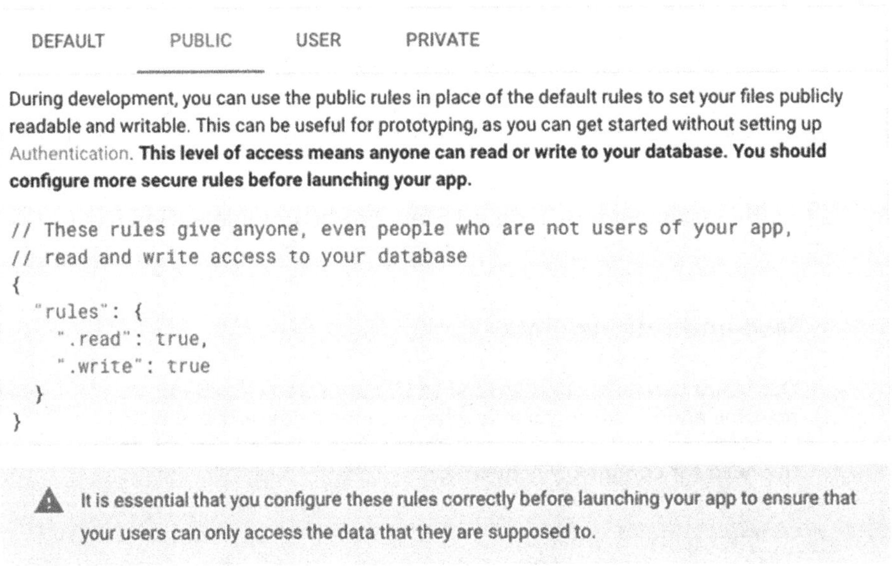

DEFAULT   PUBLIC   USER   PRIVATE

During development, you can use the public rules in place of the default rules to set your files publicly readable and writable. This can be useful for prototyping, as you can get started without setting up Authentication. **This level of access means anyone can read or write to your database. You should configure more secure rules before launching your app.**

```
// These rules give anyone, even people who are not users of your app,
// read and write access to your database
{
  "rules": {
    ".read": true,
    ".write": true
  }
}
```

⚠ It is essential that you configure these rules correctly before launching your app to ensure that your users can only access the data that they are supposed to.

Figure 1-14. Configuring Data Access Rules

These settings are used in the Firebase Console. On the top right of the browser window you'll see a link that says 'Go to Console'. Select that, or just visit https://console.firebase.google.com. This will take you directly to the console where you can edit the project. It should look something like Figure 1-15. In this case, I have a number of projects I've been working on, so don't worry if yours looks different!

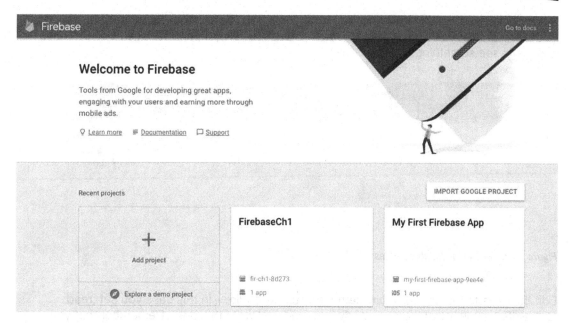

Figure 1-15. *The Firebase Console*

If you called your project FirebaseCh1, you'll see its tile here. Otherwise, choose the tile for whatever you called the app. Clicking on it will take you to the console for the app. You'll see tiles for the mobile apps in this project, as well as a list of links on the left-hand side for the elements of Firebase. See Figure 1-16.

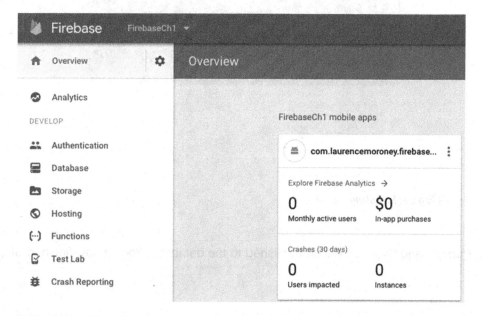

Figure 1-16. *The Firebase Console for this project*

Select 'Database' on the left-hand side, and you'll get taken to the Database settings page. At the top of this, you'll see tabs for 'Data', 'Rules', 'Backups', and 'Usage'. Select 'Rules' and you'll see something like Figure 1-17.

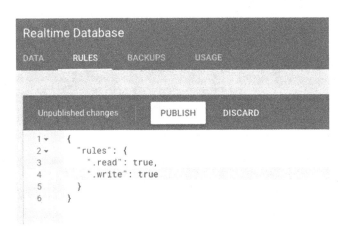

Figure 1-17. *Setting the Database Rules*

Edit the rules to match the public settings you saw earlier – in this case you set .read and .write to true, meaning everybody can read and write this data. Remember that you should never architect a public app in this way, or anybody will be able to do whatever they want to your data! But for learning and testing, it's okay for now.

Once you've done this, you'll see a 'Publish' button appears. See Figure 1-18.

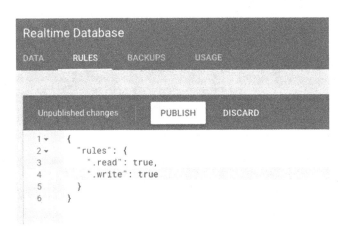

Figure 1-18. *Editing and Publishing the rules*

Press 'Publish' and the rules will be published to the database. You've now finished Step 3!

Step 4. Write to the Database

Back in the assistant you'll see that Step 4 shows you that you can write to your database along with a code snippet. Let's put this code snippet behind a button in your Android app. So, first off, in Android Studio, select the 'Project' view, and open app ➤ src ➤ main ➤ res ➤ layout. You'll see the activity_main.xml file there. This defines the user interface for your main activity. See Figure 1-19.

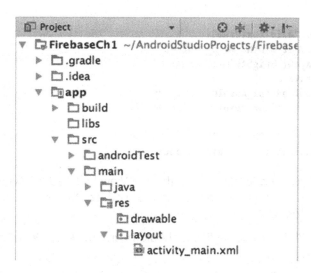

Figure 1-19. *Finding the layout file*

Open it, and the Android Studio activity editor will show. Drag and drop a button from the 'Widgets' area to your Activity. Double-click the button and change its text to 'Write Data'. Also drag and drop a TextView and set its text to 'Data'. Put these controls inside a LinearLayout that is oriented vertically, so you can be sure that they're visible at runtime.

If you click the 'Text' tab at the bottom of the window, you should see the source code for your layout. It should look something like this.

```
<?xml version="1.0" encoding="utf-8"?>
<android.support.constraint.ConstraintLayout xmlns:android="http://schemas.android.com/apk/
res/android"
    xmlns:app="http://schemas.android.com/apk/res-auto"
    xmlns:tools="http://schemas.android.com/tools"
    android:layout_width="match_parent"
    android:layout_height="match_parent"
    tools:context="com.laurencemoroney.firebasech1.MainActivity">

    <LinearLayout
        android:layout_width="134dp"
        android:layout_height="495dp"
        android:orientation="vertical"
        tools:layout_editor_absoluteX="8dp"
```

```
        tools:layout_editor_absoluteY="8dp">
        <Button
            android:id="@+id/button2"
            android:layout_width="wrap_content"
            android:layout_height="wrap_content"
            android:text="Write Data"
            tools:layout_editor_absoluteX="150dp"
            tools:layout_editor_absoluteY="42dp" />

        <TextView
            android:id="@+id/textView"
            android:layout_width="wrap_content"
            android:layout_height="wrap_content"
            android:text="Data"
            tools:layout_editor_absoluteX="162dp"
            tools:layout_editor_absoluteY="161dp" />
    </LinearLayout>

</android.support.constraint.ConstraintLayout>
```

Note that the button is called 'button2' and the TextView is called 'textView' in this layout. It's a good habit to change them to something more descriptive, but I'll keep them as they are for now for this tutorial.

Next, open your MainActivity source file. It should be in app ➤ src ➤ java ➤ [package name] ➤ MainActivity.java

You'll see that a simple boilerplate activity class has been created, and it has an onCreate method already implemented. Add a button click listener to this:

```
package com.laurencemoroney.firebasech1;

import android.support.v7.app.AppCompatActivity;
import android.os.Bundle;
import android.view.View;
import android.widget.Button;

public class MainActivity extends AppCompatActivity {
    Button dbButton;
    @Override
    protected void onCreate(Bundle savedInstanceState) {
        super.onCreate(savedInstanceState);
        setContentView(R.layout.activity_main);
        dbButton = (Button) findViewById(R.id.button2);
        dbButton.setOnClickListener(new View.OnClickListener() {
            @Override
            public void onClick(View v) {

            }
        });
    }
}
```

Now within the onClick, you can paste the code that was provided in the Firebase Assistant. Add the FirebaseDatabase and DatabaseReference code outside the onClick, and be sure to make them final, as they'll be accessed from an inner class. Then, within the onClick, set the value of the database reference to 'Hello, World!' Your code should look like this:

```
package com.laurencemoroney.firebasech1;

import android.support.v7.app.AppCompatActivity;
import android.os.Bundle;
import android.view.View;
import android.widget.Button;

import com.google.firebase.database.DatabaseReference;
import com.google.firebase.database.FirebaseDatabase;

public class MainActivity extends AppCompatActivity {
    Button dbButton;
    @Override
    protected void onCreate(Bundle savedInstanceState) {
        super.onCreate(savedInstanceState);
        setContentView(R.layout.activity_main);
        final FirebaseDatabase database = FirebaseDatabase.getInstance();
        final DatabaseReference myRef = database.getReference("message");
        dbButton = (Button) findViewById(R.id.button2);
        dbButton.setOnClickListener(new View.OnClickListener() {
            @Override
            public void onClick(View v) {
                // Write a message to the database
                myRef.setValue("Hello, World!");
            }
        });
    }
}
```

This code first creates a Firebase database object. Once this is instantiated, it then gets a DatabaseReference to a node on this database called 'message'. If this doesn't already exist, it will be created upon first write. Then, in the button's onClickListener, it will write the text 'Hello, World!' to that database reference.

You can now run the app on a device or emulator. If you don't have an emulator set up, follow the steps at https://developer.android.com/studio/run/emulator.html. Do note that when creating a virtual device, be sure to use one that has the Google APIs included.

Before pressing the button on the app though, be sure to have the Firebase Console open, with the 'Data' tab on the Realtime Database page selected. See Figure 1-20.

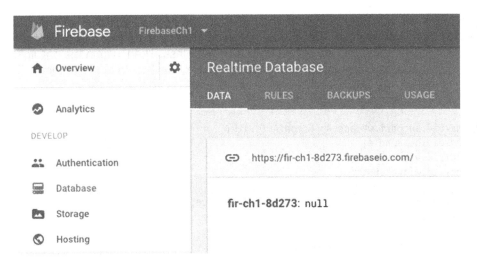

Figure 1-20. The Realtime Database Data view

You'll see that the database is empty. Now when you press the button on the app in your phone or emulator, you should see the 'Hello World' value get written! See Figure 1-21.

Figure 1-21. The Message is written to the database

This demonstrates how data is written to the Realtime Database. But because the Firebase Realtime Database is an event-driven database, you can also read data very easily by catching the event that is fired when the data changes, and reading it from there. You'll see that in the next step.

Step 5. Reading from the Database

In Step 4, when you wrote data to the database using a DatabaseReference class called 'myRef'. To read data from the database, you don't do it in the traditional way of using a query – but instead you listen for changes to this database reference, and when the change occurs, you handle it. Let's update this app by having an event listener listen for changes, and write them to the textView you created earlier.

In the assistant you'll see the code to handle this. Add this immediately below to the declaration of myRef you did earlier. You can remove the Log commands, and add the code required to use the TextView. When done your code should look like this:

```java
package com.laurencemoroney.firebasech1;

import android.support.v7.app.AppCompatActivity;
import android.os.Bundle;
import android.util.Log;
import android.view.View;
import android.widget.Button;
import android.widget.TextView;

import com.google.firebase.database.DataSnapshot;
import com.google.firebase.database.DatabaseError;
import com.google.firebase.database.DatabaseReference;
import com.google.firebase.database.FirebaseDatabase;
import com.google.firebase.database.ValueEventListener;

public class MainActivity extends AppCompatActivity {
    Button dbButton;
    TextView dataTextView;
    @Override
    protected void onCreate(Bundle savedInstanceState) {
        super.onCreate(savedInstanceState);
        setContentView(R.layout.activity_main);
        final FirebaseDatabase database = FirebaseDatabase.getInstance();
        final DatabaseReference myRef = database.getReference("message");
        // Read from the database
        myRef.addValueEventListener(new ValueEventListener() {
            @Override
            public void onDataChange(DataSnapshot dataSnapshot) {
                // This method is called once with the initial value and again
                // whenever data at this location is updated.
                String value = dataSnapshot.getValue(String.class);
                dataTextView.setText(value);
            }

            @Override
            public void onCancelled(DatabaseError error) {
                // Failed to read value
                dataTextView.setText("Error " + error.toString());
            }
        });
        dbButton = (Button) findViewById(R.id.button2);
        dbButton.setOnClickListener(new View.OnClickListener() {
            @Override
            public void onClick(View v) {
                // Write a message to the database
                myRef.setValue("Hello, World!");
            }
        });
        dataTextView = (TextView) findViewById(R.id.textView);
    }
}
```

Stop and re-run your application. You should now see that it has the words 'Hello World!' (from the previous write) in the center of the activity. To see the data read in action in realtime, go back to the console, and click on the text. Using the console, you can edit it to something else, like 'Hello, Readers!', and see what happens to the app! See Figure 1-22.

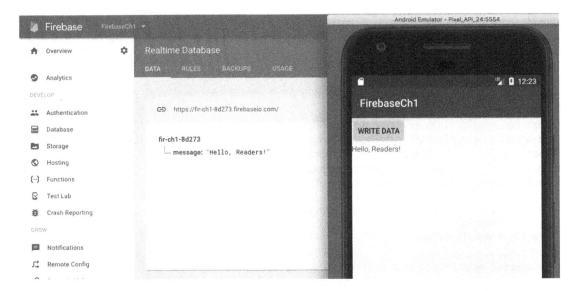

Figure 1-22. Reading from the Database

Other Steps

The rest of the steps in the assistant will help you for launching your app, or configuring ProGuard so that your database objects can be serialized on the device to prevent reverse engineering. They're worth investigating, but you don't need to go through them to learn Firebase.

Summary

In this chapter you were introduced to Firebase, including all of the tools that it gives you to build better apps, grow them, and earn from your hard work! You also saw how to get started using Android Studio and the Android Studio assistant, including how to build your first very basic database application. You saw that in order to access the data you had to open it up to the world, with everybody getting read and write access. Of course, that's not how you would want to do it in a real app, so in the next chapter we'll look at Firebase Authentication, so you can get users signed in and identified, and then give access to data to the right people at the right time!

Reference

1. Developer Economics – State of the Developer Nation report Q1, 2016 by Vision Mobile: http://vmob.me/DE1Q16.

Chapter 2

Using Authentication in Firebase

Most apps need to have some form of user identification. This allows them to set preferences, store data, and provide personalized experiences that are consistent across all of the user's devices. In order to provide this, they need to provide the facility to sign up new users, sign in existing users, manage account details, and keep all of this data secure. It's a very difficult and time-consuming process. From a user experience perspective, it's also very difficult to get right – users tend to hesitate to give out information that is personally identifiable, such as their user name, password, security questions, and anything else that, should it leak, be damaging to them. As a result, they often prefer using credentials that they have already provided to a third party, and having that third party manage the sign-in for them – so, for example, if they have a Facebook account, they would like to use Facebook to verify to your app that they are who they say they are, without needing to give you their information also.

With that in mind, Firebase Authentication has been designed to be a single SDK that allows you to grow your own authentication, use email/password authentication, or federate identity out to common providers: Google, Facebook, Twitter, and GitHub. It can also tie in with your own existing authentication system, so that users don't need to sign up all over again if you choose to use Firebase, as well as an anonymous authentication system that allows you to create temporary accounts so that users who haven't signed up with you yet can use it to work with data that's protected by security rules.

© Laurence Moroney 2017

L. Moroney, *The Definitive Guide to Firebase*, https://doi.org/10.1007/978-1-4842-2943-9_2

The Firebase Authentication APIs give you the raw code that you can use to have user sign-up and sign-in with all of the above. In addition to these libraries, Google released and open sourced a set of libraries called FirebaseUI where best practices for sign-in and sign-up, providing a consistent user experience, have been followed. You'll be using these in this chapter.

FirebaseUI

FirebaseUI is an open source library that allows you to quickly do common Firebase scenarios using best practices. One of these is Authentication, and I'd recommend using this if you've never done auth before. There are very many complex user flows when handling sign-up and sign-in, and these are handled for you in FirebaseUI.

The Android version of the open source libraries is available at https://github.com/firebase/FirebaseUI-Android.

When using Android, users may also be familiar with Smart Lock for Passwords, a technology that is used to store and retrieve credentials, enabling automatic or single tap sign-in when they return to your app. FirebaseUI handles this for you, as well as use cases such as recovering accounts, or linking different accounts.

To show how complicated the user flow process is, see Figure 2-1.

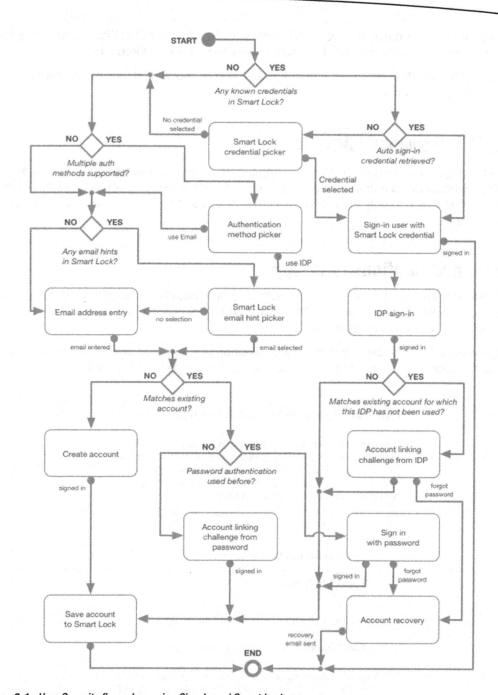

Figure 2-1. User Security flow when using Sign-In and Smart Lock

That's a lot of corner cases that you'd typically have to implement for. Thankfully you're not going to need to code all of that, because it is handled for you in FirebaseUI.

Let's get started with building our first auth app using it, and we'll do a simple Email/Password sign-up to begin.

Email/Password Sign-In

Users can sign up and sign in to Firebase apps, and get secured access to data with a simple email/password authentication scheme. You can choose to validate the email if you wish – so that they can only sign in with an email address they own, and we'll cover how to do that, too.

Create and Configure the App

To get started, create a new Android app with an empty activity in exactly the same way as you did in Chapter 1. Call it FirebaseCh2. **Note**: When doing this make sure that you use a minimum SDK version of at least 16.

Using the Firebase Assistant, find the 'Authentication' section, and open it. You'll see a number of steps. We're just going to follow the first two steps. See Figure 2-2.

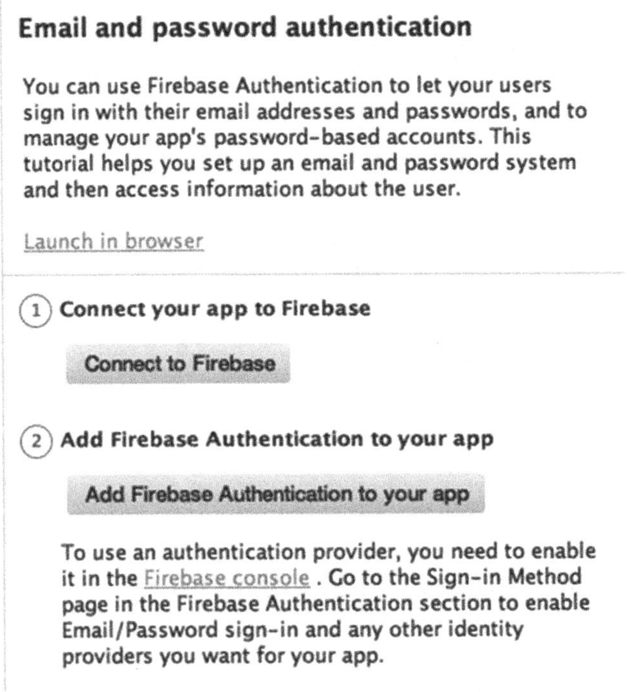

Email and password authentication

You can use Firebase Authentication to let your users sign in with their email addresses and passwords, and to manage your app's password-based accounts. This tutorial helps you set up an email and password system and then access information about the user.

Launch in browser

(1) **Connect your app to Firebase**

    Connect to Firebase

(2) **Add Firebase Authentication to your app**

    Add Firebase Authentication to your app

To use an authentication provider, you need to enable it in the Firebase console . Go to the Sign-in Method page in the Firebase Authentication section to enable Email/Password sign-in and any other identity providers you want for your app.

Figure 2-2. Getting Started with Authentication

Press the button in Step 1, and you'll be asked to Create a new Firebase project. I called mine FirebaseCh2 to match the app name. Click the 'Connect to Firebase', and a project will be created for you on the Firebase Console that your Android app will be associated with. Once this is completed, click the second button, to 'Add Firebase Authentication to your app'. This will update your build files with the Firebase Authentication dependencies.

In Step 2, you see there's a link to the Firebase Console, click on it. The console should open in your browser, and you'll see the new project that you just created. See Figure 2-3.

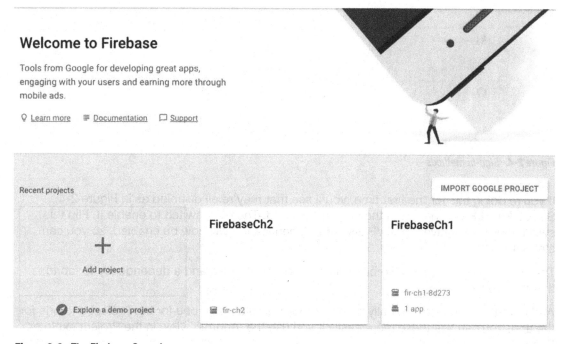

Figure 2-3. *The Firebase Console*

Open the new project (in this case FirebaseCh2) and click the 'Authentication' link on the left of the screen. At the top of the screen, you'll now see tabs for 'Users', 'Sign-In Method', and 'Email Templates'. Choose 'Sign-In Method', and you'll see the Sign-In providers that your project currently supports. See Figure 2-4.

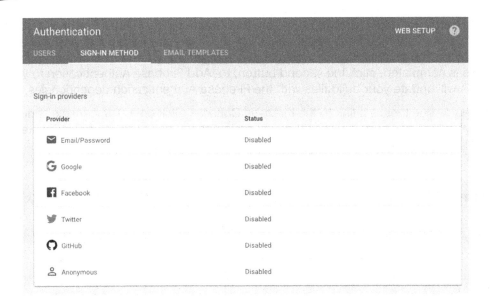

Figure 2-4. Sign-In methods

If you're doing this for the first time, you'll see that they're all disabled as in Figure 2-4. Select 'Email/Password', and the area will expand. There's a switch to enable it. Flip this switch, and click 'Save'. Email/Password authentication will now be enabled, so you can start using it!

The final step is to add the FirebaseUI open source libraries and a dependency to fabric.io that they need.

Android Studio projects typically have two build.gradle files – one for the Project and one for the app. You can see these more easily if you use the 'Android' view in the Project explorer. See Figure 2-5.

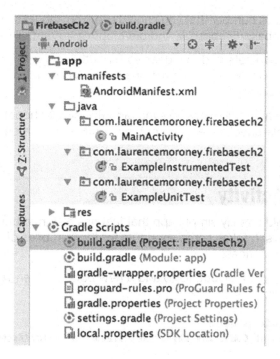

Figure 2-5. Using build.gradle

Select the *Project* one as shown in Figure 2-5. You'll find that there are several sections. Be sure to add a maven configuration for fabric.io to the **allprojects** section, like this:

```
allprojects {
    repositories {
        jcenter()
        maven { url 'https://maven.fabric.io/public' }
    }
}
```

It's a common mistake to add it to the buildscript section (because that has a jcenter() too), which will result in an error after you add the FirebaseUI libraries.

Then, in the app's build.gradle file, ass the FirebaseUI Auth libraries to the dependencies section:

```
dependencies {
    compile fileTree(dir: 'libs', include: ['*.jar'])
    androidTestCompile('com.android.support.test.espresso:espresso-core:2.2.2', {
        exclude group: 'com.android.support', module: 'support-annotations'
    })
    compile 'com.android.support:appcompat-v7:25.3.1'
    compile 'com.android.support.constraint:constraint-layout:1.0.2'
    compile 'com.google.firebase:firebase-auth:10.0.1'
    compile 'com.firebaseui:firebase-ui-auth:1.2.0'
    testCompile 'junit:junit:4.12'
}
```

Do check the latest version number that you should use. You should see this in the instructions at https://github.com/firebase/FirebaseUI-Android/blob/master/auth/README.md.

Note that you will have two sets of dependencies for auth in this file – one is the firebase-ui-auth itself, and the other is the underlying firebase-auth. As you use FirebaseUI, you'll see this pattern occurring regularly.

When you're done you should do a gradle sync, and this should hopefully have no errors. If you have some, double-check where you put the configuration information – particularly the maven one.

Code the Main Activity

In this section you'll build a really simple app that just has a sign-in button to invoke the sign-up and sign-in flows. It takes some shortcuts for the purposes of learning, and as such doesn't invoke all best practices!

First off, edit the activity_main layout file to add a new button. When you're done, your code for it should look like this:

```xml
<?xml version="1.0" encoding="utf-8"?>
<android.support.constraint.ConstraintLayout xmlns:android="http://schemas.android.com/apk/
res/android"
    xmlns:app="http://schemas.android.com/apk/res-auto"
    xmlns:tools="http://schemas.android.com/tools"
    android:layout_width="match_parent"
    android:layout_height="match_parent"
    tools:context="com.laurencemoroney.firebasech2.MainActivity">

    <Button
        android:id="@+id/signInButton"
        android:layout_width="wrap_content"
        android:layout_height="wrap_content"
        android:text="Sign In"
        tools:layout_editor_absoluteX="161dp"
        tools:layout_editor_absoluteY="143dp" />
</android.support.constraint.ConstraintLayout>
```

This will give you a basic sign-in button. Now go to the MainActivity.java class to edit the source code.

Add a couple of module level variables at the top of the class before the onCreate() function. These will handle the button, and a variable to determine the identity of the activity you will start for the sign-in. The value of RC_SIGN_IN can be any int.

```java
private static final int RC_SIGN_IN = 100;
Button signInButton;
```

Before using Firebase AuthUI, you need to initialize FirebaseAuth and check to see if there's a user already signed in. If they're signed in, you'll go to the signed-in activity and finish this one. You'll implement the signed-in activity later, then come back and edit this code to uncomment the startActivity line. So just keep it at finishing for now. Add this code to your onCreate method:

```
if(auth.getCurrentUser() != null){
    // Start signed in activity
    //startActivity(SignedInActivity.createIntent(this, null));
    finish();
}
```

Now, in the onCreate function, set up the Sign-In button, and add an onClick listener to it.

```
signInButton = (Button) findViewById(R.id.signInButton);
signInButton.setOnClickListener(new View.OnClickListener() {
    @Override
    public void onClick(View v) {

    }
});
```

In this listener you'll add the code to create a sign-in intent. This intent is provided for you by the Firebase AuthUI libraries. All you have to do is implement it. Here's the code:

```
signInButton.setOnClickListener(new View.OnClickListener() {
    @Override
    public void onClick(View v) {
        startActivityForResult(
                AuthUI.getInstance().createSignInIntentBuilder()
                    .build(),
                    RC_SIGN_IN);
    }
});
```

This builds a sign-in activity, and passes RC_SIGN_IN to it, so that when you get the response from this activity, you can check for that variable. There may be multiple activities giving you results in an Android app, so you use an identifier like this for each one. In this case we only have one – but we still need to identify it with an integer, which in this case we called RC_SIGN_IN.

When the activity has finished its work, it will send back an onActivityResult containing the request code and some data. The data is an intent, which we can use to figure out what happened. First, let's catch the onActivityResult. Here's the code:

```
@Override
protected void onActivityResult(int requestCode, int resultCode, Intent data){
    super.onActivityResult(requestCode, resultCode, data);
    if(requestCode == RC_SIGN_IN){
        handleSignInResponse(resultCode, data);
        return;
    }
}
```

This simply checks to see if the Activity was as a result of the intent we identified with RC_ SIGN_IN. If it is, it calls the handleSignInResponse() method, passing it the result code and the data.

Let's take a look at this next. It should simply do the following: If the sign-in was successful, call the 'Signed In' activity, otherwise tell us why sign-in failed. Here's the code:

```java
@MainThread
private void handleSignInResponse(int resultCode, Intent data) {
    IdpResponse response = IdpResponse.fromResultIntent(data);
    Toast toast;
    // Successfully signed in
    if (resultCode == ResultCodes.OK) {
        //startActivity(SignedInActivity.createIntent(this, response));
        finish();
        return;
    } else {
        // Sign in failed
        if (response == null) {
            // User pressed back button
            toast = Toast.makeText(this, "Sign in was cancelled!", Toast.LENGTH_LONG);
            toast.show();
            return;
        }

        if (response.getErrorCode() == ErrorCodes.NO_NETWORK) {
            toast = Toast.makeText(this, "You have no internet connection", Toast.LENGTH_LONG);
            toast.show();
            return;
        }

        if (response.getErrorCode() == ErrorCodes.UNKNOWN_ERROR) {
            toast = Toast.makeText(this, "Unknown Error!", Toast.LENGTH_LONG);
            toast.show();
            return;
        }
    }

    toast = Toast.makeText(this, "Unknown Error!", Toast.LENGTH_LONG);
    toast.show();
}
```

As you can see this code is very straightforward. If the response code was ResultCodes.OK, that means the sign-in went well, so you can start the signed-in activity. This is commented out right now, as you haven't implemented that activity yet. You'll do that in a moment, then come back and uncomment these lines.

If the response code was otherwise, then you can cast the intent to an IdpResponse class, and query its error code, giving the user a toast with a hint as to why the sign-in failed.

Before building the Signed-In activity, there's one more function you'll need to implement, and that's the ability for this activity to create an intent for itself.

Here's the code:

```
public static Intent createIntent(Context context) {
    Intent in = new Intent();
    in.setClass(context, MainActivity.class);
    return in;
}
```

This is used by the sign in activity in the case that it doesn't have a valid user. It will close itself, and return to this activity to get you to sign in again.

Create and Code the Signed-In Activity

Now let's create a simple signed-in activity. You can do this in Android Studio by right-clicking on the package containing the Main Activity. See Figure 2-6.

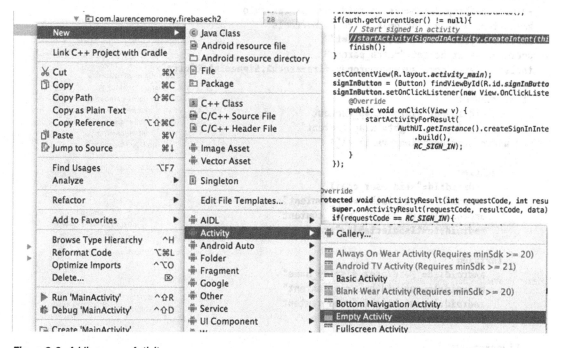

Figure 2-6. Adding a new Activity

Select New ➤ Activity ➤ Empty Activity. Call it SignedInActivity, and press Create.

Android Studio will create all the files you need – source, layout, and settings in your Android Manifest.

Go to the layout file – which should be called activity_signed_in.xml as you can see in Figure 2-7.

Figure 2-7. Layout for new Activity

Edit the layout to add two TextView controls, arranged in a LinearLayout. These will be for the user's email address and their display name.

Here's the complete code:

```xml
<?xml version="1.0" encoding="utf-8"?>
<android.support.constraint.ConstraintLayout xmlns:android="http://schemas.android.com/
apk/res/android"
    xmlns:app="http://schemas.android.com/apk/res-auto"
    xmlns:tools="http://schemas.android.com/tools"
    android:layout_width="match_parent"
    android:layout_height="match_parent"
    tools:context="com.laurencemoroney.firebasech2.SignedInActivity">

    <LinearLayout
        android:layout_width="wrap_content"
        android:layout_height="wrap_content"
        android:orientation="vertical">

        <TextView
            android:id="@+id/user_email"
            android:layout_width="wrap_content"
            android:layout_height="wrap_content"
            android:textIsSelectable="true"/>

        <TextView
            android:id="@+id/user_display_name"
            android:layout_width="wrap_content"
            android:layout_height="wrap_content"
            android:textIsSelectable="true"/>

    </LinearLayout>

</android.support.constraint.ConstraintLayout>

@Override
protected void onCreate(Bundle savedInstanceState) {
    super.onCreate(savedInstanceState);
    setContentView(R.layout.activity_signed_in);

}
```

In the onCreate for this activity you should check to see if you have a valid current user. If you don't, then you can go back to the sign-in screen by calling its createIntent function, and finishing. Here's the code:

```
if(currentUser == null){
    startActivity(MainActivity.createIntent(this));
    finish();
    return;
}
```

Now if the current user is not null, then you have a signed-in user. Let's simply get their Email Address and User Name and load them into the TextView controls. Here's the code:

```
userEmail = (TextView) findViewById(R.id.user_email);
userName = (TextView) findViewById(R.id.user_display_name);

userEmail.setText(currentUser.getEmail());
userName.setText(currentUser.getDisplayName());
```

Don't forget to declare TextView controls for userName and userEmail at the top of the class code.

Finally, you'll need a createIntent function so that this activity can be started by intent:

```
public static Intent createIntent(Context context, IdpResponse idpResponse) {
    Intent in = IdpResponse.getIntent(idpResponse);
    in.setClass(context, SignedInActivity.class);
    return in;
}
```

That's the basic code to get sign-up and sign-in with email/password addresses. Before running the code, go back to the MainActivity and uncomment the two places where you had the startActivity calls to this activity. There was one in onCreate and one in handleSignInResponse.

Explore the Sign-In Flows

Before running the app, make sure you have the following configuration in your AndroidManifest.xml file:

```
<uses-permission android:name="android.permission.INTERNET" />
```

Now run the app, and you'll see something like Figure 2-8.

Figure 2-8. The Basic Sign-In app

Press the Sign-In button, and you'll be given a basic screen asking for an Email Address. This is part of the standard UI given to you by Firebase AuthUI. See Figure 2-9.

Figure 2-9. Sign in with Email

Enter something here – it doesn't matter what Email you use, because it isn't validated yet. When you press 'Next', Firebase UI will recognize that this address isn't in the system, so it will change you to a Sign-Up form, where this Email is asked to provide a First & Last Name as well as a password. See Figure 2-10.

Figure 2-10. Signing Up for a new account

Enter values here and click 'Save'. Notice that basic Password validation is done for you. You can override the rules of this validation by editing the FirebaseUI code, as it's open source, but doing that is beyond the scope of this book.

After pressing 'Save', the account is created, and you are signed in with those credentials. The Signed-In activity will launch, and you'll see the email address and user name that you created. See Figure 2-11.

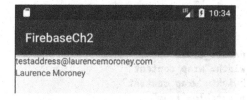

Figure 2-11. Signed in to the App

There's no sign-out yet, you'll do that next. So if you close and reopen the app, you'll see that you're still signed in.

Before doing that, go take a look at the Firebase Console. You'll see in the Authentication section, under the Users tab that this user now exists! See Figure 2-12.

Figure 2-12. Users List in Authentication Panel

Adding Sign Out

Now that the user has been able to create an account and sign into it, let's take a look at signing them out. To do this, go back to the signed-in activity and add a button to it for signing out. Here's what activity_signed_in.xml should look like:

```xml
<?xml version="1.0" encoding="utf-8"?>
<android.support.constraint.ConstraintLayout xmlns:android="http://schemas.android.com/apk/
res/android"
    xmlns:app="http://schemas.android.com/apk/res-auto"
    xmlns:tools="http://schemas.android.com/tools"
    android:layout_width="match_parent"
    android:layout_height="match_parent"
    tools:context="com.laurencemoroney.firebasech2.SignedInActivity">
    <LinearLayout
        android:layout_width="wrap_content"
        android:layout_height="wrap_content"
        android:orientation="vertical">

        <TextView
            android:id="@+id/user_email"
            android:layout_width="wrap_content"
            android:layout_height="wrap_content"
            android:textIsSelectable="true"/>

        <TextView
            android:id="@+id/user_display_name"
            android:layout_width="wrap_content"
            android:layout_height="wrap_content"
            android:textIsSelectable="true"/>
```

```
<Button
    android:layout_width="match_parent"
    android:layout_height="match_parent"
    android:id="@+id/signOutButton"
    android:text="Sign Out"/>

    </LinearLayout>
</android.support.constraint.ConstraintLayout>
```

Note the added button called signOutButton.

Then, in the SignedInActivity code, set up the button and add an onClickListener to it in your onCreate method.

```
signOutButton = (Button) findViewById(R.id.signOutButton);
signOutButton.setOnClickListener(new View.OnClickListener() {
    @Override
    public void onClick(View v) {
        signOut();
    }
});
```

This will call a function called signOut, which uses the AuthUI.getInstance().signout method. This is an asynchronous task, which returns upon completion, so you implement its onComplete. In there you will start a new MainActivity to bring you back to the sign-in screen. Here's the code:

```
public void signOut(){
    AuthUI.getInstance().signOut(this)
            .addOnCompleteListener(new OnCompleteListener<Void>() {
                @Override
                public void onComplete(@NonNull Task<Void> task) {
                    if(task.isSuccessful()){
                        startActivity(MainActivity.createIntent(SignedInActivity.this));
                        finish();
                    } else {
                        // Signout failed
                    }
                }
            });
}
```

So let's take a look at this in action. When you last ran the app you signed up a new address, and signed into it. You weren't able to sign out, so when you run the app you should see the signed-in activity, but now it will have the Sign Out button. See Figure 2-13.

Figure 2-13. Signed-In screen

Press the Sign Out button, and you should get returned to the Sign In screen. Press the sign-in button, and be sure to enter the same email address that you did earlier (e.g., testaddress@laurencemoroney.com in this case) – and you'll see that you get taken to the 'Welcome back!' screen – allowing you to sign back into that account. See Figure 2-14.

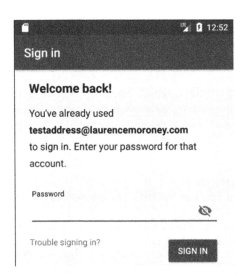

Figure 2-14. The Welcome back screen

Enter a wrong password, and you'll see that the UI gives you a message that the password is invalid. You didn't have to write any code to get this.

Resetting the Password

In Figure 2-14, you saw the Welcome back screen for users with known accounts. The users of these may have lost their passwords, so a 'Trouble Signing In' link takes you to a screen where you can have a reset password sent. See Figure 2-15.

Figure 2-15. Resetting the password

Now you may enter any email address here, but Firebase will only allow you to send to addresses that are linked to this account. This is another really nice validation feature that comes with the AuthUI code, and it's one that you don't have to implement yourself! See Figure 2-16.

Figure 2-16. Entering the wrong Email

Once you enter the right address, Firebase will send an email to the email address with reset instructions. See Figure 2-17.

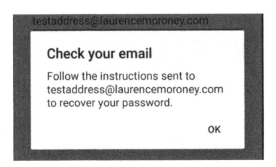

Figure 2-17. Sending the reset Email

You'll get an email with the reset instructions that looks like Figure 2-18.

Subject:	Reset your password for FirebaseCh2
From:	noreply@fir-ch2.firebaseapp.com
Date:	Thu, May 4, 2017 1:56 pm
To:	testaddress@laurencemoroney.com
Priority:	Normal
Options:	View Full Header	View Printable Version	Download this as a file	Add to Address Book	View Message Details	View as plain text

Hello,

Follow this link to reset your FirebaseCh2 password for your testaddress@laurencemoroney.com account.

https://fir-ch2.firebaseapp.com/__/auth/action?mode=resetPassword&oobCode=TAD-DfPVCwodC3JNV2aNrR3ch4k&apiKey=AIzaSyDx65gvMcbXjLwexBVdkY6aUP2JWdAm9ow

If you didn't ask to reset your password, you can ignore this email.

Thanks,

Your FirebaseCh2 team

Figure 2-18. The reset Email

Clicking on this will take you to an online form where you can enter your new password.

Adding Smart Lock for Passwords

Smart Lock for Passwords lets your users automatically sign in using credentials they have saved. It can be used for username/password as we've just implemented as well as federated identity provider credentials like you'll see later in this chapter.

Firebase AuthUI makes it very simple to do so – you simply edit your code where you created the sign-in builder to enable it using the setIsSmartLockEnabled property to true.

Here's the code:

```
signInButton.setOnClickListener(new View.OnClickListener() {
    @Override
    public void onClick(View v) {
        startActivityForResult(
                AuthUI.getInstance().createSignInIntentBuilder()
                        .setIsSmartLockEnabled(true)
                        .build(),
                        RC_SIGN_IN);
    }
});
```

Now when you run your app, if there's a Google account signed in on the device, as well as using the Email/Password sign-in, you'll see options to sign in the addresses that are saved in Smart Lock. See Figure 2-19.

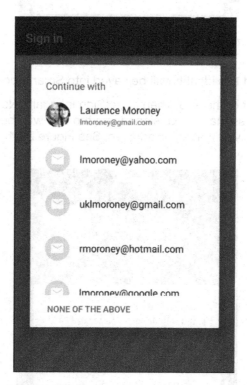

Figure 2-19. Using addresses stored in Smart Lock

If you pick one of these, then the email address underpinning it will be prepopulated as a Sign Up form, should that email not be an identity in the Email/Password set of users to begin with. But for now don't pick one, and instead select 'None of the Above'.

Sign in again with the Email and Password settings you created earlier. When you sign in successfully, you'll get a Smart Lock dialog asking if you want to save this username and password for future use. See Figure 2-20.

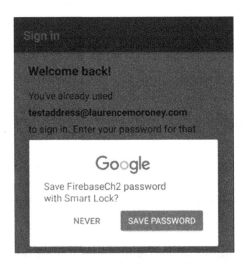

Figure 2-20. Save identity to Smart Lock

Click 'Save Password' and this identity will be saved into Smart Lock for you.

Click 'Sign Out' to sign out of the app. Then click 'Sign In' again. Now, that the app has recognized an email address that you've signed into the app with before, the Smart Lock dialog will change to show you that email address. See Figure 2-21.

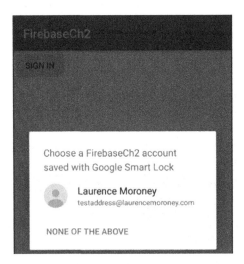

Figure 2-21. Saved identity in Smart Lock

Select this, and you'll notice that you are now signed into the app without entering a password!

Using Federated Identity Providers

So far you've seen how to set up Email and Password sign-in. Firebase also supports federated identity through providers like Google, Facebook, Twitter, and GitHub. In these scenarios, the user doesn't need to register with your site or app at all. They simply sign in with their credentials used on those sites, and they handle the process of authenticating the user and sending you verification that they are who they say they are.

Adding Sign-In with Google

In this section we'll explore how to implement Sign-In with Google, and how your users can use their Google Credentials to sign into your app.

Earlier in your main activity, on the button click listener, you created a sign-in intent builder with this code:

```
        startActivityForResult(
                AuthUI.getInstance().createSignInIntentBuilder()
                        .setIsSmartLockEnabled(true)
                        .build(),
                        RC_SIGN_IN);
    }
});
```

When you don't specify any sign-in providers, it defaults to just giving email sign-in. To add Sign-In with Google, you can simply create a list of IDP Providers, and specify which ones you want, so, for example, to use both Email and Google as providers you would update the OnClickListener code to this:

```
signInButton.setOnClickListener(new View.OnClickListener() {
    @Override
    public void onClick(View v) {
        List<AuthUI.IdpConfig> selectedProviders = new ArrayList<>();
        selectedProviders.add(new AuthUI.IdpConfig.Builder(AuthUI.EMAIL_PROVIDER).build());
        selectedProviders.add(new AuthUI.IdpConfig.Builder(AuthUI.GOOGLE_PROVIDER).build());
        startActivityForResult(
                AuthUI.getInstance().createSignInIntentBuilder()
                        .setIsSmartLockEnabled(true)
                        .setProviders(selectedProviders)
                        .build(),
                        RC_SIGN_IN);
    }
});
```

A provider is created using an IdpConfig builder, and you specify which builders you want using constants on the AuthUI object.

You may to make a modification to the Firebase Console, before you can run it – Android apps using Sign In with Google need to provide the SHA1 of their signing certificate to the console so they identify that they are who they say they are. If you had used the assistant to configure Authentication, this would have been done for you. If not, you can get your debug SHA1 by running the following command in a terminal:

```
keytool -list -v -keystore ~/.android/debug.keystore -alias androiddebugkey -storepass
android -keypass android
```

You'll see the SHA1 in the text that is returned. Then go to the Firebase Console. Beside the word 'Overview' you'll see a cog icon. Click that, and select Project Settings. In the Your Apps section, you'll see your Android app. Select that, and near the bottom you'll see where you can paste your SHA1 value. Go ahead and do that before running.

Run the app and take a look what happens! Click the Sign-In button. You might be asked to pick a Smart Lock credential – don't do that and just select 'None of the Above'. You'll now see that the sign-in activity includes a branded 'Sign in with Google' button. You didn't need to implement this – it was done for you by the FirebaseUI code simply by specifying that you want Google as a provider. See Figure 2-22.

Figure 2-22. Sign in with Google added as a provider

When you click the button, you'll get a chooser for the account that is on this phone, as you can see in Figure 2-23.

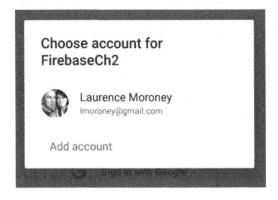

Figure 2-23. Account chooser for Google accounts

If you select the account, you'll be asked to provide basic profile info to the app. This is the standard Google dialog, provided directly by Google, so it's easier for your users to trust it. See Figure 2-24.

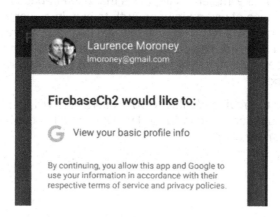

Figure 2-24. Google sign-in basic profile permission request

Tap on allow, and Google will sign you into the app, providing it with the Basic Profile details (Name and Email address), and the app will render them. Notice in this scenario that there was no need to sign **up** for the app, you just signed **in**.

Also notice, from Figure 2-23, that you had the facility to 'Add account' – which will take you through the standard Google flow for adding a new Google identity with a Gmail account. Again, all of this is handled for you by the Firebase AuthUI libraries!

You'll also see that this user is then a user for your app by browsing the Authentication section of the Firebase Console, which shows you a list of your users, as well as the provider they use to sign in. See Figure 2-25, where I have a user that signed up using Email, and another that signed up using Google!

Email	Providers	Created	Signed In	User UID ↑
testaddress@laurencemoron...	✉	4 May 2017	4 May 2017	UQmXR4nzA6fwtqS8gWk9pn1kbgr2
lmoroney@gmail.com	G	5 May 2017	5 May 2017	rPno4nQipEZrgNhn0qO8FR53t1Q2

Rows per page: 50 ▾   1-2 of 2   ‹   ›

Figure 2-25. Signed-in users

Setting up for sign-in with other providers is equally simple. You can learn about them all at https://firebase.google.com/docs/auth/.

Summary

In this chapter you learned about Firebase Auth, and in particular how the open source Firebase AuthUI libraries make implementing apps that use Firebase Auth very simple. You stepped through the process of using Firebase Auth to sign in a user with an email and password, including all the flows required to sign them up, and integrating with Smart Lock for Passwords. You then saw how easy it was to extend this to allowing sign-in with Google, with just a few lines of code. From here you can extend to other federated providers, or use anonymous providers too!

Now that you know how to provide identity to your users, this will come in really useful when you want to provide secure access to data, and you'll learn all about that, including using the realtime database in the next chapter.

Chapter 3

The Firebase Realtime Database

The Firebase Realtime Database is a NoSQL cloud-based database that syncs data across all clients in realtime, and provides offline functionality. Data is stored in the Realtime database as JSON, and all connected clients share one instance, automatically receiving updates with the newest data.

In this chapter you'll get hands-on with building a simple app that writes and reads data from the database. You'll learn how to have an app with public data, as well as how to provide user-based access to data based on users that you created and signed in with the techniques covered in Chapter 2.

Using the Firebase Realtime Database from a programming perspective is very different from what you might be used to with traditional relational databases like MySQL or SQL Server. Primarily you'll structure your data in a fundamentally different way – using JSON instead of the traditional tables and joins. You can learn more about NoSQL at en.wikipedia.org/wiki/NoSQL.

You'll also find that from an architectural perspective, your approach will differ significantly. Instead of the traditional way of building, with a database surrounded by a data access layer on which you run queries or stored procedures, which in turn you then expose via some form of endpoint to your mobile or web application, all of the code when writing for the Firebase Realtime Database is in your mobile client. It makes building and maintaining apps much simpler.

Getting Started

If you've never used this type of database before, I think the best way is to just get hands-on and give it a try. Using Android Studio, create a new Android application with an Empty Activity. Call it FirebaseCh3. See Chapter 1 for details if you haven't done this yet.

© Laurence Moroney 2017
L. Moroney, *The Definitive Guide to Firebase*, https://doi.org/10.1007/978-1-4842-2943-9_3

Using the Firebase Assistant, find the Realtime Database section, and open it by clicking on the arrow. See Figure 3-1.

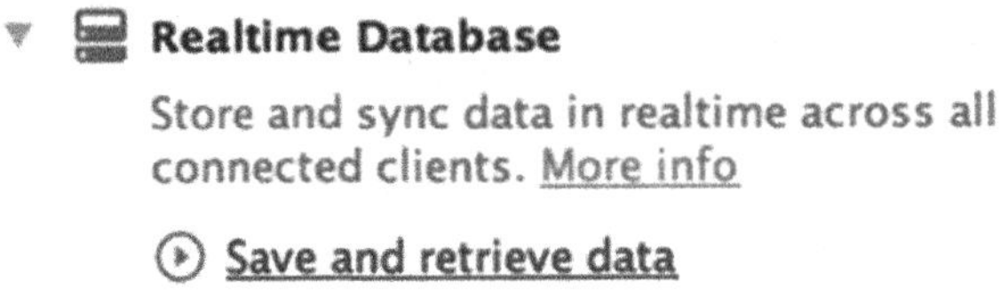

▼ 🖳 Realtime Database

Store and sync data in realtime across all connected clients. More info

⊙ Save and retrieve data

Figure 3-1. The Realtime Database in the Firebase Assistant

Click the link 'Save and retrieve data', and you'll be given a set of steps. The first of these, 'Connect to Firebase', will start a new Firebase project on the Firebase Console. When asked, create a new Firebase project called FirebaseCh3. See Figure 3-2.

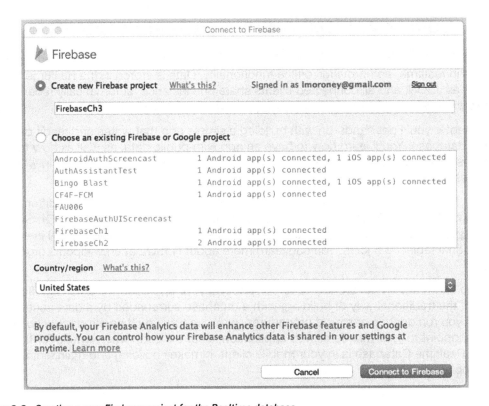

Figure 3-2. Creating a new Firebase project for the Realtime database

Once you press the Connect to Firebase button a new project will be created on the Firebase Console, and this Android App will be connected to it. For more details on this process, see Chapter 1.

Once this is complete, you'll see the Assistant is updated. Then you can do Step 2 – Adding the Realtime Database to your app. Click the button, and you'll be shown the code modifications that need to be performed. Select 'Accept Changes' and your app will be updated with the required configuration to use the Realtime Database.

For the first Apps you'll work on in this chapter, you'll just use public access to your data. Then, once you see how it all works, you'll see how to only use authenticated access to your data. Before you can do this, you'll need to do some edits on your Firebase Console project.

Visit console.firebase.google.com, and take a look at the project that you created a moment ago. The one I used (see Figure 3-2) was FirebaseCh3, so if you used the same name you should see it in the console.

Once you open the project, select 'Database' on the left, and you should see something like Figure 3-3.

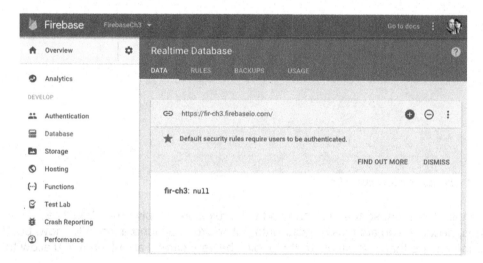

Figure 3-3. *The Realtime Database in Firebase Console*

You'll see a warning that the default security rules require users to be authenticated. Let's override those next.

Click the 'Rules' tab at the top of the screen. You'll see the set of rules on the screen, configured as a JSON document. See Figure 3-4.

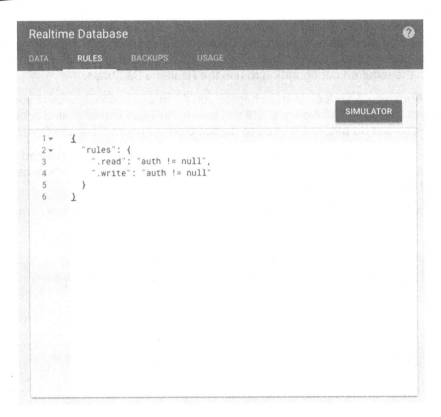

Figure 3-4. *The Realtime Database rules*

Change this document so that the read and write rules are simply 'true'. You'll see some warnings, because you are making your data public. You can ignore these for now, but if you are writing an app that is available to the public, be very careful about what you allow to be public!

See Figure 3-5 to see what your rules will look like after this step.

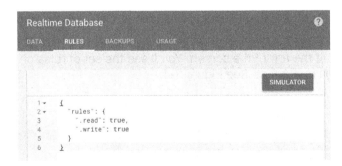

Figure 3-5. *The Realtime Database rules made public*

Don't close the browser; keep it open on the console, with the Realtime Database data tab open. You'll use that again in a moment.

Write Your First Data

Go back to your Android app, and open the layout file (res/layoutout/activitymain.xml), remove the TextView with 'Hello World', and add a button. Give the button the name 'writeButton'. Your layout file should look like this when you're done.

```xml
<?xml version="1.0" encoding="utf-8"?>
<android.support.constraint.ConstraintLayout xmlns:android="http://schemas.android.com/apk/
res/android"
    xmlns:app="http://schemas.android.com/apk/res-auto"
    xmlns:tools="http://schemas.android.com/tools"
    android:layout_width="match_parent"
    android:layout_height="match_parent"
    tools:context="com.laurencemoroney.firebasech3.MainActivity">

    <Button
        android:id="@+id/writeButton"
        android:layout_width="wrap_content"
        android:layout_height="wrap_content"
        android:text="Button"
        tools:layout_editor_absoluteX="147dp"
        tools:layout_editor_absoluteY="29dp" />

</android.support.constraint.ConstraintLayout>
```

Now go to the MainActivity.java file, and edit it.

First, in the onCreate function, you'll need to get an instance of the Firebase database that you will use to manage reading/writing data. Here's the code:

```java
FirebaseDatabase database = FirebaseDatabase.getInstance();
final DatabaseReference myRef = database.getReference("message");
```

Now create a handler for the button. In this, use the DatabaseReference object you created earlier to write a value to the database. Here's the code:

```java
writeButton = (Button) findViewById(R.id.writeButton);
writeButton.setOnClickListener(new View.OnClickListener() {
    @Override
    public void onClick(View v) {
        myRef.setValue("Hello, World");
    }
});
```

For reference, here's the full code for the MainActivity Class:

```java
package com.laurencemoroney.firebasech3;

import android.support.v7.app.AppCompatActivity;
import android.os.Bundle;
import android.view.View;
import android.widget.Button;

import com.google.firebase.database.DatabaseReference;
import com.google.firebase.database.FirebaseDatabase;

public class MainActivity extends AppCompatActivity {
    Button writeButton;
    @Override
    protected void onCreate(Bundle savedInstanceState) {
        super.onCreate(savedInstanceState);
        setContentView(R.layout.activity_main);
        FirebaseDatabase database = FirebaseDatabase.getInstance();
        final DatabaseReference myRef = database.getReference("message");
        writeButton = (Button) findViewById(R.id.writeButton);
        writeButton.setOnClickListener(new View.OnClickListener() {
            @Override
            public void onClick(View v) {
                myRef.setValue("Hello, World");
            }
        });
    }
}
```

Run the app, but don't push the button yet. Make sure you can see the database tab in the browser before doing so. The console works in the same way as the Realtime Database, so any writes done by your app will be reflected instantly on the console, with a little animation to show how it works.

Figure 3-6 shows what your app and database should look like before you press the button. Nothing has been written to the database yet, so it shows up as 'null'.

Figure 3-6. The Empty Database

Press the button, and you should see an instant update to the database, which looks like Figure 3-7.

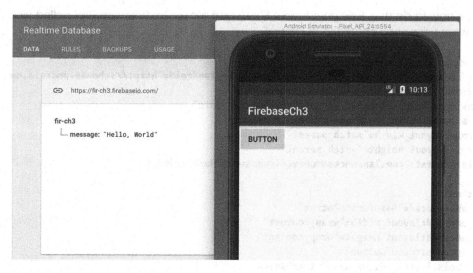

Figure 3-7. Writing your first field

Take a look at the anatomy of what was written. Remember this is a JSON structure, so it's a name-value pair. This is shown with the name 'message' and the value 'Hello, World'. To see how this was constructed, look back at the code.

When you created the Database reference, it was created with the parameter 'message':

```
final DatabaseReference myRef = database.getReference("message");
```

This determined that the name of this reference was 'message', giving us that parameter. The value of this could be a single value, or a nested structure. We simply set it to a single value – the string 'Hello World' in this code:

```
myRef.setValue("Hello, World");
```

You may also have noticed a URL at the top of the database window – in this case it's https://fir-ch3-firebaseio.com. This will give you a handy shortcut back to this screen.

Read Your First Data

In the previous section, you wrote a field to the database by creating a reference called 'message' and setting its value to "Hello, World". You saw in the console that the message was written. Let's now take a look at how data is read. This is very different from relational databases where reads are usually a 'pull' from the database where you explicitly query the data, and get a result. In the Firebase Realtime database it's more of a 'push', where the database detects a change in a field and pushes that update to you. These updates (or events) are captured in your app by a Value Event Listener. A snapshot of the data is passed to this, and you parse that to get the updated values.

Let's see how to do this. Edit your layout file to add a new TextView control called viewText. Here's what your code should look like:

```
<?xml version="1.0" encoding="utf-8"?>
<android.support.constraint.ConstraintLayout xmlns:android="http://schemas.android.com/apk/
res/android"
    xmlns:app="http://schemas.android.com/apk/res-auto"
    xmlns:tools="http://schemas.android.com/tools"
    android:layout_width="match_parent"
    android:layout_height="match_parent"
    tools:context="com.laurencemoroney.firebasech3.MainActivity">

    <Button
        android:id="@+id/writeButton"
        android:layout_width="wrap_content"
        android:layout_height="wrap_content"
        android:text="Button"
        tools:layout_editor_absoluteX="147dp"
        tools:layout_editor_absoluteY="29dp" />

    <TextView
        android:id="@+id/viewText"
        android:layout_width="wrap_content"
        android:layout_height="wrap_content"
        android:text="TextView"
        tools:layout_editor_absoluteX="162dp"
        tools:layout_editor_absoluteY="246dp" />

</android.support.constraint.ConstraintLayout>
```

Then, in your code, on your DatabaseReference, you can add a value event listener, which receives an onDataChange event. This receives a DataSnapShot, from which you can get the value of the updated field. Here's the code:

```
myRef.addValueEventListener(new ValueEventListener() {
    @Override
    public void onDataChange(DataSnapshot dataSnapshot) {
        String value = dataSnapshot.getValue(String.class);
        viewText.setText(value);
    }
    @Override
    public void onCancelled(DatabaseError error) {
        // Failed to read value
        Log.w("Ch3", "Failed to read value.", error.toException());
    }
});
```

You specify the expected class for the value that's returned in the Snapshot. In this case it's simply a string, so we use String.class. Note that the onCancelled event is expected or you'll get an error. In this case I just logged the error in this code.

Here's the complete update code for the activity including the code to set up the controls, and the required imports.

```
package com.laurencemoroney.firebasech3;

import android.support.v7.app.AppCompatActivity;
import android.os.Bundle;
import android.util.Log;
import android.view.View;
import android.widget.Button;
import android.widget.TextView;

import com.google.firebase.database.DataSnapshot;
import com.google.firebase.database.DatabaseError;
import com.google.firebase.database.DatabaseReference;
import com.google.firebase.database.FirebaseDatabase;
import com.google.firebase.database.ValueEventListener;

public class MainActivity extends AppCompatActivity {
    Button writeButton;
    TextView viewText;
    @Override
    protected void onCreate(Bundle savedInstanceState) {
        super.onCreate(savedInstanceState);
        setContentView(R.layout.activity_main);
        FirebaseDatabase database = FirebaseDatabase.getInstance();
        final DatabaseReference myRef = database.getReference("message");
        writeButton = (Button) findViewById(R.id.writeButton);
        writeButton.setOnClickListener(new View.OnClickListener() {
            @Override
            public void onClick(View v) {
```

```
                    myRef.setValue("Hello, World");
            }
        });
        viewText = (TextView) findViewById(R.id.viewText);
        myRef.addValueEventListener(new ValueEventListener() {
            @Override
            public void onDataChange(DataSnapshot dataSnapshot) {
                String value = dataSnapshot.getValue(String.class);
                viewText.setText(value);
            }
            @Override
            public void onCancelled(DatabaseError error) {
                // Failed to read value
                Log.w("Ch3", "Failed to read value.", error.toException());
            }
        });
    }
}
```

Run this app, and you'll see that the event fires right away – from your previous time running the app you set the message to be 'Hello World', and the text view that you just created has been updated to show that. See Figure 3-8.

Figure 3-8. The data is read automatically

In Firebase, data is retrieved using this asynchronous listener methodology. The listener is triggered when the data is first written, and subsequently whenever it changes. To really see the power of this, you can edit the data in the console directly by typing. Change the text from "Hello, World" to something else – and when you press Enter, you'll see that the console, and the text in the app will update instantly. See Figure 3-9.

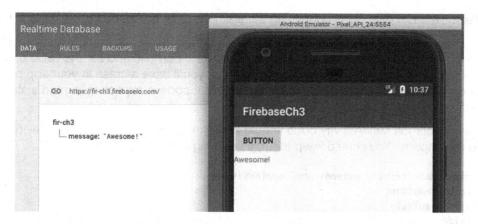

Figure 3-9. Updating Data in the Realtime Database

Now that you have done the basics of reading and writing data, let's take this to the next level, and work with structured data fields to store and retrieve something beyond basic strings.

Using Java to Structure Data

The examples you've just seen were very handy for a single data field – writing or reading a string from a database. But most applications have much more data than that, and the data will need to be structured in some way. For Firebase –JSON is used. Think of your database as a JSON tree, with data being added as children in the structure. On the client side, this maps neatly to using a Java class for storing data. When the class is written to the database it is automatically serialized into the required JSON.

Let's take a look at this in action.

Write Structured Data with a Stock Portfolio

Go to your FirebaseCh3 project, and add a new Java class called StockPortfolio. Edit its code to look like this:

```java
package com.laurencemoroney.firebasech3;

public class StockPortfolio {
    public String portfolioName;
    public String portfolioOwner;
    public String portfolioContact;

    public StockPortfolio(){}

    public StockPortfolio(String name, String owner, String contact){
        this.portfolioName = name;
        this.portfolioOwner = owner;
        this.portfolioContact = contact;
    }
}
```

This creates a basic data class containing three strings, with a constructor to initialize them.

Then, edit your MainActivity code to change the DatabaseReference from 'messages' to 'portfolios'. Add code to the onClick function to create a portfolio and set the value of myRef to it. Also, comment out the onDataChange code, or you'll have a crash in your app because you're now saving a structure to the database, but that code is expecting to read a string, and you'll get a data mismatch.

Here's what your full MainActivity code should look like. Note the changes. For brevity I have omitted the imports. You should keep them, as nothing has changed there.

```java
public class MainActivity extends AppCompatActivity {
    Button writeButton;
    TextView viewText;
    @Override
    protected void onCreate(Bundle savedInstanceState) {
        super.onCreate(savedInstanceState);
        setContentView(R.layout.activity_main);
        FirebaseDatabase database = FirebaseDatabase.getInstance();
        final DatabaseReference myRef = database.getReference("portfolios");
        writeButton = (Button) findViewById(R.id.writeButton);
        writeButton.setOnClickListener(new View.OnClickListener() {
            @Override
            public void onClick(View v) {
                StockPortfolio myFolio = new StockPortfolio("demoFolio", "lmoroney", "lm@
                hotmail.com");
                myRef.setValue(myFolio);
                //myRef.setValue("Hello, World");
            }
        });
        viewText = (TextView) findViewById(R.id.viewText);
        myRef.addValueEventListener(new ValueEventListener() {
            @Override
            public void onDataChange(DataSnapshot dataSnapshot) {
                //String value = dataSnapshot.getValue(String.class);
                //viewText.setText(value);
            }
            @Override
            public void onCancelled(DatabaseError error) {
                // Failed to read value
                Log.w("Ch3", "Failed to read value.", error.toException());
            }
        });
    }
}
```

Now run your app, and press the write button as before. You should see data added to your Realtime database that looks like Figure 3-10:

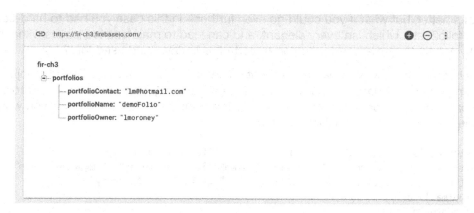

Figure 3-10. Writing the portfolio

We don't have any contents in the portfolio yet, but we can probably see an issue already – if we're going to have a collection of portfolios (as the plural in its name suggests), then we should likely need a bit more structure. Consider this code – what do you think it would do?

```
StockPortfolio myFolio = new StockPortfolio("demoFolio", "lmoroney", "lm@hotmail.com");
myRef.setValue(myFolio);
StockPortfolio myOtherFolio = new StockPortfolio("realFolio", "lmoroney",
"lmwork@hotmail.com");
myRef.setValue(myOtherFolio);
```

Because we are setting a value of myRef – the second portfolio would overwrite the first. So we need to do something a little better. The natural next step is to think of multiple portfolios as children of the 'portfolios' node. To achieve that, your code would look like this:

```
StockPortfolio myFolio = new StockPortfolio("demoFolio", "lmoroney", "lm@hotmail.com");
myRef.child("folio1").setValue(myFolio);
StockPortfolio myOtherFolio = new StockPortfolio("realFolio", "lmoroney",
"lmwork@hotmail.com");
myRef.child("folio2").setValue(myOtherFolio);
```

Running this would give you the results in Figure 3-11. (Note that I deleted previous data before running, so if you see the previous data also, it's because this new code is adding the data in a different place.)

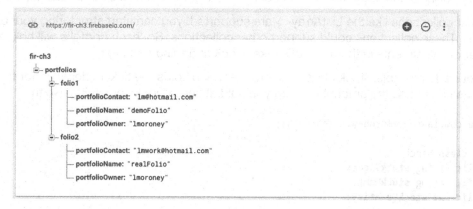

Figure 3-11. Using child nodes

This looks better, but what if you could go even further – in this case you had to hard-code 'folio1', 'folio2' etc, which isn't very elegant, and can lead to maintenance issues. What if instead you had an in-memory collection of portfolios in Java, and used that?

Here's what the code would look like for creating an ArrayList<> of StockPortfolio objects, and writing that to the database. Now, instead of hard-coding which children I want to write to, you can manage your collection of StockPortfolio objects in Java, and when you write them, Firebase will do the heavy lifting for you.

```
ArrayList<StockPortfolio> myFolios = new ArrayList<StockPortfolio>();
StockPortfolio myFolio = new StockPortfolio("demoFolio", "lmoroney", "lm@hotmail.com");
StockPortfolio myOtherFolio = new StockPortfolio("realFolio", "lmoroney",
"lmwork@hotmail.com");
myFolios.add(myFolio);
myFolios.add(myOtherFolio);
myRef.setValue(myFolios);
```

And when you run this code, you'll see something like Figure 3-12 in the Firebase Console:

Figure 3-12. Writing the collection

This looks much better – you now have a logical separation of portfolios. Indeed, Firebase has given me an index into them too, so if needed you can refer to a folio by this index (0, 1 etc.).

Now that collections like the ListArray<> are supported, you can start structuring your data logically. These collections could support other collections. So, each portfolio will hold a number of investments in them, so let's take a look at adding that next.

First, let's add a simple Stock class to our app – which holds the ticker (identifier) for the stock, its name, and the amount of them you hold. It should look something like this:

```
package com.laurencemoroney.firebasech3;

public class Stock {
    public String stockTicker;
    public String stockName;
    public int stockQuantity;
```

```java
    public Stock(){}

    public Stock(String ticker, String name, int quantity ){
        this.stockTicker = ticker;
        this.stockName = name;
        this.stockQuantity = quantity;
    }
}
```

Then, we'll add an ArrayList<> of stocks to the StockPortfolio class:

```java
package com.laurencemoroney.firebasech3;

import java.util.ArrayList;

public class StockPortfolio {
    public String portfolioName;
    public String portfolioOwner;
    public String portfolioContact;
    public ArrayList<Stock> portfolioHoldings;

    public StockPortfolio(){}

    public StockPortfolio(String name, String owner, String contact){
        this.portfolioName = name;
        this.portfolioOwner = owner;
        this.portfolioContact = contact;
    }
}
```

Now, when we press the button, let's add some stocks in hypothetical amounts to each portfolio to demonstrate this concept:

```java
ArrayList<StockPortfolio> myFolios = new ArrayList<StockPortfolio>();

StockPortfolio myFolio = new StockPortfolio("demoFolio", "lmoroney", "lm@hotmail.com");

ArrayList<Stock> myFolioHoldings = new ArrayList<Stock>();
myFolioHoldings.add(new Stock("GOOG", "Google", 100));
myFolioHoldings.add(new Stock("AAPL", "Apple", 50));
myFolioHoldings.add(new Stock("MSFT", "Microsoft", 10));
myFolio.portfolioHoldings = myFolioHoldings;

StockPortfolio myOtherFolio = new StockPortfolio("realFolio", "lmoroney",
"lmwork@hotmail.com");

ArrayList<Stock> myOtherFolioHoldings = new ArrayList<Stock>();
myOtherFolioHoldings.add(new Stock("IBM", "IBM", 50));
myOtherFolioHoldings.add(new Stock("MMM", "3M", 10));
myOtherFolio.portfolioHoldings = myOtherFolioHoldings;
```

```
myFolios.add(myFolio);
myFolios.add(myOtherFolio);
myRef.setValue(myFolios);
```

This creates an ArrayList of Stock objects for each of the portfolios, and adds some stocks to each. It then writes them out to the Database. Figure 3-13 shows the results:

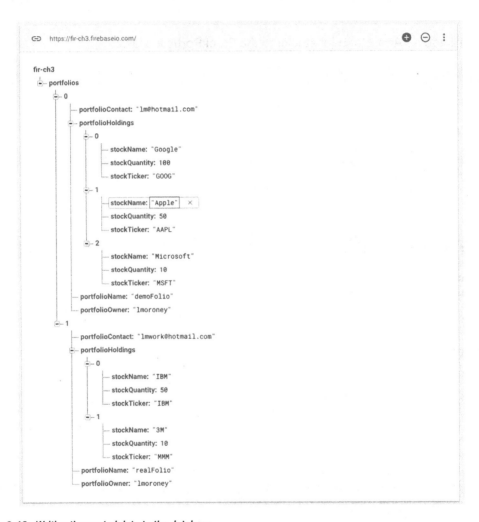

Figure 3-13. Writing the nested data to the database

You'll notice that the keys are sorted alphabetically, which is why the portfolioHoldings appear in the middle of the record. If you want to make the data more readable in the console, this is something to consider! Also, note that the same auto index was applied to the stocks, starting the count at 0 and moving up.

If you want to see the raw JSON for this, you can do so by using the URL for this data (mine as you can see in Figure 3-13 is https://fir-ch3.firebaseio.com) and adding .json at the end of the URL, so, for example: https://fir-ch3.firebaseio.com/.json.

You can see this in Figure 3-14.

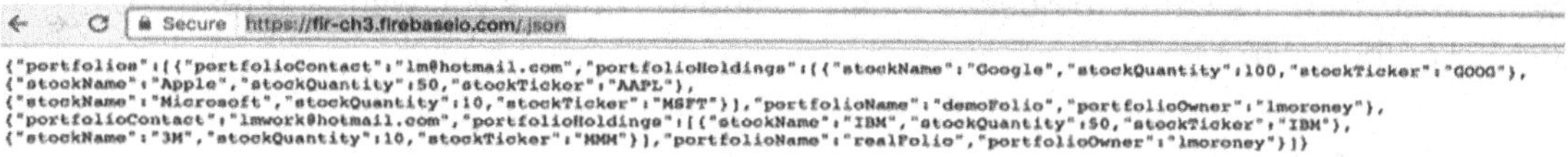

← C 🔒 Secure https://fir-ch3.firebaseio.com/.json

{"portfolios":[{"portfolioContact":"lm@hotmail.com","portfolioHoldings":[{"stockName":"Google","stockQuantity":100,"stockTicker":"GOOG"},
{"stockName":"Apple","stockQuantity":50,"stockTicker":"AAPL"},
{"stockName":"Microsoft","stockQuantity":10,"stockTicker":"MSFT"}],"portfolioName":"demoFolio","portfolioOwner":"lmoroney"},
{"portfolioContact":"lmwork@hotmail.com","portfolioHoldings":[{"stockName":"IBM","stockQuantity":50,"stockTicker":"IBM"},
{"stockName":"3M","stockQuantity":10,"stockTicker":"MMM"}],"portfolioName":"realFolio","portfolioOwner":"lmoroney"}]}

Figure 3-14. Seeing your Database as JSON

Now that we have some structured data in place, let's next take a look at reading it back from the database.

Reading Structured Data

In the previous section we wrote a collection of Stock Portfolios, each containing a collection of Stock holdings to the database. As it's not a flat structure, when it comes to reading it back, we might have several scenarios – the first, and easiest, is to read back the entire collection to memory. Let's explore that.

Earlier, when we had written just a single String to the database, we read it back in onDataChange using this code:

```
String value = dataSnapshot.getValue(String.class);
viewText.setText(value);
```

We got the value of the dataSnapshot, telling it that the contents were a string, and loaded that into the String called 'value'. We could then call setText on the viewText TextView to render this string. But now our data type is a collection of StockPortfolio objects. If we try to run this code, we'll get a crash, because what is being read back doesn't match 'String. class'.

As we're using Generics, it does add a layer of complexity to this code – when for a basic String, we could add the String.class to getValue in order to declare what we're doing, the syntax for something like ArrayList<StockPortfolio> means we need an approach that lets us declare what types we're getting back.

To achieve this you can use a GenericTypeIndicator class like this:

```
GenericTypeIndicator<ArrayList<StockPortfolio>> t = new GenericTypeIndicator<ArrayList<Stoc
kPortfolio>>() {};
```

Now that you've declared the type, you can read back the ArrayList<StockPortfolio>:

```
ArrayList<StockPortfolio> myFolios = dataSnapshot.getValue(t);
```

As we still have a TextView, we can edit it to be the name of the first folio in the list:

```
String value = myFolios.get(0).portfolioName;
viewText.setText(value);
```

Of course hard-coding the 0th portfolio in the list isn't great coding – there could be none, and you'd get an error! So be sure to check for that if you are coding your data like this. To be more efficient, it's better to query the data to find the objects you want and read them instead of the entire set.

Querying the Data

In a typical relational database, queries are powerful because they allow you to return a subset of data instead of the entire blob. The JSON structure of Firebase also allows this, but you have to rethink how you approach it. Data isn't stored in tables, so you can't say something like `SELECT * from portfolios WHERE portfolioName='demoFolio'` to retrieve the portfolio you want.

One way, would, of course be to just take the 0th branch of the portfolios field, but how would we know that the 0th branch is the one with the portfolio name 'demoFolio'?

Another way would, of course, be to read all the portfolios into memory, and throw away the ones that don't match portfolioName='demoFolio', but if you have many portfolios, and these have many holdings, you could be reading a lot of data in order to find one folio.

Firebase allows you to query using a Query object, but you don't have a language like SQL – you need to think in terms of children that you are using and matching them against a value.

So, for example, if you want the portfolio where I set the name the be demoFolio – the equivalent of `SELECT * from portfolios WHERE portfolioName='demoFolio'` – you'll create a Firebase Query object, and order it by children that match your desired value. Here's the same query, done in the Firebase way!

```
Query query = myRef.orderByChild("portfolioName").equalTo("demoFolio");
```

Because Firebase is a realtime event-driven database, you don't do a request-response type query like you do with SQL. Instead, you set up listeners for changes. Now you may not always want to get constant updates, and just read the data once (like you would with SQL), and for this you can add a listener for a single event to have the same effect.

Add a button to your app, and but an onClickListener on it that runs a query when you click on the button. Here's the code for onClick:

```
Query query = myRef.orderByChild("portfolioName").equalTo("demoFolio");
query.addListenerForSingleValueEvent(new ValueEventListener() {
    @Override
    public void onDataChange(DataSnapshot dataSnapshot) {
    }
}
```

Here you can see how the query is set up to order all results of the portfolioName field that matches the value demoFolio.

Then you add a listener for a single value event to the query, and when it returns, the onDataChange will fire.

Here's the code for that – it's very similar to what we just saw, using a GenericTypeIndicator to get the ArrayList<> back from the snapshot:

```
@Override
public void onDataChange(DataSnapshot dataSnapshot) {
    GenericTypeIndicator<ArrayList<StockPortfolio>>
    t = new GenericTypeIndicator<ArrayList<StockPortfolio>>() {};
    ArrayList<StockPortfolio> myFolios = dataSnapshot.getValue(t);
    String pName="";
    if(myFolios != null){
        pName = myFolios.get(0).portfolioName;
    }
    viewText.setText(pName);
}
```

Then we check to see if any results were returned (myFolios will be non-null), and if so, you'll get the portFolioName value from that and load it into the TextView.

Updating Data

The next step is to update data. There are lots of ways that you could do this, but the one I usually recommend is the following – you query the data that you want using the above mechanism. Then, if your data has a unique key, it's easy to update. If it doesn't – and the key has been autogenerated for you as in this instance (remember the 0,1 under portfolios, and the 0,1,2 under holdings? Those are autogenerated keys for the collections) – so we need to understand what the key is for the node that we're currently looking at. This can be obtained using an iterator. Here's the code:

```
Query query = myRef.orderByChild("portfolioName").equalTo("demoFolio");
query.addListenerForSingleValueEvent(new ValueEventListener() {
    @Override
    public void onDataChange(DataSnapshot dataSnapshot) {
        DataSnapshot nodeShot = dataSnapshot.getChildren().iterator().next();
        String key = nodeShot.getKey();
    }
}
```

Now that you have the key, it's easy to get a handle on the right child to update using myRef. child(key), but in order to update a value, you need to create a HashMap of <String,Object> containing the key that you want to update, and the value you want to update it to.

So, for example, if you want to update the portfolio owner to a new value, you would simply do this:

```
HashMap<String, Object> update = new HashMap<>();
update.put("portfolioOwner", "New Owner");
myRef.child(key).updateChildren(update);
```

Add a new button called 'Update' to your app, and add this code to its onClick listener, and take it for a spin – you'll see the field get updated when you press the button. For convenience, here's the code:

```
Button updateButton = (Button) findViewById(R.id.updateButton);
updateButton.setOnClickListener(new View.OnClickListener() {
    @Override
    public void onClick(View v) {
        Query query = myRef.orderByChild("portfolioName").equalTo("demoFolio");
        query.addListenerForSingleValueEvent(new ValueEventListener() {
            @Override
            public void onDataChange(DataSnapshot dataSnapshot) {
                DataSnapshot nodeShot = dataSnapshot.getChildren().iterator().next();
                String key = nodeShot.getKey();
                HashMap<String, Object> update = new HashMap<>();
                update.put("portfolioOwner", "New Owner");
                myRef.child(key).updateChildren(update);
            }

            @Override
            public void onCancelled(DatabaseError databaseError) {

            }
        });
    }
});
```

Deleting Data

You've created, retrieved, updated data. Now it's time to finish the CRUD acronym, and learn how to delete data. Doing this is very similar to the updating of data that you saw in the previous step, but instead of getting the key and updating the value of the data at that key using a HashMap, you simply remove the child using removeValue() on its reference. Let's take a look:

```
Button deleteButton = (Button) findViewById(R.id.deleteButton);
deleteButton.setOnClickListener(new View.OnClickListener() {
    @Override
    public void onClick(View v) {
        Query query = myRef.orderByChild("portfolioName").equalTo("demoFolio");
        query.addListenerForSingleValueEvent(new ValueEventListener() {
            @Override
            public void onDataChange(DataSnapshot dataSnapshot) {
                DataSnapshot nodeShot = dataSnapshot.getChildren().iterator().next();
                String key = nodeShot.getKey();
                myRef.child(key).removeValue();
            }
```

```
        @Override
        public void onCancelled(DatabaseError databaseError) {

        }
    });
}
});
```

You'll notice in this case that you query the data to find the folio where the name is 'demoFolio', and then from there you derive its key in the database. Then all you have to do is remove the value of the child that matches that key and the entire node will be removed. You can do similarly for fields, etc.

Summary

In this chapter you got an introduction to the Firebase Realtime Database – and you saw how it can be used as a fully functioning database that gives you realtime capabilities to build a very responsive app. You saw how your data was structured as a JSON table, and how with a little rethinking you could perform queries just like those in SQL. You also learned about value event listeners that will execute when your data changes, so you can update the state of your application, or their SQL-like cousin – the listener for single value events that can be used to run queries. You then saw how you can find fields within a database and update or delete them! This chapter touches on what you can do with the Firebase Realtime DB, but there's a whole lot more to discover! In the next chapter, we'll look at the next type of storage – Firebase Cloud Storage, which can be used to store large files like images or videos in the cloud with a simple way to use API!

Chapter 4

Cloud Storage for Firebase

In Chapter 3 you looked at the Realtime database for Firebase that allowed you to have a codeless back end to your apps requiring data, and which gave an event-driven model that gave you responsive updates to your app when data changed. In this chapter you'll go beyond data into how to store files in the scalable cloud infrastructure provided by Firebase.

It's designed for storing objects as opposed to data – so it's perfect if your app needs to store and serve user-generated content like pictures or videos. It's built on top of Google Cloud Storage, so the SDKs inherit functionality from there – such as gracefully handling loss of connection when uploading or downloading files.

In order to ensure that your files are secured, it also integrates with Firebase Authentication (see Chapter 2) so that you can provide access to files based on your app requirements – and aspects of the files such as name, size, type, etc., can be used in a declarative security model to provide access.

Because Cloud Storage for Firebase uses Google Cloud Storage, you can also build apps for the Google Cloud Platform that can access them. This is a common scenario, where you may have a web app and a mobile app, each of which require access to the files.

Building an App with Cloud Storage for Firebase

Create a new Android App with the empty activity template, and use the Firebase Assistant to configure it for Storage. See Figure 4-1.

© Laurence Moroney 2017
L. Moroney, *The Definitive Guide to Firebase*, https://doi.org/10.1007/978-1-4842-2943-9_4

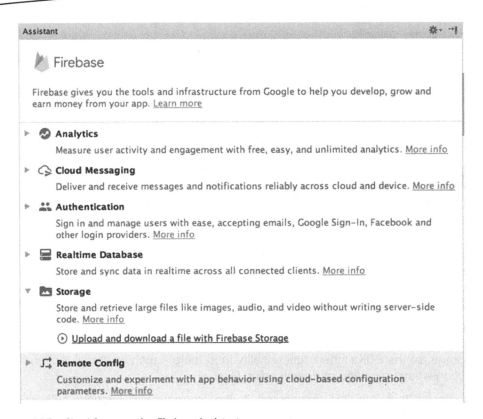

Figure 4-1. Adding Cloud Storage using Firebase Assistant

Follow the steps to connect the app to a new Firebase project, and then add Firebase storage to your app.

You're now ready to upload or download files from Cloud Storage for Firebase. Let's build a simple app that allows you to take a picture with the device camera, and then upload it to Firebase!

Create a new App with an empty activity in the usual manner, and connect this to a Firebase project called FirebaseChapter4.

Enable Anonymous Authentication

Before you can use Storage, you'll need authentication on your Firebase project. This can be anonymous authentication, so let's set that up first.

On the Firebase Console, within your project, select the Authentication tab on the left, and then pick 'Sign-In Method' at the top of the screen. You'll see a list of sign-in providers, with 'Anonymous' as one of the options. See Figure 4-2.

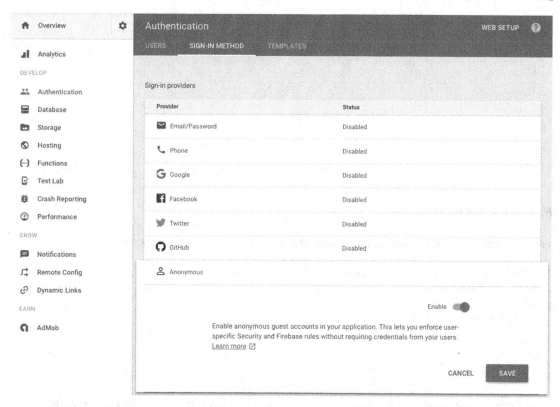

Figure 4-2. Setting up Anonymous authentication

Now that Anonymous authentication is set up, you'll next enable access to your Cloud Storage bucket for anonymous users.

Set Storage Rules

Next up you'll have to enable the anonymous users to read or write from this bucket. Do note that these actions will allow anyone to read or write from your bucket. You should set up authenticated (non-Anonymous) users before releasing any application. To do this, on your Firebase Console, select the 'Storage' tab, and pick 'Rules' from the top of the screen. Change the content to allow read, write for all users.

You'll do this with the following code. See Figure 4-3.

```
service firebase.storage {
  match /b/{bucket}/o {
    match /{allPaths=**} {
      allow read, write;
    }
  }
}
```

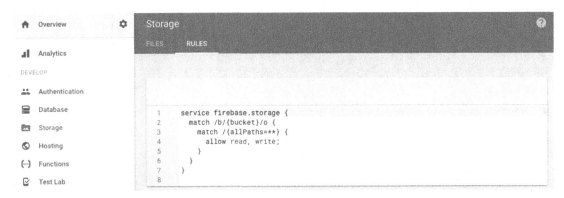

Figure 4-3. Setting the Storage Rules

When using a non-Anonymous authenticated user, the rules would look like this:

```
// Only authenticated users can read or write to the bucket
service firebase.storage {
  match /b/{bucket}/o {
    match /{allPaths=**} {
      allow read, write: if request.auth != null;
    }
  }
}
```

Now that you have set up your user and the rules, let's now look at the app and how to create it.

Editing the Layout

First off, let's create the layout. It will need two buttons – the first is a sign-in button that signs in with Anonymous authentication. The second is one that takes a picture using the onboard camera, and uploads it to Cloud Storage.

Here's the full layout file, including the two buttons:

```xml
<?xml version="1.0" encoding="utf-8"?>
<android.support.constraint.ConstraintLayout xmlns:android="http://schemas.android.com/apk/
res/android"
    xmlns:app="http://schemas.android.com/apk/res-auto"
    xmlns:tools="http://schemas.android.com/tools"
    android:layout_width="match_parent"
    android:layout_height="match_parent"
    tools:context="com.laurencemoroney.firebasechapter4.MainActivity">

    <LinearLayout
        android:layout_width="match_parent"
        android:layout_height="match_parent"
        android:orientation="vertical">
        <Button android:id="@+id/loginButton"
            android:text="Sign In"
            android:layout_height="wrap_content"
```

```
        android:layout_width="wrap_content">
    </Button>
    <Button
        android:layout_width="wrap_content"
        android:layout_height="wrap_content"
        android:text="Take Picture"
        android:id="@+id/takePictureButton"
        android:enabled="false"/>

</LinearLayout>

</android.support.constraint.ConstraintLayout>
```

Note that the take picture button is disabled, it will be enabled once the user signs in. Next, let's take a look at the code for these.

Editing the Code for Anonymous Sign-In

First off, you'll need to implement the sign-in button so an anonymous authenticated user can sign in. To do this, you'll need the following code.

You'll need a FirebaseAuth object called mAuth. Define this on the class level, and then, in onCreate get an instance of FirebaseAuth:

```
mAuth = FirebaseAuth.getInstance();
```

Next you'll implement the signInButton, and on its click you'll call a function called doSignIn():

```
signInButton = (Button) findViewById(R.id.loginButton);
signInButton.setOnClickListener(new View.OnClickListener() {
    @Override
    public void onClick(View v) {
        doSignIn();
    }
});
```

Now, in order to get an anonymous sign in, you use the mAuth object like this:

```
private void doSignIn() {
    mAuth.signInAnonymously().addOnSuccessListener(this, new OnSuccessListener<AuthResult>()
{
        @Override
        public void onSuccess(AuthResult authResult) {
            takePictureButton.setEnabled(true);
        }
    }).addOnFailureListener(this, new OnFailureListener() {
        @Override
        public void onFailure(@NonNull Exception e) {
            String foo = e.getLocalizedMessage();
        }
    });

}
```

For more details on the auth programming model, see Chapter 2. Ultimately, this will set up an onSuccessListener for the sign-in. When the sign-in is successful, the take picture button will be enabled; otherwise it will stay disabled.

Taking a Photo with the Onboard Camera

The take picture button is disabled by default, but once the user signs in it will become enabled. At that point the user can take a picture using it, and the picture will be uploaded to Cloud Storage. Let's now take a look at how to take a picture.

First of all, you'll need to wire up the Take Picture button. Here's the code:

```
takePictureButton = (Button) findViewById(R.id.takePictureButton);
takePictureButton.setOnClickListener(new View.OnClickListener() {
    @Override
    public void onClick(View v) {
        takePictureAndUpload();
    }
});
```

When the user taps on the button the **takePictureAndUpload()** method will be called. Let's take a look at this:

```
private void takePictureAndUpload() {
    Intent cameraIntent = new Intent(MediaStore.ACTION_IMAGE_CAPTURE);
    startActivityForResult(cameraIntent, CAMERA_REQUEST);
}
```

Taking a picture is very simple – you just create a new intent using MediaStore.ACTION_ IMAGE_CAPTURE, and start an activity for its result. You pass an int to this (in this case CAMERA_REQUEST), which you can check for in the activity result. You may have multiple activities giving callbacks, so you set up an integer to identify each one. In this case, I set a CAMERA_REQUEST constant with the value 1. When the activity result comes back, it will pass back this code, so I can check against that to make sure it's the right activity result. That will look like this:

```
protected void onActivityResult(int requestCode, int resultCode, Intent data){
    if ((requestCode == CAMERA_REQUEST) && (resultCode == Activity.RESULT_OK)){
        ...
}
```

In the case of the camera taking a picture the 'data' field will contain the picture. To get the picture from this as a byte array, you use the following code:

```
Bundle extras = data.getExtras();
Bitmap imageBitmap = (Bitmap) extras.get("data");
ByteArrayOutputStream stream = new ByteArrayOutputStream();
imageBitmap.compress(Bitmap.CompressFormat.JPEG, 100, stream);
byte[] imageData = stream.toByteArray();
```

Now that you have the picture as a byte array, you can upload it to Firebase Storage. You'll see that in the next section.

Uploading the Image to Cloud Storage

In the previous section you got the image from the camera as a byte array. You can now upload this to Cloud Storage.

First of all you'll need an instance of storage:

```
FirebaseStorage storage = FirebaseStorage.getInstance();
```

Next you'll need to get a StorageReference for this:

```
StorageReference storageRef = storage.getReference();
```

Your image will then be a child for this storage reference. In this case I'm just hard-coding it as a child called 'image.jpg'. In a real scenario you'd need to generate a filename, based on the timestamp or something else that makes it more unique.

```
StorageReference imageRef = storageRef.child("image.jpg");
```

You can call the putBytes method on the imageRef to upload the image. This gives you an UploadTask datatype that handles it asynchronously for you. Here's an example:

```
UploadTask uploadTask = imageRef.putBytes(imageData);
uploadTask.addOnFailureListener(new OnFailureListener() {
    @Override
    public void onFailure(@NonNull Exception e) {
        String ex = e.getLocalizedMessage();
    }
}).addOnSuccessListener(new OnSuccessListener<UploadTask.TaskSnapshot>() {
    @Override
    public void onSuccess(UploadTask.TaskSnapshot taskSnapshot) {
        String url = taskSnapshot.getDownloadUrl().toString();
    }
});
```

That's it for this sample. As you can see it's pretty straightforward - you sign in anonymously, and once singed in, you can take a picture with the onboard camera and upload it.

For convenience, here's the entire code for the MainActivity.java class:

```
package com.laurencemoroney.firebasechapter4;

import android.app.Activity;
import android.content.Intent;
import android.graphics.Bitmap;
import android.provider.MediaStore;
import android.support.annotation.NonNull;
import android.support.v7.app.AppCompatActivity;
import android.os.Bundle;
import android.view.View;
import android.widget.Button;
```

```java
import com.google.android.gms.tasks.OnFailureListener;
import com.google.android.gms.tasks.OnSuccessListener;
import com.google.firebase.auth.AuthResult;
import com.google.firebase.auth.FirebaseAuth;
import com.google.firebase.storage.FirebaseStorage;
import com.google.firebase.storage.StorageReference;
import com.google.firebase.storage.UploadTask;

import java.io.ByteArrayInputStream;
import java.io.ByteArrayOutputStream;

public class MainActivity extends AppCompatActivity {
    private static final int CAMERA_REQUEST = 1;
    Button signInButton, takePictureButton;
    FirebaseAuth mAuth;

    @Override
    protected void onCreate(Bundle savedInstanceState) {
        super.onCreate(savedInstanceState);
        setContentView(R.layout.activity_main);
        mAuth = FirebaseAuth.getInstance();

        signInButton = (Button) findViewById(R.id.loginButton);
        signInButton.setOnClickListener(new View.OnClickListener() {
            @Override
            public void onClick(View v) {
                doSignIn();
            }
        });

        takePictureButton = (Button) findViewById(R.id.takePictureButton);
        takePictureButton.setOnClickListener(new View.OnClickListener() {
            @Override
            public void onClick(View v) {
                takePictureAndUpload();
            }
        });
    }

    private void doSignIn() {
        mAuth.signInAnonymously().addOnSuccessListener(this, new
        OnSuccessListener<AuthResult>() {
            @Override
            public void onSuccess(AuthResult authResult) {
                takePictureButton.setEnabled(true);
            }
        }).addOnFailureListener(this, new OnFailureListener() {
            @Override
            public void onFailure(@NonNull Exception e) {
                String foo = e.getLocalizedMessage();
            }
        });

    }
```

```java
private void takePictureAndUpload() {
    Intent cameraIntent = new Intent(MediaStore.ACTION_IMAGE_CAPTURE);
    startActivityForResult(cameraIntent, CAMERA_REQUEST);
}

protected void onActivityResult(int requestCode, int resultCode, Intent data){
    if ((requestCode == CAMERA_REQUEST) && (resultCode == Activity.RESULT_OK)){
        Bundle extras = data.getExtras();
        Bitmap imageBitmap = (Bitmap) extras.get("data");
        ByteArrayOutputStream stream = new ByteArrayOutputStream();
        imageBitmap.compress(Bitmap.CompressFormat.JPEG, 100, stream);
        byte[] imageData = stream.toByteArray();

        FirebaseStorage storage = FirebaseStorage.getInstance();
        StorageReference storageRef = storage.getReference();
        StorageReference imageRef = storageRef.child("image.jpg");

        UploadTask uploadTask = imageRef.putBytes(imageData);
        uploadTask.addOnFailureListener(new OnFailureListener() {
            @Override
            public void onFailure(@NonNull Exception e) {
                String ex = e.getLocalizedMessage();
            }
        }).addOnSuccessListener(new OnSuccessListener<UploadTask.TaskSnapshot>() {
            @Override
            public void onSuccess(UploadTask.TaskSnapshot taskSnapshot) {
                String url = taskSnapshot.getDownloadUrl().toString();
            }
        });

    }
  }
}
```

Once you have the url of the file, you can then persist it if needed in the Firebase Realtime Database (Chapter 3), or store it in some other way.

> **Note**   In this example, while an upload task was used, the image upload was still initiated from the main thread by having it running off a button's onClick. A more efficient way to do this would be to use a background service in Android. That's beyond the scope of this book, but recommended for real-world apps. You can learn more about these at: developer.android.com/training/run-background-service.

Let's take a look at the app in action.

Running the App

The Android Emulator allows you to emulate a camera, so we can try out the application to see an image being captured and uploaded to Cloud Storage.

Let's run the app and try it out.

Figure 4-4 shows the app when you first run it.

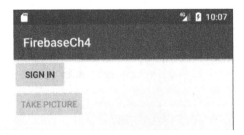

Figure 4-4. *Running the App*

Clicking the 'Sign In' button will sign you in anonymously, enabling the 'Take Picture' button. When you click that you'll get a bouncing square over an animated background. You can see this in Figure 4-5.

Figure 4-5. *The Camera Emulator*

Click the blue circle in the center, and the animation will stop. You'll see a tick to its right and a cross to its left. See Figure 4-6.

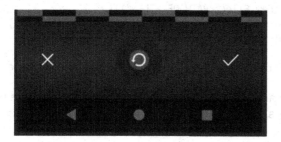

Figure 4-6. Taking a picture

Click the tick button, and you'll be returned to the home screen after the image upload begins. To see if it uploaded, check out the Firebase Console. In the storage section, you'll see a 'Files' tab, and here you can see the image that has been uploaded!

Figure 4-7. The uploaded image in Cloud Storage

You can select the image to see a preview. See Figure 4-8.

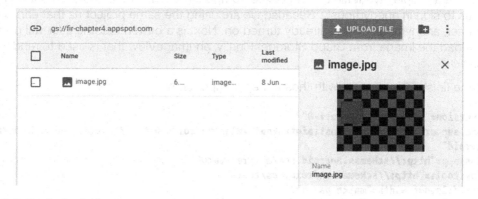

Figure 4-8. Previewing the image

In this example, the putBytes() method was used to upload the image byte by byte. If the image was stored as a local file, you culd use the putFile() method in a similar way:

```
Uri file = Uri.fromFile(new File("<PATH OF FILE>"));
StorageReference fileRef = storageRef.child(file.getLastPathSegment());
uploadTask = fileRef.putFile(file);

// Use same listeners for onFailure and onSuccess as previous example
```

Additionally if you have access to a stream for the data – perhaps the most versatile way, as it can be used for files, in-memory data and other examples, then you would perform the upload like this:

```
InputStream stream = new FileInputStream(new File("<PATH OF FILE>"));
StorageReference fileRef = storageRef.child(file.getLastPathSegment());
uploadTask = fileRef.putStream(stream);

// Use same listeners for onFailure and onSuccess as previous example
```

Remember that in addition to this, you also have the ability to pause, resume, and cancel uploads with the methods of those names.

Building an App to Download from Cloud Storage

Let's create another app that will download the file from Cloud Storage. In the usual manner, create an app with an empty activity. Use the Firebase Assistant to connect it to the same project as the previous app in this chapter – you can have multiple apps in one Firebase project.

Similar to the previous app, use the assistant to add Firebase Storage to your app. This will set up all your dependencies correctly.

Edit the Layout File

Let's create a simple layout file that has three components. The first is a sign-in button that allows us to sign in anonymously. Because we are using the same project as that earlier in the chapter, anonymous auth is already turned on. Next is a button that the user will press to download the image from Cloud Storage. Finally, an ImageView that is used to render the image.

Here's the finished Layout file with these three components:

```
<?xml version="1.0" encoding="utf-8"?>
<android.support.constraint.ConstraintLayout xmlns:android="http://schemas.android.com/apk/
res/android"
    xmlns:app="http://schemas.android.com/apk/res-auto"
    xmlns:tools="http://schemas.android.com/tools"
    android:layout_width="match_parent"
    android:layout_height="match_parent"
    tools:context="com.laurencemoroney.firebasech4_2.MainActivity">
```

```xml
<LinearLayout android:orientation="vertical"
    android:layout_height="wrap_content"
    android:layout_width="wrap_content">
    <Button
        android:layout_width="wrap_content"
        android:layout_height="wrap_content"
        android:id="@+id/LoginButton"
        android:text="Log In"/>
    <Button
        android:layout_width="wrap_content"
        android:layout_height="wrap_content"
        android:id="@+id/GetPictureButton"
        android:text="Get Picture"
        android:enabled="false" />
    <ImageView
        android:layout_width="wrap_content"
        android:layout_height="wrap_content"
        android:id="@+id/ShowPicture" />
</LinearLayout>

</android.support.constraint.ConstraintLayout>
```

Edit your activity_main.xml to match this.

Coding the App

In your MainActivity.java you'll now write the code that does the following:

- When the user clicks sign in, start off a sign-in flow, which upon completion will enable the 'Get Picture' button.

- When the user clicks the Get Picture button, download the image and render it in the ImageView.

Let's look at the sign-in first. The code for this is very straightforward. First you'll wire the button up to the view, and call the doSignIn() function when the user clicks on it:

```java
LoginButton = (Button) findViewById(R.id.LoginButton);
LoginButton.setOnClickListener(new View.OnClickListener() {
    @Override
    public void onClick(View v) {
        doSignIn();
    }
});
```

The doSignIn() function then starts an anonymous sign in flow. If it completes, the GetPictureButton will be enabled, so the user can click it.

```java
private void doSignIn() {
    mAuth.signInAnonymously().addOnSuccessListener(this, new OnSuccessListener<AuthResult>()
    {
        @Override
```

```java
            public void onSuccess(AuthResult authResult) {
                GetPictureButton.setEnabled(true);
            }
    }).addOnFailureListener(this, new OnFailureListener() {
        @Override
        public void onFailure(@NonNull Exception e) {
            String foo = e.getLocalizedMessage();
        }
    });

}
```

It's as simple as that!

For the GetPictureButton, you'll first wire it up to the view, and call the downloadPicture() function when the user clicks on it.

```java
GetPictureButton = (Button) findViewById(R.id.GetPictureButton);
GetPictureButton.setOnClickListener(new View.OnClickListener() {
    @Override
    public void onClick(View v) {
        downloadPicture();

    }
});
```

The downloadPicture() function then downloads the image from storage to a local file, and then loads that file into the ImageView:

```java
private void downloadPicture(){
    FirebaseStorage storage = FirebaseStorage.getInstance();
    StorageReference storageRef = storage.getReference();
    StorageReference imageRef = storageRef.child("image.jpg");
    try {
        final File localFile = File.createTempFile("image", "jpg");
        imageRef.getFile(localFile).addOnSuccessListener(new OnSuccessListener<FileDownload
        Task.TaskSnapshot>() {
            @Override
            public void onSuccess(FileDownloadTask.TaskSnapshot taskSnapshot) {
                // Local file has been created, load it into ImageView
                Bitmap myBitmap = BitmapFactory.decodeFile(localFile.getAbsolutePath());

                ImageView myImage = (ImageView) findViewById(R.id.ShowPicture);

                myImage.setImageBitmap(myBitmap);
            }
        }).addOnFailureListener(new OnFailureListener() {
            @Override
            public void onFailure(@NonNull Exception e) {
                String foo = e.getLocalizedMessage();
            }
        });
```

```
    } catch (Exception ex){
        String foo = ex.getLocalizedMessage();
    }
}
```

Let's take a look at what this is doing step by step.

First, it initializes Storage, getting a reference to it, and then using this to determine a reference to the image as a child of the main reference, called 'image.jpg'. Note that it's hard-coded here for simplicity, because in the previous step we used the same hard-coded name.

```
FirebaseStorage storage = FirebaseStorage.getInstance();
    StorageReference storageRef = storage.getReference();
    StorageReference imageRef = storageRef.child("image.jpg");
```

Then it creates a file on the device called image.jpg:

```
final File localFile = File.createTempFile("image", "jpg");
```

Once you have this, you can now call the getFile() method on the StorageReference – in this case imageRef like this:

```
imageRef.getFile(localFile)
```

You should add an onSuccessListener() and onFailureListener() to this to handle the callbacks as getFile is an asynchronous operation. Let's look at the onSuccessListener:

```
imageRef.getFile(localFile).addOnSuccessListener(new OnSuccessListener<FileDownloadTask.
TaskSnapshot>() {
    @Override
    public void onSuccess(FileDownloadTask.TaskSnapshot taskSnapshot) {
        // Local file has been created, load it into ImageView
        Bitmap myBitmap = BitmapFactory.decodeFile(localFile.getAbsolutePath());

        ImageView myImage = (ImageView) findViewById(R.id.ShowPicture);

        myImage.setImageBitmap(myBitmap);
    }
```

In this case once the file has successfully downloaded, you simply create a Bitmap object from the local file, and then load that into the ImageView using its setImageBitmap method.

Now, when you run the app, you'll see that the image gets downloaded and rendered. See Figure 4-9.

Figure 4-9. *Loading the Picture from Cloud Storage*

For convenience, here's the entire source file for the activity:

```java
package com.laurencemoroney.firebasech4_2;

import android.graphics.Bitmap;
import android.graphics.BitmapFactory;
import android.support.annotation.NonNull;
import android.support.v7.app.AppCompatActivity;
import android.os.Bundle;
import android.view.View;
import android.widget.Button;
import android.widget.ImageView;

import com.google.android.gms.tasks.OnFailureListener;
import com.google.android.gms.tasks.OnSuccessListener;
import com.google.firebase.auth.AuthResult;
import com.google.firebase.auth.FirebaseAuth;
import com.google.firebase.storage.FileDownloadTask;
import com.google.firebase.storage.FirebaseStorage;
import com.google.firebase.storage.StorageReference;

import java.io.File;

public class MainActivity extends AppCompatActivity {

    Button LoginButton, GetPictureButton;
    FirebaseAuth mAuth;

    @Override
    protected void onCreate(Bundle savedInstanceState) {
        super.onCreate(savedInstanceState);
        setContentView(R.layout.activity_main);

        mAuth = FirebaseAuth.getInstance();

        LoginButton = (Button) findViewById(R.id.LoginButton);
        LoginButton.setOnClickListener(new View.OnClickListener() {
            @Override
            public void onClick(View v) {
                doSignIn();
            }
        });
```

```java
        GetPictureButton = (Button) findViewById(R.id.GetPictureButton);
        GetPictureButton.setOnClickListener(new View.OnClickListener() {
            @Override
            public void onClick(View v) {
                downloadPicture();


            }
        });
    }
    private void doSignIn() {
        mAuth.signInAnonymously().addOnSuccessListener(this, new OnSuccessListener
        <AuthResult>() {
            @Override
            public void onSuccess(AuthResult authResult) {
                GetPictureButton.setEnabled(true);
            }
        }).addOnFailureListener(this, new OnFailureListener() {
            @Override
            public void onFailure(@NonNull Exception e) {
                String err = e.getLocalizedMessage();
            }
        });


    }

    private void downloadPicture(){
        FirebaseStorage storage = FirebaseStorage.getInstance();
        StorageReference storageRef = storage.getReference();
        StorageReference imageRef = storageRef.child("image.jpg");
        try {
            final File localFile = File.createTempFile("image", "jpg");
            imageRef.getFile(localFile).addOnSuccessListener(new OnSuccessListener<File
            DownloadTask.TaskSnapshot>() {
                @Override
                public void onSuccess(FileDownloadTask.TaskSnapshot taskSnapshot) {
                    // Local file has been created, load it into ImageView
                    Bitmap myBitmap = BitmapFactory.decodeFile(localFile.getAbsolutePath());

                    ImageView myImage = (ImageView) findViewById(R.id.ShowPicture);

                    myImage.setImageBitmap(myBitmap);
                }
            }).addOnFailureListener(new OnFailureListener() {
                @Override
                public void onFailure(@NonNull Exception e) {
                    String err = e.getLocalizedMessage();
                }
            });
        } catch (Exception ex){
            String err = ex.getLocalizedMessage();
        }
    }

}
```

While in this case you downloaded the image to display it on your Android device, there are libraries such as Glide and Picasso that can use the URL of the image to display it directly, and persisting the image URL to the Realtime Database upon upload would allow you to do this. Additionally, the FirebaseUI libraries (see Chapter 2 where they are used in Auth scenarios for download instructions) provide a FirebaseImageLoader() class that can be used to access an image directly from Firebase Storage.

Reading Metadata

When a file is in Cloud Storage for Firebase, you'll be able to read and/or update its metadata. Let's update the app to view some of the metadata for this image so you can see how it works.

Update the Layout File

You'll update the layout file to add a new button to fetch the metadata and a TextView in which you can render this data.

Here's the full layout file including the new controls:

```
<?xml version="1.0" encoding="utf-8"?>
<android.support.constraint.ConstraintLayout xmlns:android="http://schemas.android.com/apk/
res/android"
    xmlns:app="http://schemas.android.com/apk/res-auto"
    xmlns:tools="http://schemas.android.com/tools"
    android:layout_width="match_parent"
    android:layout_height="match_parent"
    tools:context="com.laurencemoroney.firebasech4_2.MainActivity">
<LinearLayout android:orientation="vertical"
    android:layout_height="wrap_content"
    android:layout_width="wrap_content">
    <Button
        android:layout_width="wrap_content"
        android:layout_height="wrap_content"
        android:id="@+id/LoginButton"
        android:text="Log In"/>
    <Button
        android:layout_width="wrap_content"
        android:layout_height="wrap_content"
        android:id="@+id/GetPictureButton"
        android:text="Get Picture"
        android:enabled="false" />
    <Button
        android:layout_width="wrap_content"
        android:layout_height="wrap_content"
        android:id="@+id/GetMetadataButton"
        android:text="Get Metadata"
        android:enabled="false"/>
```

```xml
<ImageView
    android:layout_width="wrap_content"
    android:layout_height="wrap_content"
    android:id="@+id/ShowPicture" />
<TextView
    android:layout_width="wrap_content"
    android:layout_height="wrap_content"
    android:id="@+id/ShowPath"/>
</LinearLayout>

</android.support.constraint.ConstraintLayout>
```

When the user signs into the app, they'll be able to download an image. When the image is finished downloading, they'll access the metadata, so the GetMetaDataButton is disabled until the image is finished. Thus, in the onSuccess for the image download, you should add code to enable the button:

```
GetMetadataButton.setEnabled(true);
```

Let's now take a look at the code for the GetMetaDataButton. In your onCreate, you'll need to initialize it and the TextView that will render its results:

```java
GetMetadataButton = (Button) findViewById(R.id.GetMetadataButton);
GetMetadataButton.setOnClickListener(new View.OnClickListener() {
    @Override
    public void onClick(View v) {
        getMetadata();
    }
});
ShowPathTextView = (TextView) findViewById(R.id.ShowPath);
```

When the user touches the button, the getMetadata() function is called. Let's take a look at that:

```java
private void getMetadata(){
    FirebaseStorage storage = FirebaseStorage.getInstance();
    StorageReference storageRef = storage.getReference();
    StorageReference imageRef = storageRef.child("image.jpg");
    imageRef.getMetadata().addOnSuccessListener(new OnSuccessListener<StorageMetadata>() {
        @Override
        public void onSuccess(StorageMetadata storageMetadata) {
            String url = storageMetadata.getDownloadUrl().toString();
            ShowPathTextView.setText(url);
        }
    }).addOnFailureListener(new OnFailureListener() {
        @Override
        public void onFailure(@NonNull Exception e) {
            String foo = e.getLocalizedMessage();
        }
    });
}
```

As with the image upload/download it creates a reference to Firebase Storage, and uses that to get a reference to this image. Then, once you have a reference to the image, you can call getMetadata() on that reference. This is an asynchronous function that will call back to its onSuccess if it completes successfully. A StorageMetadata object is passed to this, and from that you can access metadata about the object in storage. In this case I call the getDownloadUrl() method to get the URL to download.

Figure 4-10 shows this in action, where you can see the downloaded URL.

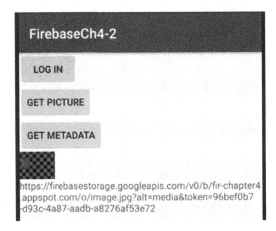

Figure 4-10. *Accessing metadata for a file in Storage*

Next Steps

Because Cloud Storage for Firebase is built on top of Google Cloud Storage, there's a whole lot more you can do in GCS. You may have noticed, for example, that I used a hard-coded file name for upload and download. If you want to access files in Cloud Storage for Firebase, you have to know their names. Typically, upon upload, you would write data to the realtime database with the file name and URI, and you could read it back from there if you wanted to know all the files in storage. Google Cloud Storage is a lower-level API, which offers you things such as listing the files in a particular storage bucket. It's beyond the scope of this book to go into it in detail, but you can learn more at https://cloud.google.com/storage/.

Summary

In this chapter you took a look at Cloud Storage for Firebase, a powerful, simple and cost-effective object storage service built for massive scale. You saw how to use it to upload and download files, as well as access their metadata, and you saw how the underlying asynchronous model – which provides service regardless of network quality – was available with a very simple programming model. Being able to store files in the cloud is pretty cool, and you'll extend this in the next chapter into building a web site that runs in the cloud using Firebase Hosting!

Using Firebase Hosting

Firebase Hosting is designed to provide fast, globally cached and secure hosting for your web app. It's used for web sites that host static files – such as HTML, JavaScript, CSS, and more. This gives you the ability to build and host a progressive web app with the likes of Angular.

It works natively with SSL, so you don't need to handle registering certificates in order to get an HTTPS connection. Content in Firebase hosting is edge-cached on solid state devices at a variety of Content Delivery networks around the world, giving your users a fast connection wherever they are. It also provides multiple snapshots of your site, so you can roll back to previous versions at a moment's notice.

Deployment to Firebase Hosting is handled using the Firebase Command Line Interface (CLI). This will be the first time you've seen that in this book, so you'll first look at installing and using it, before then building a simple site that takes advantage of Firebase Hosting's performance.

The Firebase CLI

The Firebase Command Line Interface (CLI) is a tool for managing some aspects of Firebase Development including Firebase Hosting, Functions, and more. You'll need it for this chapter.

Installing the Firebase CLI

The Firebase Command Line Interface (CLI) requires Node.js on your development machine. So if you don't have it already, you can download it from nodejs.org. This installs the Node Package Manager (npm) tool that is used to install the Firebase CLI.

Once you have npm, you can install the Firebase tools with this command:

```
sudo npm install -g firebase-tools
```

© Laurence Moroney 2017
L. Moroney, *The Definitive Guide to Firebase*, https://doi.org/10.1007/978-1-4842-2943-9_5

Once it completes, you'll need to associate it with your Firebase account. You do this by logging in from the command line with this command:

```
firebase login
```

You'll notice that a URL gets generated in the command line window, and your browser may open to a page asking you to sign in. See Figure 5-1.

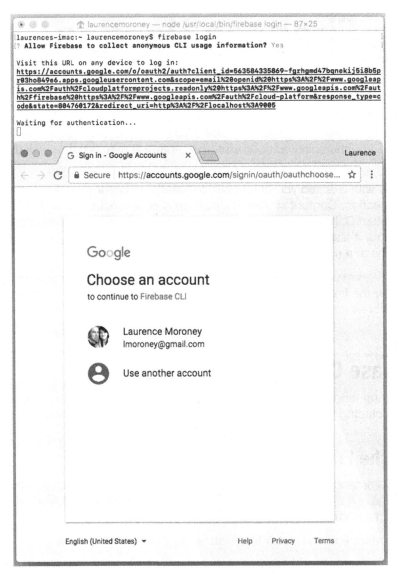

Figure 5-1. Authenticating with Firebase CLI

Be sure to sign in with the same account that you use for your Firebase Console projects. This will give you the ability to access them with the CLI. After signing in, you'll be asked to give the CLI various permissions as shown in Figure 5-2.

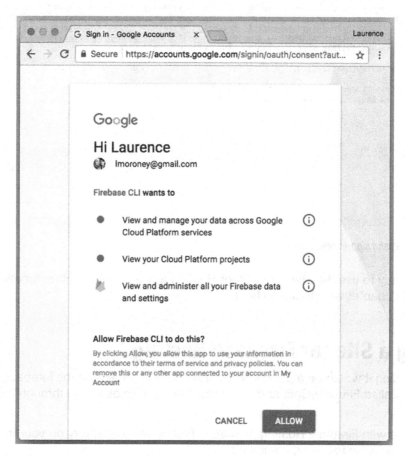

Figure 5-2. Giving the CLI permissions

If you agree to grant these permissions, click 'Allow', and you'll see a message saying the Firebase CLI login was successful, and you can close the browser window. In your terminal you'll see that you successfully signed in. See Figure 5-3.

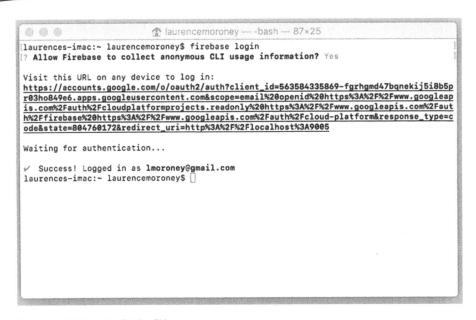

Figure 5-3. Successful sign-in with the CLI

You're now ready to use the Firebase CLI for Hosting and a variety of other functions, but for the rest of this chapter we'll focus on hosting.

Creating a Site for Firebase Hosting

Before continuing it would be a good idea to create a new project on the Firebase Console. I created one called FirebaseCh5, and you'll see it referred to as we go through the next steps.

To create a site with Firebase Hosting, you must first create a directory on your machine for it. You do this with the following command:

```
firebase init
```

This will give you a screen with a number of options – to create a database, to use Cloud Functions for Firebase, or to use Hosting. For this chapter you're going to use the third option: Hosting. See Figure 5-4. Use the arrow keys to navigate up and down the list, and press the space bar to select your desired features.

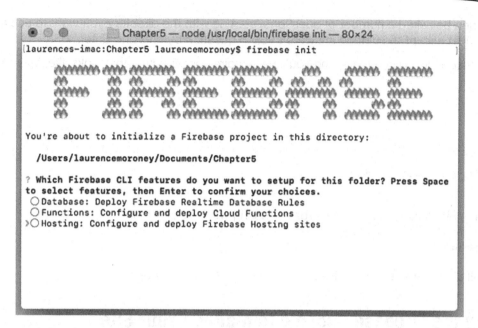

Figure 5-4. Using the CLI to set up hosting

Do note the directory that the project will be initialized in. You should be in that directory and run Firebase init from there to be sure.

You'll be asked to select the default Firebase project for this directory. Use the one that you created for this chapter (in my case FirebaseCh5) and press Enter. See Figure 5-5.

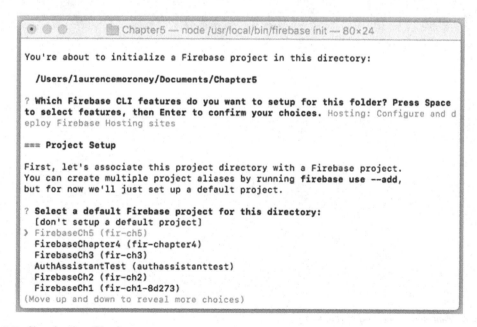

Figure 5-5. Choosing your Directory

You'll then be asked a number of questions, starting with the directory you want to use as public. Just accept the default answers to each question by pressing Enter.

Your initialization will complete, and you'll have a directory structure that looks like Figure 5-6.

▼ 📁 Chapter5	Today, 8:15 AM	--	Folder
📄 firebase.json	Today, 8:14 AM	46 bytes	Plain Text File
▼ 📁 public	Today, 8:14 AM	--	Folder
📄 404.html	Today, 8:14 AM	2 KB	HTML
📄 index.html	Today, 8:14 AM	4 KB	HTML

Figure 5-6. Your Directory Structure

You can now deploy this site to Firebase hosting with this command:

```
firebase deploy
```

This will upload the template files to your Firebase hosting account.

Using the Firebase Console to Manage Your Site

If you open your Firebase Console (console.firebase.google.com) and navigate to your project – in this case fir-ch5 as show in in Figure 5-5 – you can then see how to manage your web site. Click the hosting link on the left, and you'll see details on the site, including its domain and deployment history. See Figure 5-7.

Figure 5-7. Managing the hosting of your site

First off, you'll see that the site is hosted at the <project-name>.firebaseapp.com site, in this case fir-ch5.firebaseapp.com. Go take a look at that URL, and you'll see the default site that was created for you by the CLI.

You can also connect a domain name to it by clicking on the 'Connect Domain' button. We'll step through that later in this chapter. Finally, you can see your deployment history, so you can manage which version of the site you should run as the 'live' master.

A Real-World Example: Handling Zoomable Images

Open Seadragon is an open source viewer for high resolution zoomable images. It's built in pure JavaScript, so it may be perfect for our needs! Here's an example of a site built using it – it's called a million pages in one: http://labs.statsbiblioteket.dk/zoom/.

It provides a newspaper image, which when zoomed in on provides a grid of thousands more newspaper images. These can be zoomed in on in the same way, hence the name a million pages in one.

In this section you'll build a web site that hosts an image containing 100 million pixels, and see how fast it is handled using Firebase hosting.

Preparing the Image

You can download the image at this link: https://storage.googleapis.com/firebase-resources/skbook.png.

In order to use it with Open Seadragon, you'll need to slice the image up into tiles at various zoom levels. One open source tool that may be helpful is available in Python called deepzoom.py. You can download it here: https://github.com/openzoom/deepzoom.py.

Note, on many systems you may need to 'pip install image' in order to get the image slicer to work. If you encounter errors in the follow steps, give that a try.

If you use deepzoom.py, after installing, you'll see an examples directory containing a folder called 'helloworld'. Copy the image into that folder, and edit the helloworld.py script like this:

```python
#!/usr/bin/env python
# -*- coding: utf-8 -*-

import deepzoom

# Specify your source image
SOURCE = "sk10x10-3.png"

# Create Deep Zoom Image creator with weird parameters
creator = deepzoom.ImageCreator(tile_size=128, tile_overlap=2, tile_format="png",
                                image_quality=0.8, resize_filter="bicubic")

# Create Deep Zoom image pyramid from source
creator.create(SOURCE, "sk.dzi")
```

Once this is done, you can execute this code with:

```
./helloworld.py
```

The image is larger than the limit that Python imaging can handle, so you'll get a DecompressionBobWarning. That's ok; you can ignore it and continue. It should take a few minutes to complete the slicing of the image.

Once it's done, you'll see a directory called sk_files containing multiple subdirectories. You'll also see an 'sk.dzi' file, which is the index into all the tiles. See Figure 5-8.

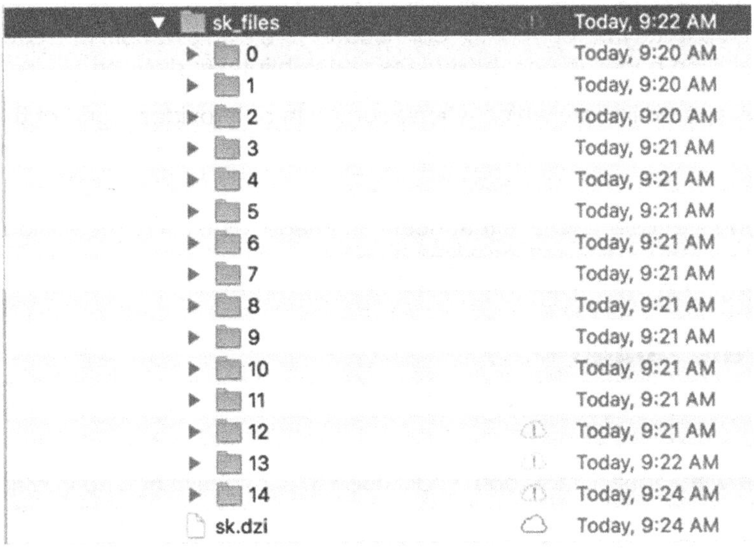

▼ 🗀 sk_files		Today, 9:22 AM
▶ 🗀 0		Today, 9:20 AM
▶ 🗀 1		Today, 9:20 AM
▶ 🗀 2		Today, 9:20 AM
▶ 🗀 3		Today, 9:21 AM
▶ 🗀 4		Today, 9:21 AM
▶ 🗀 5		Today, 9:21 AM
▶ 🗀 6		Today, 9:21 AM
▶ 🗀 7		Today, 9:21 AM
▶ 🗀 8		Today, 9:21 AM
▶ 🗀 9		Today, 9:21 AM
▶ 🗀 10		Today, 9:21 AM
▶ 🗀 11		Today, 9:21 AM
▶ 🗀 12		Today, 9:21 AM
▶ 🗀 13		Today, 9:22 AM
▶ 🗀 14		Today, 9:24 AM
🗋 sk.dzi		Today, 9:24 AM

Figure 5-8. The Processed Image

Copy all of these into the 'public' folder that you created with the Firebase CLI earlier.

You next need to edit the index.html file to use Open Seadragon and point it at this file.

Creating the Page

In the public folder, you'll have an index.html file. Open it, and replace its contents with this code:

```
<!DOCTYPE html>
<meta charset="utf-8">
<title>Index Page</title>
<html>
<head>
        <script type="text/javascript" src="https://openseadragon.github.io/openseadragon/
        openseadragon.min.js"></script>
                <style>
```

```
        body > div {
                position: absolute;
                top: 0;
                bottom: 0;
                left: 0;
                right: 0;
                display: flex;
                justify-content: space-around;
                align-items: center;
                flex-wrap: wrap;
                background-color: #FAFAFA;
                                }
        </style>
</head>
<body>
  <div id="openseadragon1"></div>
  <script>
    var viewer = OpenSeadragon({
      id: 'openseadragon1',
      prefixUrl: 'https://openseadragon.github.io/openseadragon/images/',
      tileSources: 'sk.dzi',
        maxZoomLevel: 200
    });
  </script>
</html>
```

This does a number of things. First of all it loads the openseadragon javascript libraries in the initial script tag. Then, it created a style for the body that fills the available space. Then within a div called 'openseadragon1' it points the Open Seadragon library at sk.szi that we've just created.

The prefixUrl parameter is used to load the UI controls for 'Home', 'Zoom In', 'Zoom Out', etc. You'll see them in a moment.

From the terminal, now issue the 'firebase deploy' command. You'll see that the tiled files will upload. It may take some time because there are several thousand files. See Figure 5-9.

```
[laurences-imac:public laurencemoroney$ firebase deploy                                    ]

=== Deploying to 'fir-ch5'...

i  deploying hosting
i  hosting: preparing public directory for upload...
✔  hosting: 8391 files uploaded successfully
i  starting release process (may take several minutes)...

✔  Deploy complete!

Project Console: https://console.firebase.google.com/project/fir-ch5/overview
Hosting URL: https://fir-ch5.firebaseapp.com
laurences-imac:public laurencemoroney$ []
```

Figure 5-9. Deploying the OpenSeadragon-based site to Firebase Hosting

Now, if you return to the Firebase Console, you'll see the new site in the deployment history. See Figure 5-10.

Figure 5-10. *Updated Deployment History*

You can now visit the site to see it in action – the URL is on the hosting page. In this case it's fir-ch5.firebaseapp.com

As an example of how detailed the image is, you can zoom in on the character's eye to see a reflection of what was behind the virtual camera when this image was rendered, as well as fine detail like eyelashes and skin pores! See Figure 5-11.

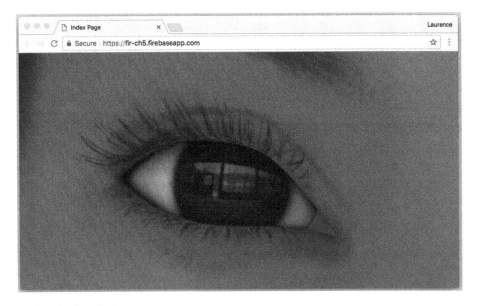

Figure 5-11. *Zooming into the image*

You'll also see how fast and fluid the downloading of the image tiles is thanks to Firebase Hosting's edge caching. In many cases it will be seamless.

Mapping a Domain Name to Your Site

The Firebase Console also allows you to map a domain name to your site with the Connect Domain button. Let's take a look at how this works. In this step, I'll show how to register a domain name at https://domains.google, and then use that domain on this site.

When you visit the Google Domains site while logged into your Google Account, you can search for a domain name to see if it is available. I used firebasebook0ch5.com and got the results from Figure 5-12.

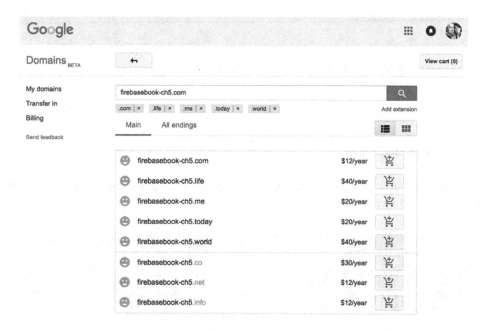

Figure 5-12. Getting a Domain on Google Domains

As it was available, I purchased it. Once that was done, I could see in the 'My Domains' section that the domain was available for editing. See Figure 5-13.

DOMAIN	WEBSITE	EMAIL	DNS	SETTINGS	EXPIRES
firebasebook-ch5.com +⚎	▤	✉	▤	⚙	364 days

Figure 5-13. The Domain name in Google Domains

Leave this window open; you'll need it in a moment. Go to the Firebase Console, and press the 'Connect Domain' button.

You'll be asked for the domain name. Enter it exactly as you registered it – in this case firebasebook-ch5.com. You can leave the 'Redirect' check box unchecked. See Figure 5-14.

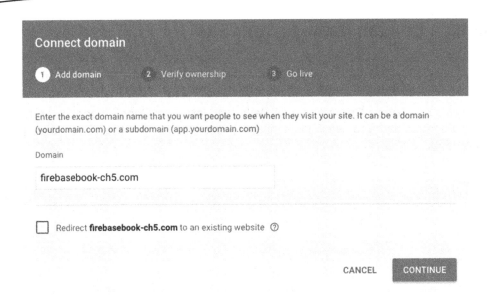

Figure 5-14. *Mapping a domain name*

Press Continue and you'll be asked to verify ownership of the site. This will involve adding a number of 'A' records as shown in Figure 5-15.

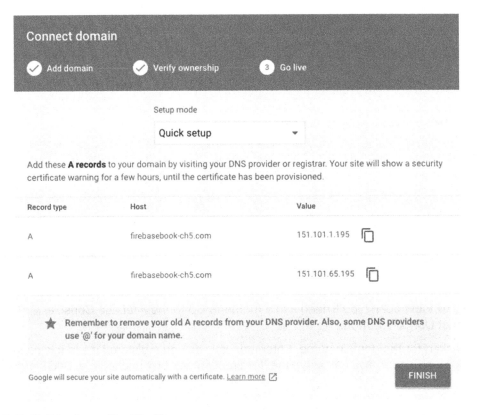

Figure 5-15. *Verifying Ownership of the Site*

Now on the Google Domains site, for your domain, click the button in the DNS column, and scroll to the bottom of the page. You'll see a section called 'Custom resource records'; add a single record containing both IP addresses that the Firebase Console recommended as shown in Figure 5-16.

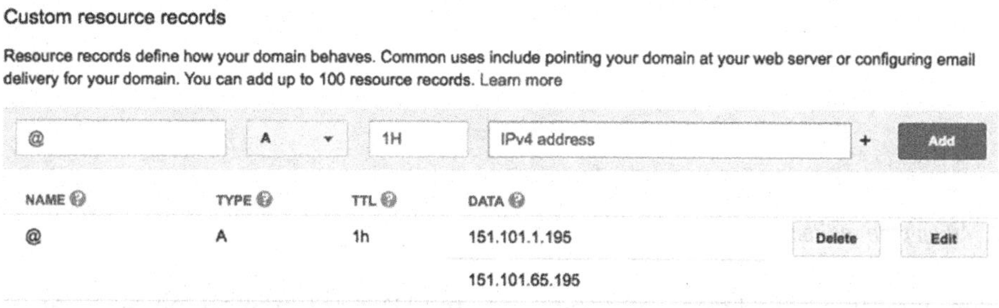

Figure 5-16. *Adding the DNS settings for your domain name*

Note that this is a single record, and not two separate ones. When adding the IP address, you'll see a small '+' to the right of the text field. Use that to add the second one.

It will take some time for Firebase to set up the domain for HTTPS – which can take up to two hours. While it's working on this, you'll see 'Pending' in the domain name field in the console. See Figure 5-17.

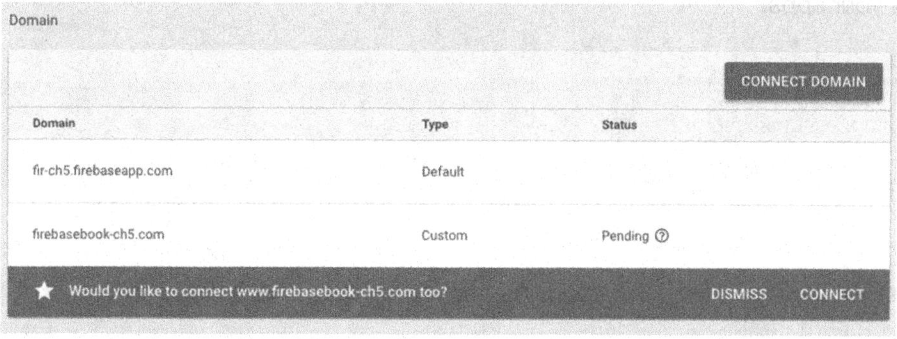

Figure 5-17. *Adding the domain name*

You'll notice that Firebase also asks you if you want to add the 'www' prefix. Press 'Connect' to do this by setting up a redirect.

When you do this, you'll see another record added to the Domains list. See Figure 5-18.

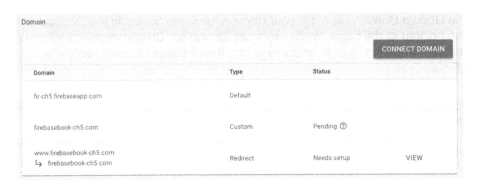

Figure 5-18. Adding the redirect

Once you've done this, you'll also need to update the DNS settings on the registrar.

Summary

In this chapter you got a taste of Firebase Hosting, and how you can use it to build web sites using static HTML and JavaScript. You saw how you can use these to create a responsive, fluid site using Open Seadragon. You also saw how you can manage your site, including setting up a domain name and a redirect. In the next chapter, you'll switch gears back to mobile development, focusing on how to use Firebase Test Lab for Android to do automatic testing of your apps.

Chapter 6

Using Test Lab for Android

Because of the sheer diversity of Android devices, with many types available in many different countries, testing an app on Android can be very difficult to do. The goal for the Firebase Test Lab for Android is to give you a cloud-based infrastructure where a wide variety of devices is available. Instead of managing and maintaining these diverse devices yourself, the goal is to give you a place where you upload your app and a suite of basic tests, including navigation, entering data, clicking buttons, etc., is performed on that app for you. There are two main types of test – automated (or Robo) tests where the infrastructure intelligently works its way through your app; and user-defined, where you can specify what to test and how.

When the tests are run, you'll get a report back from Firebase Test Lab showing you how your app performed, including screenshots, stack traces, and more.

In this chapter you'll take a look at how to use Test Lab, and as an example, you'll test the popular open source application Friendly Chat using it. So first, let's get up and running with Friendly Chat.

Getting the App

Friendly Chat can be downloaded from https://github.com/firebase/friendlychat-android. You'll see a folder in this called 'android', which contains the finished Android version of the app. When you open this, you'll likely see an error that the app wouldn't compile because of a missing google-services.json file. You can fix that by connecting the app to a Firebase project. The easiest way to do that is with the assistant. Open it, and in the Analytics section, click on the 'Log an Analytics event' as shown in Figure 6-1.

© Laurence Moroney 2017
L. Moroney, *The Definitive Guide to Firebase*, https://doi.org/10.1007/978-1-4842-2943-9_6

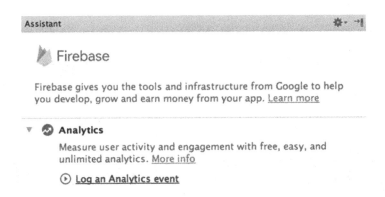

Figure 6-1. Using the Assistant to connect to Firebase

When you click this, you'll see the familiar 'Connect to Firebase' button. Use that to connect to an existing project or create a new one. I used a new project that I called 'FirebaseCh6'. Once the project is created and connected, a gradle sync will make that error go away. But before you can run the app, there are a couple of things you need to do in the Firebase Console.

Enabling Authentication

Friendly Chat uses a signed-in identity to provide information on who is saying what, and as such it needs Firebase Authentication to sign a user in. You'll use Google Sign-In for this, so in Firebase Console, choose 'Authentication' on the left, and then select 'Sign-In Method'. Pick 'Google', and set it to 'Enabled'. Your console should look like Figure 6-2 when you're done.

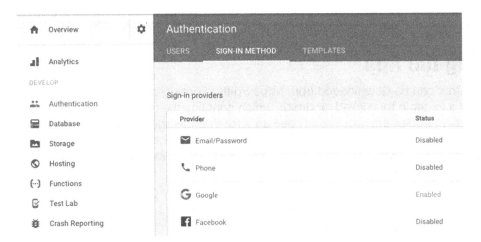

Figure 6-2. Enabling Google Authentication

Now when you run the app, you'll need to sign in with a Google Account. Test Lab will provide one for you automatically.

Enabling Database Rules

Friendly Chat lets authenticated users chat with each other by writing their messages as fields in a database. Every user can then see all the fields in the database using similar processes to what we saw in Chapter 3.

To do this, the rules on the database should allow reading and writing only to authenticated users. You can find this in the 'Database' section of the Firebase Console under 'rules'. They should be set by default, but if you need to change them, Figure 6-3 shows what the setting should be for this example.

Figure 6-3. Setting the Database Rules

Once this is done, you should be able to run and launch the app.

Using Friendly Chat

You can see Friendly Chat in Figure 6-4. It's a basic chat application that allows multiple users to sign in and chat with each other. In this case two users are signed in and chatting with each other. Each user will have an identical view of the chat.

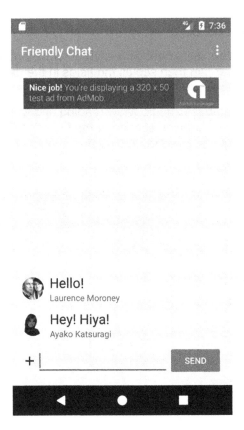

Figure 6-4. *Friendly Chat in Action*

Now that we have a working app, let's take a look at what will happen when we test it using Test Lab for Android!

First Steps: Testing Your APK

Now that you've compiled Friendly Chat, the next step is to prepare it for testing on Test Lab for Android. You do this by finding the APK. In Android Studio, under the Build menu, you'll see an option that reads 'Build APK'. Select this, and the app will build in the usual way. When it's complete, Android Studio will give you a little popup telling you that the build is complete, along with a link to open it in the appropriate file manager for your operating system. See Figure 6-5.

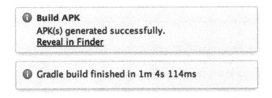

Figure 6-5. *Finding your APK*

Now that you have your APK, you can upload it to Test Lab for Android to run the basic Robo tests so you can see the possibilities. To do this, open your project on the Firebase Console (if you followed this chapter, you would have created one when you were linking Friendly Chat to Firebase in the 'Getting the App' section), and find the 'Test Lab for Android' link on the left. See Figure 6-6.

Figure 6-6. *Test Lab for Android*

If you have run any tests previously, they'll show up in the list that you can see in Figure 6-6. To start a new test, click the 'Run a Test' button, and select 'Run a Robo test' from the ensuing popup.

You'll then upload your APK, and when it's done, press the 'Continue' button. You'll then be able to pick which physical and which virtual devices you want to run your test on. Using the free tier, you are restricted in the amounts of these you can use each day as shown in Figure 6-7.

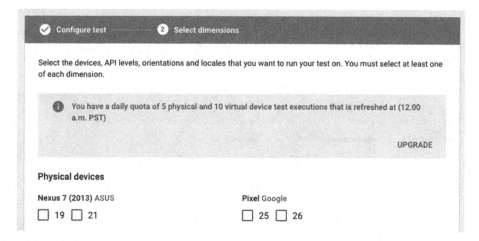

Figure 6-7. *Choosing your devices*

Choose a few devices, but don't use up your quota yet as you'll be doing more tests later. Be sure to check the Orientation as both Landscape and Portrait. When done, click the 'Start Tests' button at the bottom of the screen.

A new 'Matrix' screen will open up, showing the status of the tests. See Figure 6-8.

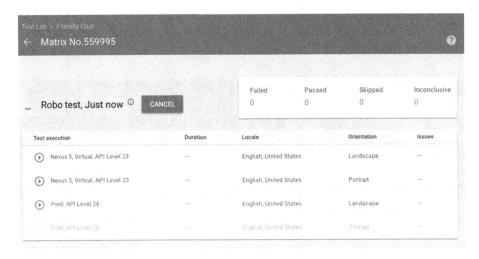

Figure 6-8. *Running Robo tests*

An arrow to the left of the device (as shown in the first three lines in Figure 6-8) determines that the test is executing. Give it a few moments and it will change to check marks, and you'll receive an email from Firebase notifying you.

Once the test is complete it will change to a check box, and then you can select one of the tests to see what happened. If you haven't changed Friendly Chat, you should see that all tests have passed. Select one of the tests to view the details. You'll then see something like Figure 6-9.

Figure 6-9. *Inspecting Test Lab reports*

There are a number of tabs:

- **Logs** gives you raw logs that were captured from the test. You can pick which types of logs you can see, defaulting ot 'Warning and Higher'. When the list is styled, you can see icons denoting what was captured – with the red 'E' for errors. Not that none of these errors caused the app to fail or crash, and the test passed.

- **Screenshots** show you which screenshots were captured. These are really useful in showing you how the Robo test worked its way around your app. If you take a look at the screenshots for Friendly Chat, for example, you'll see that it signed in successfully, but then only worked on the context menu, trying to do an app invite. This helps you craft your own tests – by figuring out what the Robo tests didn't cover.

- **Activity map** shows you how the Robo test flowed through the different activities, showing how the screenshots link together.

- **Videos** shows you a video that was captured of the test. Again, this can be used to help you tweak the tests to ensure that everything you want to be covered is done. For example, if you play back the FriendlyChat test, you'll see that it successfully hit the sign in button to sign into the app, but it then didn't know how to send a message, and was only able to acchess the 'Share' menu item. In the next section we'll look at how you can get it to test a core part of FriendlyChat – sending a message.

- **Performance** will only work on physical device tests. It shows you a chart of how the device CPU, Memory, and Network behaved correlated to a video of the test. So, for example, in Figure 6-10, you can see that by clicking on a CPU spike, the video automatically moved to that part of the test, so I could see what caused the spike!

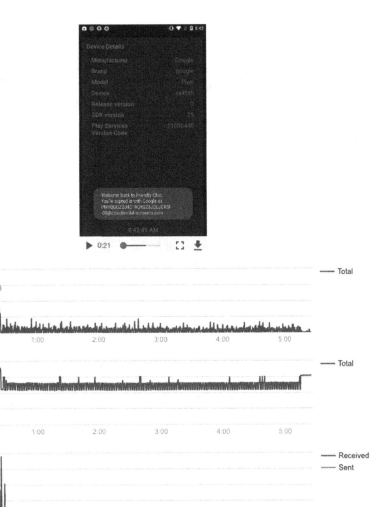

Figure 6-10. Correlating Performance with activity

So, while this test was useful, it was also limited. Let's see how we can customize test lab to run tests of our choosing – which we will do by having it send a message to FriendlyChat!

Creating Custom Tests

There are a number of ways that you can customize your testing, but let's first look at the Robo test, and how you can fix it to handle the issue we had in the previous section – that the core scenario in our App – actually chatting – is tested.

When you create a new test, turn on the advanced options at the bottom of the 'Test Dimensions' screen. You'll see that there are several options there – including 'Test Timeout', 'Max Depth', 'Test Account Credentials', and 'Additional Fields'.

You can use the 'Additional Fields' setting to enter text in the chat box. To do this, go back to your source code in Android Studio, and open the resource XML for your main activity. You should find it in res/layout/activity_main.xml.

After a quick inspection, you'll see that the input EditText is calld 'messageEditText'. See Figure 6-11.

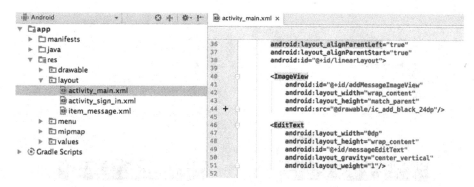

Figure 6-11. Finding the EditText field

Now, in Test Lab, you can specify this name, and the value that you want entered in the test run. See Figure 6-12.

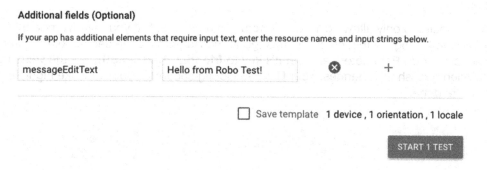

Figure 6-12. Customizing your test

Now when you run the test, the robot will attempt to edit text in that field. The user 'Nuage Laboratories' signed in and started entering text into the chat as you can see in Figure 6-13.

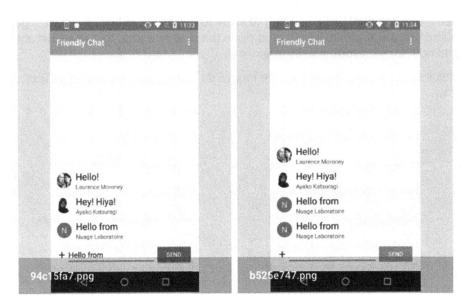

Figure 6-13. Customizing the tests

You'll notice that the text was truncated to just 'Hello from'. This is because Friendly Chat uses Remote Config to specify message length. You can learn more about Remote Config in Chapter 10.

The app defaults to only allowing 10 characters in a message, but you can override this using Remote Config. To test changing this, go to the Remote Config section of the Firebase Console, click 'Add Parameter', and set it's key to **friendly_msg_length.** Set the value to 40, and then publish the changes. Your Remote Config section should look like Figure 6-14 when you're done.

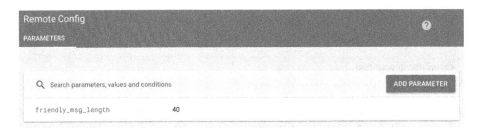

Figure 6-14. Setting Remote Config

Run the app locally to ensure that it works, and you should be able to enter a much longer message – see Figure 6-15.

Figure 6-15. Using Remote Config

Now that we know we can send a long message, try the Robo test again. Don't forget to set the text in the advanced options. Look back to Figure 6-12 for details on this.

Once you run the test, you can now look at the screenshots to see that not only did the app update its EditText length via Remote Config correctly – the robot test entering a long text field worked perfectly. See Figure 6-16.

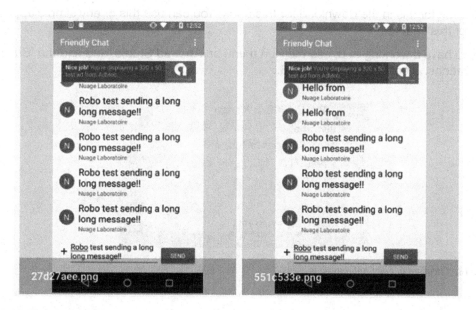

Figure 6-16. Custom Robo Test

This step involved building an app, finding the APK, and uploading it manually. But with Test Lab for Android you can also test directly from within Android Studio. Let's try that next.

Testing from Android Studio

To test from within Android Studio, let's build a simple app that has input and output so we can see how it works. It's a simple tip calculator, where you enter a value, and the app calculates what the tip should be using a number of different buttons, each with a percentage. You can see it in Figure 6-17.

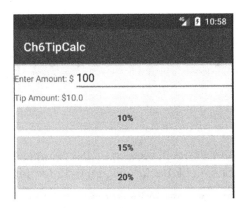

Figure 6-17. A Tip Calculator App

The full code for it is in the download for this book. You can use this or any simple app for the rest of this chapter.

When you have a working app, use the Run menu on Android Studio, and find the 'Build Configurations…' entry. See Figure 6-18.

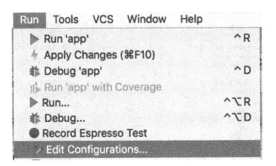

Figure 6-18. Choosing to Edit Configurations

When you select this, you'll get the Run/Debug configurations dialog. This dialog allows you to set up a testing configuration. See Figure 6-19.

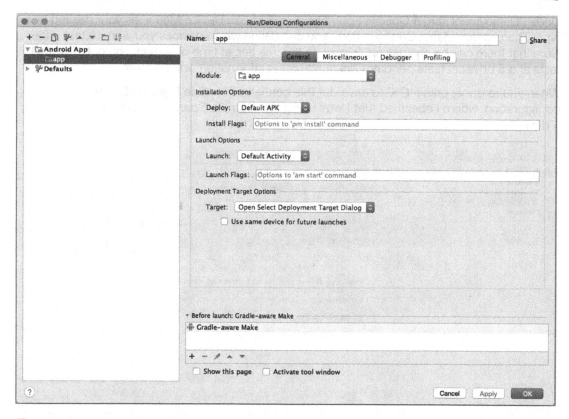

Figure 6-19. Run/Debug Configurations

On the top left-hand side of the dialog you'll see a '+'. Click on it, and a list with a number of options will pop up. From this list choose 'Android Instrumented Tests'. See Figure 6-20.

Figure 6-20. Adding a new Instrumented Test

Once you've done this, you'll need to fill out the details for the Instrumented Test. First off give it a name – in Figure 6-21, you'll see I named it TestTipCalc. Then you need to select a module. Typically this will be the 'app' module, as you want to test the app.

Under 'Deployment Target Options', put 'Firebase Test Lab Device Matrix' as your desired test type. Then, under 'Matrix Configuration', you can define which devices you want to test under. Note that there can be charges for Testing. In the free tier, at time of writing, you get 10 virtual tests and 5 physical tests per day. Click the 'Pricing Information' link for more details.

When you're done, press 'OK' to save out this configuration. See Figure 6-21 for my configuration, where I specified that I was using the 'Sample Spark Configuration' of 4 devices.

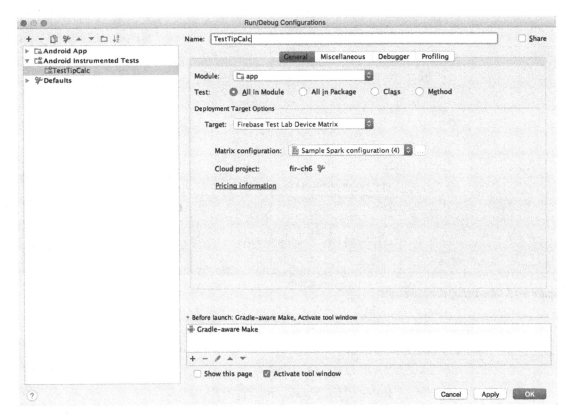

Figure 6-21. *Setting up an Instrumented Test*

Now, return to Android Studio, and in the configurations drop-down on the main toolbar (which probably reads 'app' right now), select the test configuration you just set up. In my case, I have 'TestTipCalc', and will select that. See Figure 6-22.

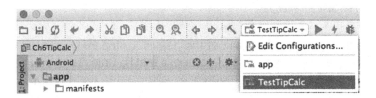

Figure 6-22. *Choosing the Instrumented Test*

Once you've done this, press the 'Run' button. You'll see that the tests will launch, and you'll get status in the Run window. See Figure 6-23.

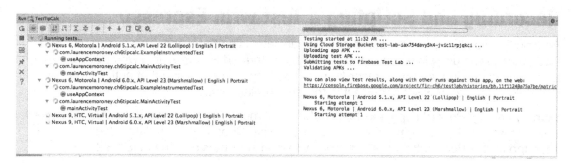

Figure 6-23. Running the tests

After a few minutes, the tests will stop. You'll see that there's a link to the tests in the results window. Click on it and you'll be taken to the Firebase Console with the tests open in the Test Lab section.

In this case I did the spark test with four devices, and you can see in Figure 6-24 that they all passed.

Test Lab > Ch6TipCalc				
← Matrix No 735595				

	Failed	Passed	Skipped	Inconclusive
✓ Instrumentation test, 7 minutes ago ①	0	4	0	0

Test execution	Duration	Locale	Orientation	Issues
✓ Nexus 9, Virtual, API Level 23	10 sec	English	Portrait	–
✓ Nexus 6, API Level 23	11 sec	English	Portrait	–
✓ Nexus 9, Virtual, API Level 22	8 sec	English	Portrait	–
✓ Nexus 6, API Level 22	9 sec	English	Portrait	–

Figure 6-24. The tests passed

By clicking through the tests, you can inspect the test cases, including seeing logs and videos of the test being performed. You can use these to tweak your tests to see if you have a false positive, as I did in this case.

With the tip calculator app you have the ability to type in a number, and then press buttons to calculate the tip. I didn't do any of these in this instrumented test – so all the app did was launch the app, and record that it did it successfully!

Let's take a look at scripting a test using Espresso in the next section.

Recording and Scripting a Test with Espresso

Android Studio allows you to record app interactivity using Espresso. This generates Java Code that will be used in testing, and Test Lab for Android is compatible with this code. It's as simple as running your app, recording your activity, and assigning that activity to a test. Let's take a look at how we can use it in the tip calculation app.

Start by finding 'Record Espresso Test' in the 'Run' menu. Once you've done this, you'll be asked to launch the app in the emulator or on-device. Choose the emulator. You'll see that your app and a 'Record Your test' window will open side-by-side. See Figure 6-25.

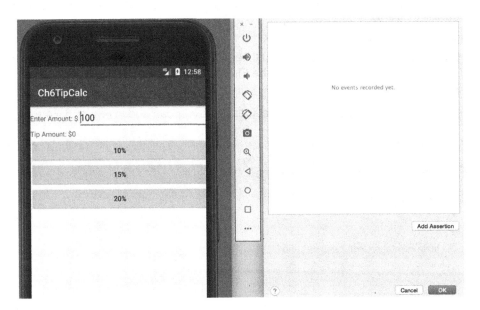

Figure 6-25. *Recording a test with Espresso*

Now start using the app. Push the tip buttons, or change the amount. You'll see that the 'Record Your Test' window will update with your activity. In the case of the tip app, I introduced a deliberate error – I can type text in the amount window, so when I do that, and try to calculate a tip, the app will crash. See Figure 6-26.

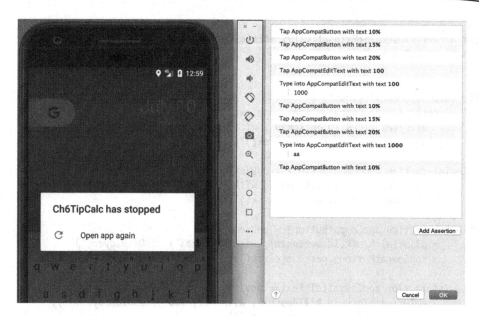

Figure 6-26. Recording Activity including a crash

Press OK, and you'll be asked to name the Test Class. It should default to MainActivityTest, so you can keep that. Take a look at the code that is generated for you – you will see that the class contains a number of commands in the constructor that match the actions you took in the emulator. Here's the code for the test in Figure 6-26:

```
package com.laurencemoroney.ch6tipcalc;

import android.support.test.espresso.ViewInteraction;
import android.support.test.rule.ActivityTestRule;
import android.support.test.runner.AndroidJUnit4;
import android.test.suitebuilder.annotation.LargeTest;

import org.junit.Rule;
import org.junit.Test;
import org.junit.runner.RunWith;

import static android.support.test.espresso.Espresso.onView;
import static android.support.test.espresso.action.ViewActions.click;
import static android.support.test.espresso.action.ViewActions.closeSoftKeyboard;
import static android.support.test.espresso.action.ViewActions.replaceText;
import static android.support.test.espresso.matcher.ViewMatchers.isDisplayed;
import static android.support.test.espresso.matcher.ViewMatchers.withId;
import static android.support.test.espresso.matcher.ViewMatchers.withText;
import static org.hamcrest.Matchers.allOf;

@LargeTest
@RunWith(AndroidJUnit4.class)
public class MainActivityTest {
```

```java
@Rule
public ActivityTestRule<MainActivity> mActivityTestRule = new ActivityTestRule<>
(MainActivity.class);

@Test
public void mainActivityTest() {
    ViewInteraction appCompatButton = onView(
            allOf(withId(R.id.button10), withText("10%"), isDisplayed()));
            appCompatButton.perform(click());

    ViewInteraction appCompatButton2 = onView(
            allOf(withId(R.id.button15), withText("15%"), isDisplayed()));
            appCompatButton2.perform(click());

    ViewInteraction appCompatButton3 = onView(
            allOf(withId(R.id.button20), withText("20%"), isDisplayed()));
            appCompatButton3.perform(click());

    ViewInteraction appCompatEditText = onView(
            allOf(withId(R.id.billAmount), withText("100"), isDisplayed()));
            appCompatEditText.perform(click());

    ViewInteraction appCompatEditText2 = onView(
            allOf(withId(R.id.billAmount), withText("100"), isDisplayed()));
            appCompatEditText2.perform(replaceText("1000"), closeSoftKeyboard());

    ViewInteraction appCompatButton4 = onView(
            allOf(withId(R.id.button10), withText("10%"), isDisplayed()));
            appCompatButton4.perform(click());

    ViewInteraction appCompatButton5 = onView(
            allOf(withId(R.id.button15), withText("15%"), isDisplayed()));
            appCompatButton5.perform(click());

    ViewInteraction appCompatButton6 = onView(
            allOf(withId(R.id.button20), withText("20%"), isDisplayed()));
            appCompatButton6.perform(click());

    ViewInteraction appCompatEditText3 = onView(
            allOf(withId(R.id.billAmount), withText("1000"), isDisplayed()));
            appCompatEditText3.perform(replaceText("aa"), closeSoftKeyboard());

    ViewInteraction appCompatButton7 = onView(
            allOf(withId(R.id.button10), withText("10%"), isDisplayed()));
            appCompatButton7.perform(click());

}

}
```

Now when you run the test, you'll see that the interactions you recorded using Espresso are tested against. In this case, the entire test failed because of the text I added. See Figure 6-27.

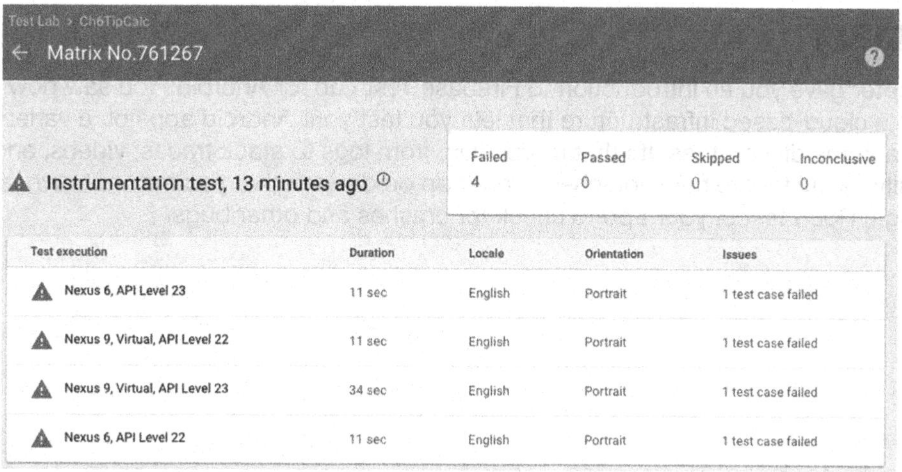

Figure 6-27. Failed Tests

But what's really nice about how Espresso generates Java code is that I can go into my code and edit it, without re-recording all the tests again. So, if you're doing the same testing as I did, you can find this code:

```
ViewInteraction appCompatEditText = onView(
        allOf(withId(R.id.billAmount), withText("100"), isDisplayed()));
        appCompatEditText.perform(click());

ViewInteraction appCompatEditText2 = onView(
        allOf(withId(R.id.billAmount), withText("100"), isDisplayed()));
        appCompatEditText2.perform(replaceText("aa"), closeSoftKeyboard());
```

Delete it, and then re-run the tests. You will see that the test passes, and you can check that it's the correct one by clicking on any of the tests and inspecting the results. As you can see in Figure 6-28, the test 'MainActivityTest', which was the one scripted in Espresso succeeded!

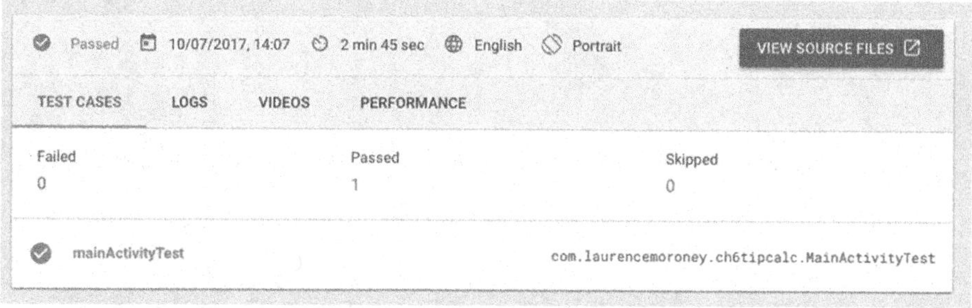

Figure 6-28. Passing Espresso test

Of course this is a very trivial case, and when you build apps that navigate between multiple activities, or perform tasks like signing in, you have the tools at your disposal to see how your app will behave on multiple devices!

Summary

This chapter gave you an introduction to Firebase Test Lab for Android. You saw how it provides a cloud-based infrastructure that lets you test your Android apps on a variety of devices and the different results that it provides, from logs to stack traces, videos, and more. It's a really useful tool to help you check your app on devices that you may not own, as well as having a Robo test of your app to check for crashes and other bugs.

Understanding Crashes

One of the themes of Firebase is to understand App Quality, and part of this is knowing when and why your app is crashing when people around the world are using it. To this end, the Crash Reporting functionality of Firebase is available as a way to help you understand which users are having problems, complete with stack traces of those problems. After releasing Firebase Crash Reporting, an acquisition by Google brought Fabric and its Crashlytics product into the Firebase family. The guidance is that if you haven't yet started to use Crash Reporting in your apps, that you should begin with Crashlytics. To that end, I'll be covering Crashlytics in this chapter.

Note that this is for *client*-side crashes only. If you are writing any server code outside of Firebase, then Google Stackdriver Error Reporting is available, but it is beyond the scope of this book.

Getting Started with Crashlytics

On the Firebase Console, create a new project. I called mine FirebaseCh7. For most of the chapters in this book you've been doing this using the Firebase Assistant in Android Studio, but in this case, do it directly at console.firebase.google.com. Click the 'Crash Reporting' tab, and you'll be given two options – to use 'Fabric's Crashlytics' or 'Crash Reporting'. See Figure 7-1.

© Laurence Moroney 2017

L. Moroney, *The Definitive Guide to Firebase*, https://doi.org/10.1007/978-1-4842-2943-9_7

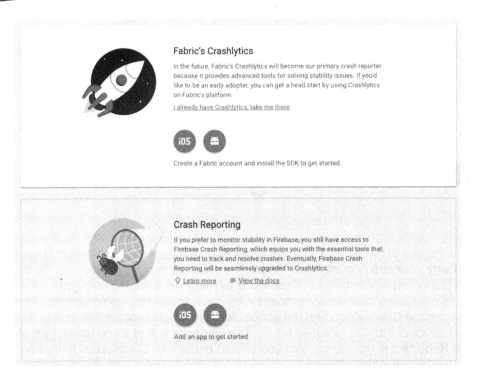

Figure 7-1. Choosing your crash reporting methodology

When Crashlytics becomes the primary crash reporter, the options may look different, but we'll follow this flow for now.

You'll see in the Crashlytics section that there are icons for iOS and Android. Select the Android one, and you'll be taken to the Crashlytics site. You're greeted by a dialog that mentions your need to create a Fabric account and install the Crashlytics SDK. You'll do the installation in the next step, but beforehand make sure you sign up and sign in to a Fabric account.

Installing Crashlytics

Create a new app in Android Studio using the empty activity template as before. Don't link it to a Firebase project yet. Android Studio projects have two build.gradle files. Make sure that you use the *Project* file, and not the *App* one to make these edits. See Figure 7-2.

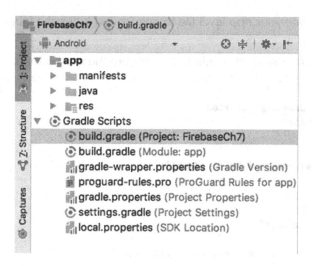

Figure 7-2. Your build.gradle files

Be sure to update the **project** level file to include the fabric tools on the classpath. Here's what your full file should look like:

```
// Top-level build file where you can add configuration options common to all sub-projects/
modules.

buildscript {

    repositories {
        google()
        jcenter()
        maven { url 'https://maven.fabric.io/public'}
    }
    dependencies {
        classpath 'com.android.tools.build:gradle:3.0.0-beta2'
        classpath 'io.fabric.tools:gradle:1.+'

        // NOTE: Do not place your application dependencies here; they belong
        // in the individual module build.gradle files
    }
}

allprojects {
    repositories {
        google()
        jcenter()
    }
}

task clean(type: Delete) {
    delete rootProject.buildDir
}
```

Next you need to update your **app** level file to ensure that it has the fabric and Crashlytics dependencies.

This requires you to add the io.fabric plug-in, configure the maven repository location, and implement the dependency. Here's what the file should look like when you're done:

```
apply plugin: 'com.android.application'
apply plugin: 'io.fabric'

repositories {
    maven { url 'https://maven.fabric.io/public'}
}
android {
    compileSdkVersion 26
    buildToolsVersion "26.0.1"
    defaultConfig {
        applicationId "com.laurencemoroney.firebasech7"
        minSdkVersion 15
        targetSdkVersion 26
        versionCode 1
        versionName "1.0"
        testInstrumentationRunner "android.support.test.runner.AndroidJUnitRunner"
    }
    buildTypes {
        release {
            minifyEnabled false
            proguardFiles getDefaultProguardFile('proguard-android.txt'), 'proguard-rules.pro'
        }
    }
}

dependencies {
    implementation fileTree(dir: 'libs', include: ['*.jar'])
    implementation 'com.android.support:appcompat-v7:26.0.1'
    implementation 'com.android.support.constraint:constraint-layout:1.0.2'
    testImplementation 'junit:junit:4.12'
    androidTestImplementation 'com.android.support.test:runner:1.0.0'
    androidTestImplementation 'com.android.support.test.espresso:espresso-core:3.0.0'
    compile('com.crashlytics.sdk.android:crashlytics:2.6.8@aar'){
        transitive = true;
    }
}
```

You'll probably see that a gradle sync fails at this point. Don't worry, because you still need to add your API key to the Android Manifest before you can continue. To get the API key, log into your account on Fabric.io. If you don't have one already, make sure you sign up for one. When you're signed in, click the 'Settings' icon in the top right.

You'll see a screen offering to tailor your experience, showing 'Apps', 'Organizations', 'Account', and 'Notifications. See Figure 7-3.

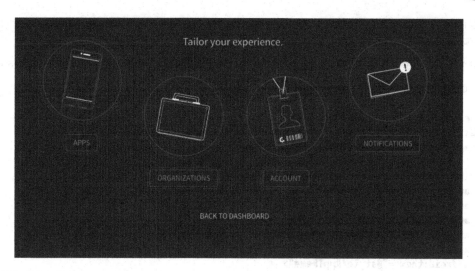

Figure 7-3. Fabric Options

Select 'Organizations', and you'll see a list of organizations in this console. If you've just signed up, you'll see <Your Name>'s projects like in Figure 7-4.

Figure 7-4. Organizations list

Click on this and you'll be taken to a card listing your projects, including users, apps, and more. At the bottom of the title, there's a link to the API key. Click on this. See Figure 7-5.

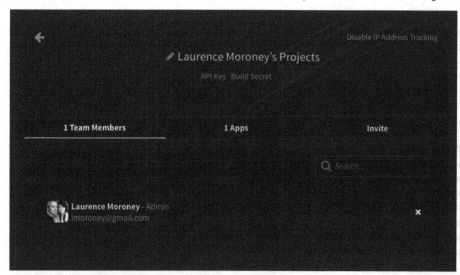

Figure 7-5. Getting your API key

Click on the API key link, and your API key will be revealed. Copy it to the clipboard and return to Android Studio.

Update your Android Manifest file to add metadata for the API Key and Internet permissions.

When you're done it should look like this:

```xml
<?xml version="1.0" encoding="utf-8"?>
<manifest xmlns:android="http://schemas.android.com/apk/res/android"
    package="com.laurencemoroney.firebasech7">

    <application
        android:allowBackup="true"
        android:icon="@mipmap/ic_launcher"
        android:label="@string/app_name"
        android:roundIcon="@mipmap/ic_launcher_round"
        android:supportsRtl="true"
        android:theme="@style/AppTheme">
        <activity android:name=".MainActivity">
            <intent-filter>
                <action android:name="android.intent.action.MAIN" />

                <category android:name="android.intent.category.LAUNCHER" />
            </intent-filter>
        </activity>
        <meta-data
            android:name="io.fabric.ApiKey"
            android:value="<Your API KEY>"
            />
    </application>
    <uses-permission android:name="android.permission.INTERNET" />
</manifest>
```

Now go to your layout file, and add a button. Here's the code:

```xml
<?xml version="1.0" encoding="utf-8"?>
<android.support.constraint.ConstraintLayout xmlns:android="http://schemas.android.com/apk/res/android"
    xmlns:app="http://schemas.android.com/apk/res-auto"
    xmlns:tools="http://schemas.android.com/tools"
    android:layout_width="match_parent"
    android:layout_height="match_parent"
    tools:context="com.laurencemoroney.firebasech7.MainActivity">

    <TextView
        android:layout_width="wrap_content"
        android:layout_height="wrap_content"
        android:text="Hello World!"
        app:layout_constraintBottom_toBottomOf="parent"
        app:layout_constraintLeft_toLeftOf="parent"
        app:layout_constraintRight_toRightOf="parent"
        app:layout_constraintTop_toTopOf="parent" />
```

```xml
<Button
    android:layout_width="match_parent"
    android:layout_height="match_parent"
    android:text="Crash now!"
    android:id="@+id/crashButton" />

</android.support.constraint.ConstraintLayout>
```

Finally, in your code you'll need to instantiate Crashlytics with Fabric using `Fabric.with(this, new Crashlytics())` and implement a crash by clicking the button – it will simply throw a runtime exception. Here's the code:

```java
package com.laurencemoroney.firebasech7;

import android.support.v7.app.AppCompatActivity;
import android.os.Bundle;
import android.view.View;
import android.widget.Button;

import com.crashlytics.android.Crashlytics;

import io.fabric.sdk.android.Fabric;

public class MainActivity extends AppCompatActivity {

    @Override
    protected void onCreate(Bundle savedInstanceState) {
        super.onCreate(savedInstanceState);
        Fabric.with(this, new Crashlytics());
        setContentView(R.layout.activity_main);
        Button crashButton = (Button) findViewById(R.id.crashButton);
        crashButton.setOnClickListener(new View.OnClickListener() {
            @Override
            public void onClick(View view) {
                throw new RuntimeException("Ch7 Crashed!");
            }
        });
    }
}
```

Run the app and you'll see something like Figure 7-6.

Figure 7-6. Running the app

Press the button, and the app will crash; see Figure 7-7.

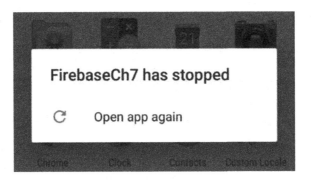

Figure 7-7. The app crashes

Now return to your Crashlytics console, and go to the dashboard. You'll see a list of crashes, grouped into crash types. Because you only have this one, there should be one entry on the list. See Figure 7-8.

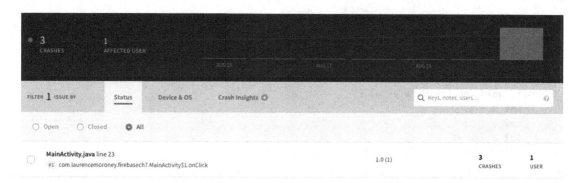

Figure 7-8. Exploring the dashboard

You can already see that the crash is in MainActivity.java, and it's in an onClick. This helps you debug the crash if it happens on somebody else's device. Click on the crash, and more detail will open up. From here you can see details about the device and its operating system, as well as more details on the crash itself. Here we can see it's a runtime exception. See Figure 7-9.

Figure 7-9. Exploring the crash details

Click the 'Raw Text' link, and you'll get a full stack trace of the crash, which should look like this:

```
Fatal Exception: java.lang.RuntimeException: Ch7 Crashed!
        at com.laurencemoroney.firebasech7.MainActivity$1.onClick(MainActivity.java:23)
        at android.view.View.performClick(View.java:5637)
        at android.view.View$PerformClick.run(View.java:22429)
        at android.os.Handler.handleCallback(Handler.java:751)
        at android.os.Handler.dispatchMessage(Handler.java:95)
        at android.os.Looper.loop(Looper.java:154)
        at android.app.ActivityThread.main(ActivityThread.java:6119)
        at java.lang.reflect.Method.invoke(Method.java)
        at com.android.internal.os.ZygoteInit$MethodAndArgsCaller.run(ZygoteInit.java:886)
        at com.android.internal.os.ZygoteInit.main(ZygoteInit.java:776)
```

Now go back to your code, and change the onClick handler to this:

```
Button crashButton = (Button) findViewById(R.id.crashButton);
crashButton.setOnClickListener(new View.OnClickListener() {
    @Override
    public void onClick(View view) {
        int x = 1;
        int y = 0;
        int z = x/y;
    }
});
```

Run the app and press the button again. This time the app will crash because of the divide by zero error. On the Crashlytics console, you'll now see that there are two entries – it groups the entries based on error type. Select the second one, and you'll see the exception details – including the fact that it's a divide by zero error are available to you. The exception on the console will look like this:

```
Fatal Exception: java.lang.ArithmeticException: divide by zero
        at com.laurencemoroney.firebasech7.MainActivity$1.onClick(MainActivity.java:25)
        at android.view.View.performClick(View.java:5637)
        at android.view.View$PerformClick.run(View.java:22429)
        at android.os.Handler.handleCallback(Handler.java:751)
        at android.os.Handler.dispatchMessage(Handler.java:95)
        at android.os.Looper.loop(Looper.java:154)
        at android.app.ActivityThread.main(ActivityThread.java:6119)
        at java.lang.reflect.Method.invoke(Method.java)
        at com.android.internal.os.ZygoteInit$MethodAndArgsCaller.run(ZygoteInit.java:886)
        at com.android.internal.os.ZygoteInit.main(ZygoteInit.java:776)
```

At the time of writing, the Crashlytics console is still separate from the Firebase one. That may change over time, but the principle – having rich, remote, crash reporting – should stay the same.

Using Firebase Crash Reporting

Should you want to use Firebase Crash Reporting (which at time of writing you could do alongside Fabric's Crashlytics), you can easily do so to. Keeping the same app as earlier, use the Firebase Assistant to link it. Then run the app, press the button, and get the crash. In the Firebase Console, you can then see the crash. See Figure 7-10.

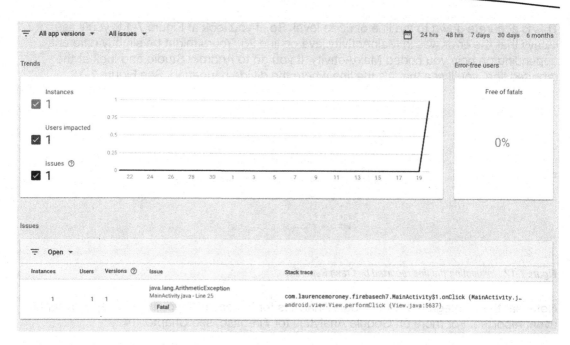

Figure 7-10. Exploring the crash in Firebase Crash Reporting

You can click on the crash to get a detailed stack trace, which, similar to the Crashlytics one, showed that this error was caused by a Divide by Zero exception. See Figure 7-11.

Figure 7-11. Stack Trace

This is accurate down to the line of code level. So, if you look at Figure 7-11, you'll see it says that the error was in MainActivity.java on line 25. Yours might be slightly different, depending on how you coded MainActivity. If you go to Android Studio and look at the reported line, you'll see that it's the line where the divide happened. See Figure 7-12.

```
13
14          @Override
15 ●↑ ⊡     protected void onCreate(Bundle savedInstanceState) {
16              super.onCreate(savedInstanceState);
17              Fabric.with( context: this, new Crashlytics());
18              setContentView(R.layout.activity_main);
19              Button crashButton = (Button) findViewById(R.id.crashButton);
20       ⊡     crashButton.setOnClickListener(new View.OnClickListener() {
21                  @Override
22 ●↑             public void onClick(View view) {
23                      int x = 1;
24                      int y = 0;
25    |               int z = x/y;
26                  }
27       ⊡     });
```

Figure 7-12. Inspecting the line reported by Crash Reporting

Note that this is integrated with Google Analytics for Firebase, so you'll get an app_exception event reported. For more on Google Analytics for Firebase, see Chapter 14.

Summary

In this chapter you got a taste of how remote crash reporting works in Firebase. You saw both Crashlytics, which will be the method of choice going forward; and the original Firebase Crash reporting work. Both provide a console where crashes will be reported, giving you the ability to inspect what is going on with your user's apps and figure out what's causing them to crash, so you can fix them and push new versions!

Chapter 8

Cloud Functions for Firebase

Cloud Functions for Firebase lets you run code on a cloud-based back end in response to events triggered by some of Firebase features and/or HTTPS requests. You'll code using Node.js, and the code is stored and executed on Google's cloud in a managed environment. The goal is to help you avoid managing middleware servers and just focus on the code. Scaling happens automatically because the code runs on the Google Cloud Platform. It's based on Google Cloud Functions, which you can learn about at https://cloud.google.com/functions/docs. This book will focus on how these functions work on Firebase.

Building a Test App

To work with Functions, you're going to use a simple Android App that receives notifications from functions. You'll use this to test things such as changes in the database or auth state. These cause 'triggers' to fire, and you'll soon write code that uses Firebase Cloud Messaging in a function to send a notification when the trigger is hit.

To get started, create a new Android App, and connect it to a Firebase Project in the usual way. In this case, I created a new one called FirebaseCh8. Using the Firebase Assistant, select 'Notifications' and follow the steps to set your app up to receive notifications.

Add a service to your app called 'MyFirebaseMessagingService'. This will receive the message from Firebase, and create a device notification for it.

Here's the code:

```
package com.laurencemoroney.chapter8dbtriggers;

import android.app.NotificationManager;
import android.app.PendingIntent;
import android.app.Service;
import android.content.Context;
import android.content.Intent;
import android.media.RingtoneManager;
import android.net.Uri;
```

L. Moroney, *The Definitive Guide to Firebase*, https://doi.org/10.1007/978-1-4842-2943-9_8

```java
import android.os.IBinder;
import android.support.v4.app.NotificationCompat;

import com.google.firebase.messaging.FirebaseMessagingService;
import com.google.firebase.messaging.RemoteMessage;

public class MyFirebaseMessagingService extends FirebaseMessagingService {
    public MyFirebaseMessagingService() {
    }

    @Override
    public void onMessageReceived(RemoteMessage remoteMessage){
        if(remoteMessage.getNotification() != null){
            sendNotification(remoteMessage.getNotification().getBody());
        }
    }

    private void sendNotification(String messageBody) {
        Intent intent = new Intent(this, MainActivity.class);
        intent.addFlags(Intent.FLAG_ACTIVITY_CLEAR_TOP);
        PendingIntent pendingIntent = PendingIntent.getActivity(this, 0 /* Request code */,
        intent,
                PendingIntent.FLAG_ONE_SHOT);

        Uri defaultSoundUri= RingtoneManager.getDefaultUri(RingtoneManager.TYPE_NOTIFICATION);
        NotificationCompat.Builder notificationBuilder = new NotificationCompat.Builder(this)
                .setContentTitle("FCM Message")
                .setContentText(messageBody)
                .setAutoCancel(true)
                .setSound(defaultSoundUri)
                .setContentIntent(pendingIntent);

        NotificationManager notificationManager =
                (NotificationManager) getSystemService(Context.NOTIFICATION_SERVICE);

        notificationManager.notify(0 /* ID of notification */, notificationBuilder.build());
    }

}
```

Ensure that this service can receive messages by making sure it is configured in AndroidManifest.xml. Here's what that file should look like:

```xml
<?xml version="1.0" encoding="utf-8"?>
<manifest xmlns:android="http://schemas.android.com/apk/res/android"
    package="com.laurencemoroney.chapter8dbtriggers">

    <application
        android:allowBackup="true"
        android:icon="@mipmap/ic_launcher"
        android:label="@string/app_name"
        android:roundIcon="@mipmap/ic_launcher_round"
```

```
    android:supportsRtl="true"
    android:theme="@style/AppTheme">
    <activity android:name=".MainActivity">
        <intent-filter>
            <action android:name="android.intent.action.MAIN" />

            <category android:name="android.intent.category.LAUNCHER" />
        </intent-filter>
    </activity>

    <service
        android:name=".MyFirebaseMessagingService"
        android:enabled="true"
        android:exported="true">
        <intent-filter>
            <action android:name="com.google.firebase.MESSAGING_EVENT" />
        </intent-filter>
    </service>
</application>

</manifest>
```

Finally, in your main Activity you should create a button, and upon the user pressing that button, the app should subscribe to an FCM topic (more on these in Chapter 9) called 'Chapter8'.

```
final Button registerButton = (Button) findViewById(R.id.registerButton);
registerButton.setOnClickListener(new View.OnClickListener() {
    @Override
    public void onClick(View v) {
        FirebaseMessaging.getInstance().subscribeToTopic("Chapter8");
        registerButton.setEnabled(false);
    }
});
```

Now when you run the app and press the button, it will register the app to receive notifications in the Chapter8 topic. To test this, run the app, and press the button. Then press the home button to put the app in the background.

Using the Firebase Console, navigate to the project that this app is associated with, and select 'Notifications'. Click the 'Send your first Message' button, and you'll be taken to the notifications composer. On here, select 'Topic' and enter the value 'Chapter8'. Make sure that this matches the string that you used in the onClick event for the button when you subscribed the app to a topic. You may see a warning that this topic doesn't yet exist. It's okay to ignore that. See Figure 8-1.

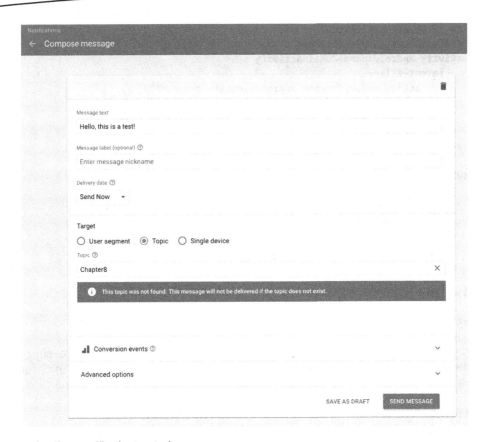

Figure 8-1. Sending a notification to a topic

Type something in the message text, and click 'Send Message'. You'll be asked to review the message. Click 'Send'. If you set your app up properly, you should see a notification appear at the top of the screen. See Figure 8-2.

Figure 8-2. The Notification appears at the top of the screen

Drag down on the notification and you'll see the details, including the text that you specified in the Notification Composer. See Figure 8-3.

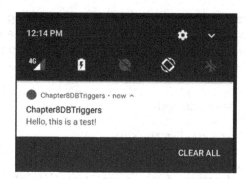

Figure 8-3. The Notification Details

With this app you'll see how database and other triggers work. You'll look at them soon, but first, make sure you're ready to start programming with functions.

The Firebase CLI and Functions

When programming with Cloud Functions for Firebase, you'll need the Firebase Command Line Interface (or CLI), which handles the uploading and updating of functions in the Firebase Cloud structure for you. If you don't have it already, take a look back at Chapter 5 where there are details on installing it.

Once you have it installed, make a directory that you're going to work in, for example, Chapter8Functions, change to this directory and issue this command:

```
firebase init
```

You'll get options to pick Database, Functions, or Hosting. See Figure 8-4.

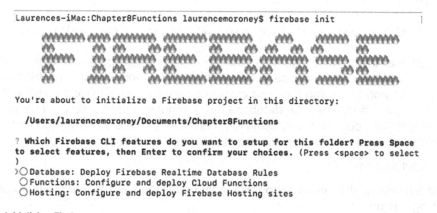

Figure 8-4. Initializing Firebase

Move the arrow to Functions, and press space to highlight it. Then press Enter to finish the initialization. When it's done, you'll see that firebase.json and a functions directory are installed in your folder.

So, before moving into detail on triggers, let's take a look at writing a simple database trigger, so that if a field is written, a function will execute. You'll use the same test app from the previous section, but this time, instead of the notification being sent from the Firebase Console, you'll create a function that sends a Firebase Cloud Messaging notification to the app instead.

Open index.js and edit it to have this code:

```
const functions = require('firebase-functions');
const admin = require('firebase-admin');
admin.initializeApp(functions.config().firebase);
exports.sendNotifications = functions.database.ref('/data/{fieldtocheck}').onWrite(event =>
{
        const textVal = event.data.val();
        console.log(textVal);

        const payload = {
                notification: {
                        title: "Notification from Functions",
                        body: textVal
                }
        };
        var topic="Chapter8";
        return admin.messaging().sendToTopic(topic, payload)
                .then(function(response){
                        console.log("Successfully sent message", response);
                })
                .catch(function(error){
                        console.log("Error sending message", error);
                });
});
```

Note this line of code:

```
exports.sendNotifications = functions.database.ref('/data/{fieldtocheck}').onWrite(
```

This specifies that the sendNotifications code should run when the field '/data/fieldtocheck' and its children get written. In this case we create a notification – which is a JSON payload containing a title and body, and then use admin.messaging().sendToTopic to send that payload to a topic. Thus, when the database field changes, a notification will be sent to the topic 'Chapter8'. As you built the Android app earlier to get messages sent to that topic – it will be rendered in your Android device or emulator as a notification.

Let's test it out and see.

From your terminal, in the directory containing firebase.json and the 'functions' folder, issue the following command:

```
firebase deploy --only functions
```

This will upload your functions to the cloud. Remember you edited index.js in the 'functions' directory, so you should see that being uploaded. See Figure 8-5.

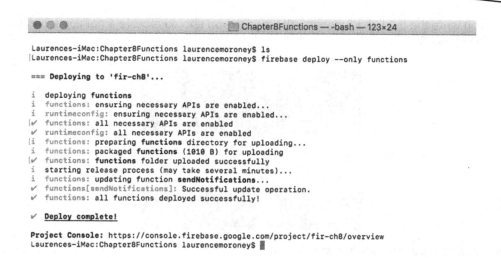

Laurences-iMac:Chapter8Functions laurencemoroney$ ls
[Laurences-iMac:Chapter8Functions laurencemoroney$ firebase deploy --only functions

=== Deploying to 'fir-ch8'...

i deploying functions
i functions: ensuring necessary APIs are enabled...
i runtimeconfig: ensuring necessary APIs are enabled...
✔ functions: all necessary APIs are enabled
✔ runtimeconfig: all necessary APIs are enabled
[i functions: preparing functions directory for uploading...
i functions: packaged functions (1010 B) for uploading
[✔ functions: functions folder uploaded successfully
i starting release process (may take several minutes)...
i functions: updating function sendNotifications...
✔ functions[sendNotifications]: Successful update operation.
✔ functions: all functions deployed successfully!

✔ Deploy complete!

Project Console: https://console.firebase.google.com/project/fir-ch8/overview
Laurences-iMac:Chapter8Functions laurencemoroney$ █

Figure 8-5. Deploying the Function

Once it's deployed, launch the Android app that you created earlier, and press its 'Register' button to ensure that it is ready to receive notifications.

Now, you'll see from the code that the function is triggered by the field /data/fieldtocheck being written, so go to the console and edit that field in the Realtime Database section. See Figure 8-6.

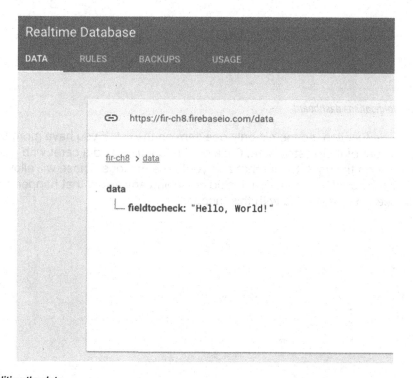

Figure 8-6. Editing the data

When you write the field, the function will fire, and you should receive a notification in the app. See Figure 8-7.

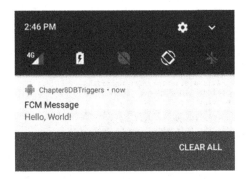

Figure 8-7. *Receiving a notification on data write*

Check out notifications on the Dashboard, and you'll see what happened here. Pick 'Notifications' on the left of the Firebase Console, and select the Dashboard tab. You should see something like Figure 8-8.

Functions BETA				
DASHBOARD	LOGS	USAGE		
				Current billing period ▾
				Jul 1 – Jul 31, 2017 (GMT-7)
Function	Event		Executions	Median run time
`sendNotifications`	ref.write /data/fieldtocheck		28	171.35 ms

Figure 8-8. *The Notifications dashboard*

We only have one function, so there's only one item on the list. If you have more than one, you'll see a number of them listed here. Click on the function, and a caret with a popup menu will appear on the right. Select that and you'll see the logs. These will allow you to check on the behavior of your function, including seeing any errors that happened. See Figure 8-9 to see what happened with this function:

Q Search logs		≡ All functions ▾	All log levels ▾		‖
Time ↓	Level	Function	Event message		
12 Jul 2017					
2:45:17.437 pm	⚑	sendNotif...	Function execution took 1273 ms, finished with status: `ok`		
2:45:17.431 pm	ⓘ	sendNotif...	Successfully sent message (messageId: 7792422083582707000)		
2:45:16.630 pm	ⓘ	sendNotif...	Hello, World!		
2:45:16.165 pm	⚑	sendNotif...	▶ Billing account not configured. External network is not accessible and quotas are severely...		
2:45:16.165 pm	⚑	sendNotif...	Function execution started		

Figure 8-9. *Logs for the functions*

As you'll see on the third line, there's a 'Hello, World!' in the logs. This comes from the line in the function code that read

```
console.log(textVal);
```

Now let's take a look at what happens when a function fails. Edit your index.js code to this, changing the body of the notification:

```
const functions = require('firebase-functions');
const admin = require('firebase-admin');
admin.initializeApp(functions.config().firebase);
exports.sendNotifications = functions.database.ref('/data/fieldtocheck').onWrite(event => {
        const textVal = event.data.val();
        console.log(textVal);

        const payload = {
                notification: {
                        title: "Notification from Functions",
                        body: event.data
                }
        };
        var topic="Chapter8";
        return admin.messaging().sendToTopic(topic, payload)
                .then(function(response){
                        console.log("Successfully sent message", response);
                })
                .catch(function(error){
                        console.log("Error sending message", error);
                });
});
```

Note that the syntax uses the concept of JavaScript and *promises* to handle the asynchronous result of the operation. In this case, the sendToTopic returns a promise, which, if completed, will run the code in the *then* clause, and if failing, will run the code in the *catch* clause.

Redeploy it from terminal with

```
firebase deploy --only functions
```

Then go to the Database from Firebase Console and change the data field. You won't get a notification. Check out the logs, and you should see something like Figure 8-10.

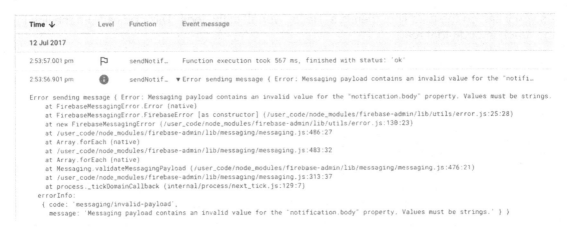

Figure 8-10. Seeing the error in Logs

From this you can see that there was something wrong with the payload. Using the logs like this is a very useful way to test and debug your functions to ensure they're working correctly.

Now that you've had a primer in functions and been hands-on in getting them to work, let's now take a look at the various options you have for starting functions – also known as Triggers.

Triggers

Firebase functions run in response to various triggers happening within the Firebase environment. For example – when a field in a database is written – this could trigger a function to execute. Or, for example, if a new user signs up that causes an auth trigger to execute, you could execute a function that sends a message to welcome them. The process of writing for Cloud Functions for Firebase follows this structure. In this chapter you'll explore many of the triggers that are available in Firebase, seeing how you can program actions that take place in response to them.

Realtime Database Triggers

The first set of triggers to explore will be those that happen when events happen on the Realtime Database. Firebase supports four triggers on data:

- onCreate() : This triggers when new data is created in the realtime database
- onUpdate() : This triggers when data is updated in the realtime database
- onDelete() : This triggers when data is deleted in the realtime database
- onWrite() : This triggers when data is created, destroyed or changed

As you saw in the previous section with the onWrite trigger, you were able to cause a notification to be sent when data was written to the 'fieldtocheck' node in the database. Of course this is a trivial example, where you triggered off of a single field. When using the Realtime Database the path specifications that you use to set off a trigger will match all uses of that path – so, for example, in the above case we matched on data/fieldtocheck and all of its children.

Let's change our functions file now to use all four triggers: creating, writing, updating, and deleting. Here's the code:

```
const functions = require('firebase-functions');
const admin = require('firebase-admin');
admin.initializeApp(functions.config().firebase);
exports.sendNotificationOnUpdate = functions.database.ref('/data/{fieldtocheck}').
        onUpdate(event => {
        doNotification("Updated: ", event);
        });

exports.sendNotificationOnWrite = functions.database.ref('/data/{fieldtocheck}').
        onWrite(event => {
        doNotification("Wrote: ", event);
});

exports.sendNotificationOnCreate = functions.database.ref('/data/{fieldtocheck}').
        onCreate(event => {
        doNotification("Created: ", event);
});

exports.sendNotificationOnDelete = functions.database.ref('/data/{fieldtocheck}').
        onDelete(event => {
        doNotification("Deleted: ", event);
});

function doNotification(message, event){
        const textVal = event.data.val();
        console.log(JSON.stringify(textVal));

        const payload = {
                notification: {
                        title: "Notification from Functions",
                        body: message + JSON.stringify(textVal)
                }
        };
        var topic="Chapter8";
        return admin.messaging().sendToTopic(topic, payload)
                .then(function(response){
                        console.log("Successfully sent message", response);
                })
                .catch(function(error){
                        console.log("Error sending message", error);
                });
}
```

Once done, don't forget to upload them to Firebase from your terminal with:

```
firebase deploy --only functions
```

Now edit your data to look like Figure 8-11.

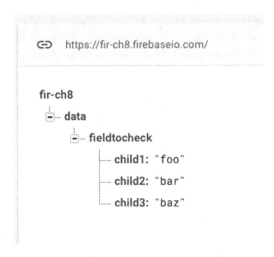

Figure 8-11. Updating the data

You'll see from your app that two triggers have fired – see Figure 8-12.

Figure 8-12. Notifications received from creating the data

As you can see there were two triggers – one for the creation of the data, telling us what was created, and one for the writing of the data, telling us what was written!

Now edit the data – say changing child1 to 'foo foo'.

You'll again see two notifications – one notifying us that the data was updated, and another telling us that the data was written. See Figure 8-13.

Figure 8-13. Notifications sent when data is updated

And of course when you delete – you'll also get two notifications. Delete the 'fieldtowrite' node, and you'll notice that the data node also vanishes. It has no data, and no children, so it doesn't need to exist. Once you've done this, you'll see two notifications. See Figure 8-14.

Figure 8-14. Notifications sent when data is deleted

Now you can see that the matching node was deleted, so we get the deleted notification. The content is null because we deleted it, so there's nothing there. We also get the write notification.

Thus, the 'write' notification will always file when something happens matching your path. The others will fire based on the appropriate event, be it creating, updating. or deleting! To understand how the path matching for the reference works, check out the Firebase documentation here: https://firebase.google.com/docs/reference/js/firebase.database. Reference.

Storage Triggers

In Chapter 4 you looked at Firebase Cloud Storage, which provides a cloud scale storage infrastructure for your files. When users access files in storage, it can cause a trigger to fire so you can do something with the file. For example – perhaps a user uploads a file and the file has inappropriate content – when this happens your function could test the file using Google APIs to see if the content was ok, and if not, it could do something like blurring the image, or notifying the user that you are going to delete it. In this section we'll look at how Storage Triggers can be used to fire a function, and what metadata you should use.

Storage triggers have a single trigger: onChange, which is used like this:

```
exports.checkStorageChanges = functions.storage.object().onChange(event =>{
});
```

In this case, no object is specified, so the default object – the root storage area – is used. You can create your own storage buckets in Firebase storage by pressing the caret button to the right of the 'Upload File' button as shown in Figure 8-15.

Figure 8-15. Creating a storage bucket

In this case I created a storage bucket called 'fir-ch8-faves'. To detect a change in this, you have to modify the code slightly to check for the bucket name like this:

```
exports.checkFavoritesChanges = functions.storage.bucket('fir-ch8-faves').object().
        onChange(event =>{
});
```

Here is the new index.js file, and how it should look with support for the storage functions added. You'll notice that when something is uploaded to either the default bucket or the fir-ch8-faves one, then the notification will be sent:

```
const functions = require('firebase-functions');
const admin = require('firebase-admin');
admin.initializeApp(functions.config().firebase);

exports.checkStorageChanges =
functions.storage.object().onChange(event =>{
                doStorageNotification("Default Bucket: ", event);
});
```

```
exports.checkFavoritesChanges =
functions.storage.bucket('fir-ch8-faves').object().onChange(event =>{
            doStorageNotification("Favorites Bucket: ", event);
});

function doStorageNotification(message, event){
        const obj = event.data;
        const filepath = obj.name;
        const resourceState = obj.resourceState;
        var status = "Updated: ";
        if(resourceState == 'not_exists'){
                status = "Deleted: ";
        }
        console.log(filepath);
        const payload = {
                notification: {
                        title: "Notification from Functions",
                        body: status + filepath
                }
        };
        var topic="Chapter8";
        return admin.messaging().sendToTopic(topic, payload)
                .then(function(response){
                        console.log("Successfully sent message", response);
                })
                .catch(function(error){
                        console.log("Error sending message", error);
                });
}
```

Try it for yourself – using the Firebase Console, upload a file to the default bucket, and then also upload one to the fir-ch8-faves bucket. If you're still running the sample app, you should see multiple notifications appear! See Figure 8-16.

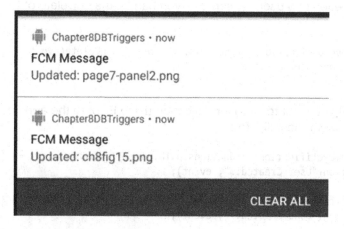

Figure 8-16. Notifications on storage changes

Now you may have noticed the code that determines things such as a change or an update in the files.

The **event** contains a **data** property whose **name** property is the name of the file. It also contains a **resourcestate** string that contains either 'exists' or 'not_exists'. If the former, the file has either been uploaded or updated; if the latter, it has been deleted. You can also use the **bucket** property to get the details on the bucket, the **contentType** to get more details on the type of content that triggered the function to run.

A common scenario is that you might want to process a file before it gets exposed to end users. So, for example, if you've built an app that allows users to upload a file, you might want to check if the file has any inappropriate content before other users see it. A walkthrough of a scenario using functions to do this – where it calls the cloud vision API to determine if the content has issues, and if so, uses ImageMagick to blur the image – can be found in the Cloud Functions for Firebase codelab here: https://codelabs.developers.google.com/codelabs/firebase-cloud-functions/#8. Note that you will have to enable billing on your cloud console project to use the Cloud Vision API.

Authentication Triggers

You can also have functions execute in response to triggers on Auth events. You can learn more about Firebase Auth in Chapter 2. Authentication triggers in Cloud Functions for Firebase will fire when a user is created and when a user is deleted. You can use these to, for example, send a welcome message to a user when they first sign up, or, if they delete their account, you can send them a goodbye, or a message to encourage them to sign back up again.

To handle the creation of a user you simply use the onCreate of the user() object like this:

```
exports.sendWelcomeNotification = functions.auth.user().onCreate(event => {

});
```

To handle the deletion of a user, it's similar – you handle the onDelete of the user() object like this:

```
exports.sendGoodbyeNotification = functions.auth.user().onDelete(event => {
  doAuthNotification("User Deleted: ", event);
});
```

So, for example if you want to send a notification using FCM to the app you've been building in this chapter, you can do it like this:

```
exports.sendWelcomeNotification = functions.auth.user().onCreate(event => {
  doAuthNotification("User Created: ", event);
});
exports.sendGoodbyeNotification = functions.auth.user().onDelete(event => {
  doAuthNotification("User Deleted: ", event);
});
```

```
function doAuthNotification(message, event){
        const user = event.data;
        const email = user.email;
        const payload = {
                notification: {
                        title: "Notification from Functions",
                        body: message + email
                }
        };
        var topic="Chapter8";
        return admin.messaging().sendToTopic(topic, payload)
                .then(function(response){
                        console.log("Successfully sent message", response);
                })
                .catch(function(error){
                        console.log("Error sending message", error);
                });
}
```

Note that the event data contains a user property, which is a UserRecord object. You can then query its properties – such as displayName, email, verified, or photoURL when appropriate. To learn more about this object and its properties, check it out at: https://firebase.google.com/docs/reference/functions/functions.auth.UserRecord.

If you don't have the test app for this chapter running, run it now.

Add the code above to your index.js, and deploy it as before. Now, in Firebase Console, go to the Authentication section, and enable Email/Password authentication. For more details on this, see Chapter 2.

Then, go to the Users tab, and manually add a user and password. See Figure 8-17.

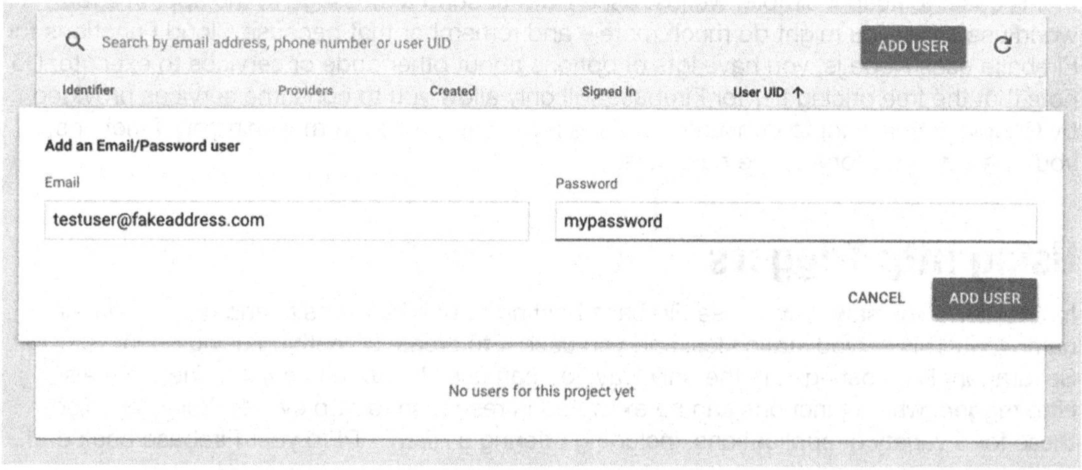

Figure 8-17. Adding a test user

When you're done, press Add User, and in a few moments, you should receive a notification in the test app. See Figure 8-18.

Figure 8-18. *Receiving the notification when a new user is created*

And of course, if you delete this user in the console, you'll see the deletion message on your app. See Figure 8-19.

Figure 8-19. *Receiving the Deletion notification*

In this case, to keep it simple, we just used FCM to send a message to the app. In a real-world use case, you might do much more – and remember that because Cloud Functions for Firebase uses Node.js, you have lots of options about other code or services to execute. Do note that the free pricing tier for Firebase will only allow you to consume services provided by Google. If you want to consume services from third parties from within your functions, you'll have to be in one of the paid tiers.

Using Http Triggers

In Chapter 5 you saw how to use Firebase hosting to build a web site and map a domain name to it. This served static files, and you used it to create something using open Seadragon. But hosting isn't the only way you can use Http with Firebase. There are also Http triggers where functions can be executed in response to http events. You could use these for a variety of applications, including offering a REST API to your Firebase back end.

How they work is simple: the functions.https namespace supports an onRequest trigger, which takes objects for the request and the response. You simply code a function that handles this, and sends something back in the response. You'll also send a status code, using standard HTTP response codes (found here: https://en.wikipedia.org/wiki/List_of_HTTP_status_codes), so – for example: a 200 code indicates success, so you can respond to a simple call like this:

```
exports.sendHelloWorld = functions.https.onRequest((req, res) =>{
        res.status(200).send("Hello, World!");
});
```

After deploying, you can access the function at https://us-central1-<your-project-name>.cloudfunctions.net/sendHelloWorld.

Note that the end of the URL (in this case 'sendHelloWorld') should match your function name exactly.

You can see this in operation in Figure 8-20.

Figure 8-20. Running the HTTP function

Now of course, this is a very simple scenario – and typically when you call an endpoint, you probably want to pass parameters to get it to do something interesting. Parameters are received in the request object. So, for example, if you wanted to update 'Hello World' to give a message to a person named in an input parameter on the querystring, you would update the function to read it from req.query.<parametername> like this:

```
exports.sendHelloWorld = functions.https.onRequest((req, res) =>{
        const myname=req.query.name;
        res.status(200).send("Hello, World to: " + myname);
});
```

Now when you run it, you'll see the name in the output. See Figure 8-21.

Figure 8-21. Using a querystring for input parameter

If you prefer to POST your request, that's also pretty easy to implement. The parameters on the request object will vary based on how you are posting them. So, for example, if I want to POST parameters using 'text/plain' encoding, then the parameters are simply the request body. So for example if I want to POST this:

```
curl -X POST -H "Content-Type:text/plain" https://us-central1-fir-ch8.cloudfunctions.net/
sendHelloWorld -d Bob
```

The function to handle it would look like this:

```
exports.sendHelloWorld = functions.https.onRequest((req, res) =>{
        const myname=req.body;
        res.status(200).send("Hello, World to: " + myname + "\n");
});
```

But typically when you post, you'll either do it using a form that contains string-encoded parameters, or you will post a JSON document containing your parameters. Let's look at coding for each of these. First, a post with a form, send using type application/x-www-form-urlencoded:

```
curl -X POST -H "Content-Type:application/x-www-form-urlencoded" https://us-central1-fir-
ch8.cloudfunctions.net/sendHelloWorld -d "name=Bob&age=99"
```

In this case, the parameters will create objects on the request object that you can parse – so, the code to handle this would look like this:

```
exports.sendHelloWorld = functions.https.onRequest((req, res) =>{
        const myname=req.body.name;
        const age = req.body.age;
        res.status(200).send("Hello, World to: " + myname + ", you are " +
                            age + " years old.\n");
});
```

See how there's a req.body.name and a req.body.age – these are created based on the fact that I had name and age parameters in the data string (see "name=Bob&age=99" in the curl request above)

It's increasingly common to use JSON to pass data in a post. Let's take a look at how we would handle this – so, for example, consider this POST:

```
curl -X POST -H "Content-Type:application/json" https://us-central1-fir-ch8.cloudfunctions.
net/sendHelloWorld -d '{"name":"Bob", "age":99}'
```

The good news is that the same process is used to handle this type of encoding, so the same function can be used to parse the parameters. See the result in Figure 8-22.

```
[laurences-imac:Chapter8Functions laurencemoroney$ curl -X POST -H "Content-Type:application/json" \
|> https://us-central1-fir-ch8.cloudfunctions.net/sendHelloWorld \
|> -d '{"name":"Bob", "age":99}'
Hello, World to: Bob, you are 99 years old.
laurences-imac:Chapter8Functions laurencemoroney$ ▮
```

Figure 8-22. Passing JSON to a function

Http Triggers with Hosting

In Chapter 5 you saw how to build a web site with Firebase hosting. You can also use http triggers on your hosting account by specifying them using your firebase.json file.

In the project directory you've been using for this chapter, re-run

```
firebase init
```

Choose the hosting option, and when you've gone through the steps your firebase.json file should look like this:

```
{
  "hosting": {
    "public": "public"
  }
}
```

You'll need to edit this to point to your function from hosting. So, let's first create a simple 'Hello World' function that writes 'Hello Word to the browser:

```
exports.helloWebWorld = functions.https.onRequest((req, res) => {
        res.status(200).send("Hello, World!");
});
```

Now, in order to have this triggered when you visit your firebase hosting-based web site, you need to edit your firebase.json file to add a reference to this function. Here's an example:

```
{
  "hosting": {
    "public": "public",
    "rewrites" : [ {
            "source": "/helloworld", "function": "helloWebWorld"
    }]
  }
}
```

Note the 'rewrites' section, which is a json list, where you specify the source URI, and the name of the function to run when you hit it. So, in this case when someone hits /helloworld, the function will execute.

Up to now when deploying, you've used

```
firebase deploy --only functions
```

But because you've edited the firebase.json file, it's not just functions anymore, so be sure to use:

```
firebase deploy
```

It's okay to use --only functions after this point *unless* you edit the firebase.json file again. Remember that will not be redeployed if you use --only functions.

Once it's deployed, you can try the URL in your browser. See Figure 8-23:

Figure 8-23. *Running the Function with Firebase hosting*

Handling parameters is exactly the same as it was with the non web-mapped functions, so, for example if you want to handle parameters on the querystring, you would simply update the function to this:

```
exports.helloWebWorld = functions.https.onRequest((req, res) => {
      const myname = req.query.name;
      const age = req.query.age;
      res.status(200).send("Hello, World to: " + myname + ", you are " + age +
      " years old.\n");
});
```

And then, after deploying, you can pass the parameters in the querystring like in Figure 8-24.

POST parameters will also work in exactly the same way as earlier in this chapter.

Figure 8-24. *Using Parameters*

Other Triggers

In addition to everything you've seen in this chapter, you can also use triggers for events in Google Analytics for Firebase (see Chapter 14), so that when a condition is met, a function will execute. Google Analytics for Firebase can be used to collect a number of common events (listed here: https://support.google.com/firebase/answer/6317485) as well as events that you define and write code for. There's more details on them in Chapter 14. To trigger a function on Analytics, you simply write a function to capture it, by setting the name of the analytic as a parameter to the functions.analytics.event("") like this:

```
exports.handleUserEngagement = functions.analytics.event('screen_view').onLog(event => {
    // do something
});
```

Additionally, if you use the Google Cloud Platform, there's functionality called Google Pub/Sub that provides a globally distributed message bus that scales on-demand. Going into it is beyond the scope of this book, but If you use it, you can trigger functions based on the Pub/Sub's topic name like this:

```
exports.helloPubSub = functions.pubsub.topic('topic-name').onPublish(event => {

});
```

Summary

In this chapter you got a look at Cloud Functions for Firebase and how their triggering mechanism works. You saw how to create functions that act on a variety of triggers. You also used Firebase Cloud Messaging to send notifications once a trigger was hit. In the next chapter, you'll go into more detail on FCM, including how to build your own simple FCM server!

Chapter 9

Firebase Cloud Messaging

Firebase Cloud Messaging is designed to provide connection to your devices via messages and notifications. It's intended to be reliable, with 98% of messages delivered to connected devices in 500ms or less, as well as massively scalable, with an infrastructure that delivers over a trillion messages each week. Being able to deliver messages is one thing, but being able to effectively target them at the right users to avoid unwanted notification 'spam' is another, and Firebase Cloud Messaging offers you a variety of methods to give you fine-grained control.

- You could send a message to *all* your users.

- You could send a message to a *single* user.

- You could send a message to an audience defined using Google Analytics for Firebase. You'll learn more about this technology in Chapter 14.

- You could send a message to a *topic* that users opt into.

- You can use the FCM API to define message *groups* and send messages to them.

In addition to having tools to choose who to send messages to, you can also control how they are delivered – for example, setting priorities, expiration dates, and more. You can also track how they are received, and understand the conversion rate.

There's two main ways that you can send messages – one is with a notification composer built into the Firebase console, and the other is to roll your own server that uses the FCM API to dispatch messages on your behalf. You'll look into both in this chapter.

Building an App to Receive Notifications

Let's start by building an app that can receive notifications from Firebase. Create a new Android Studio app based on the empty activity template. Using the Firebase Assistant, open the 'Cloud Messaging' node and follow the instructions to 'Set Up Firebase Cloud Messaging' – see Figure 9-1. (For more details on using the assistant, see the full walkthrough in Chapter 1.)

© Laurence Moroney 2017

L. Moroney, *The Definitive Guide to Firebase*, https://doi.org/10.1007/978-1-4842-2943-9_9

Figure 9-1. Set Up Cloud Messaging

For now you only need to follow steps 1 and 2, to connect your app to Firebase and Add FCM to your app. When you're done, your assistant should look like Figure 9-2.

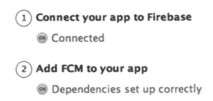

Figure 9-2. Assistant settings

At this point, you can run your app, and when it's running, put the app into the background on either your phone or emulator. In other words, make sure you see something other than the app – the home screen, or another app, for example.

Once that's done, go to the Firebase Console and open the project that you created when connecting your app to Firebase. In this case, mine is called 'Chapter 9'.

Select the 'Notifications' tab, and you'll see something like Figure 9-3.

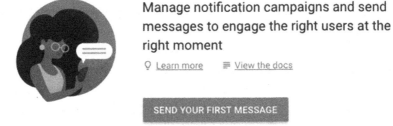

Figure 9-3. Starting with Notifications and Cloud Messaging

Click the 'Send your first message' button, and you'll get the message composer. Enter some details, but for the 'Target', make sure you select 'User Segment', and ensure that you pick 'App', and the name of the app you created. This is how you target *all* users of an app. Of course there's only one user at the moment, and that's you. See Figure 9-4.

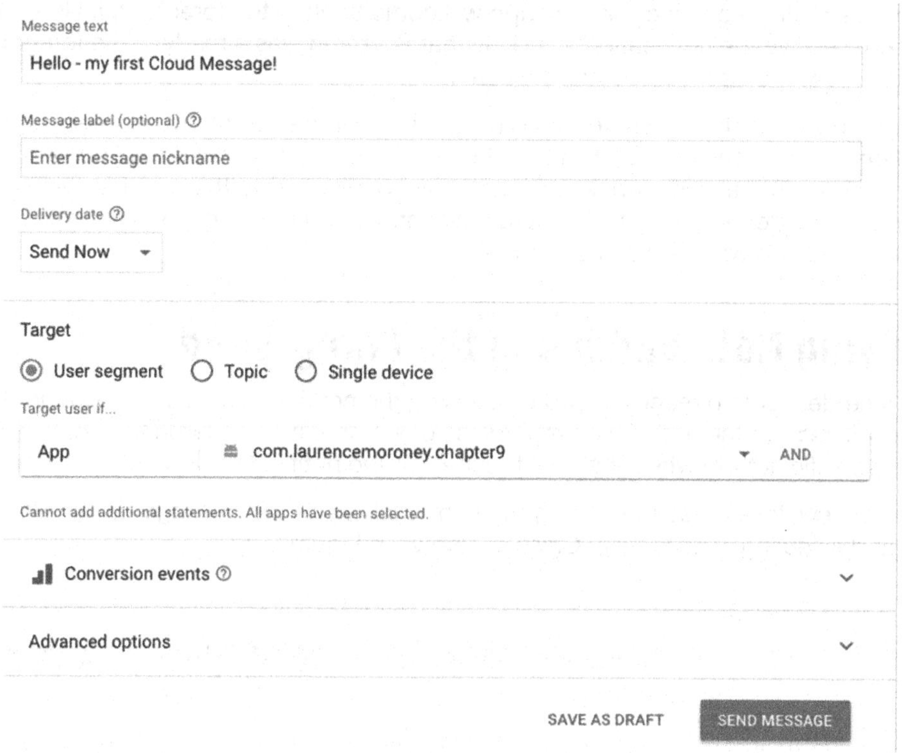

Message text

Hello - my first Cloud Message!

Message label (optional) ⓘ

Enter message nickname

Delivery date ⓘ

Send Now   ▾

Target

◉ User segment   ○ Topic   ○ Single device

Target user if...

App   ☰ com.laurencemoroney.chapter9   ▾   AND

Cannot add additional statements. All apps have been selected.

▮ Conversion events ⓘ   ⌄

Advanced options   ⌄

                                    SAVE AS DRAFT   SEND MESSAGE

Figure 9-4. Composing a Cloud Message

Press the 'Send Message' button, and a notification will appear on your device at the top of the screen. The default icon is a circle. See Figure 9-5.

Figure 9-5. Receiving the notification

Swipe it down, and you'll see the message, which matches what you typed in the composer. See Figure 9-6.

Figure 9-6. The Notification

Touch on the notification, and then the app will come back to the foreground. Note that if you did **not** receive the notification, it's likely that your app was already in the foreground. Make sure it's in the background and try again.

This scenario demonstrates where Cloud Messaging can be used to send re-engagement notifications. Of course, it's a bit limited – the notification only works if the app is in the background, so, in the next step, let's look at how to take that to the next level – when the app is in the foreground you can receive a notification, and when the user activates that notification, the app will open a specific activity.

Receiving Notifications in the Foreground

To go a little deeper into receiving and processing the notification, let's now extend the app so that it will receive the notification regardless of whether it's backgrounded or not, and will launch a specific activity when the user touches on the notification.

First, add a new Java Class to your app by right-clicking on the package name in Android Studio, and selecting New ➤ Java Class as shown in Figure 9-7.

Figure 9-7. Add a new Java Class

In the 'Create New Class' dialog, call it FCMReceiver, and make sure its superclass is **com. google.firebase.messaging.FirebaseMessagingService**.

You'll need to configure your Android Manifest for this receiver, by adding this as a service. The code to do this is here:

```
<service
    android:name=".FCMReceiver"
    android:enabled="true"
    android:exported="true">
    <intent-filter>
        <action android:name="com.google.firebase.MESSAGING_EVENT" />
    </intent-filter>
</service>
```

This sets up the class that you just created as the intent filter for a Messaging Event from Firebase. Thus it will catch messages from FCM for you. In a moment you'll see how to process that message and turn it into a notification on the device. For convenience, your full Android Manifest file should look like this:

```
<?xml version="1.0" encoding="utf-8"?>
<manifest xmlns:android="http://schemas.android.com/apk/res/android"
    package="com.laurencemoroney.chapter9">

    <application
        android:allowBackup="true"
        android:icon="@mipmap/ic_launcher"
```

```
        android:label="@string/app_name"
        android:roundIcon="@mipmap/ic_launcher_round"
        android:supportsRtl="true"
        android:theme="@style/AppTheme">
        <activity android:name=".MainActivity">
            <intent-filter>
                <action android:name="android.intent.action.MAIN" />

                <category android:name="android.intent.category.LAUNCHER" />
            </intent-filter>
        </activity>
        <service
            android:name=".FCMReceiver"
            android:enabled="true"
            android:exported="true">
            <intent-filter>
                <action android:name="com.google.firebase.MESSAGING_EVENT" />
            </intent-filter>
        </service>
    </application>

</manifest>
```

The class that you created extended the FirebaseMessagingService, so it needs to override the **onMessageReceived** method. This receives a RemoteMessage containing details of the cloud message. Let's take a look at a simple override for this:

```
package com.laurencemoroney.chapter9;

import android.util.Log;

import com.google.firebase.messaging.FirebaseMessagingService;
import com.google.firebase.messaging.RemoteMessage;

public class FCMReceiver extends FirebaseMessagingService {
    private static final String TAG = "Ch9";
    @Override
    public void onMessageReceived(RemoteMessage remoteMessage) {
        // Check if message contains a data payload.
        if (remoteMessage.getData().size() > 0) {
            Log.d(TAG, "Message data payload: " + remoteMessage.getData());
        }

        // Check if message contains a notification payload.
        if (remoteMessage.getNotification() != null) {
            Log.d(TAG, "Message Notification Body: " +
                        remoteMessage.getNotification().getBody());
        }

        String message = remoteMessage.getNotification().getBody();

        sendNotification(message);
    }
}
```

This code will receive the remote message, and check if it contains some data and a notification, logging as appropriate. If there's a text message within the notification it will turn that into a string and pass it to the 'sendNotification' method. You'll implement that shortly.

Implementing the Notification Activity

The sendNotification method will render an Android notification in the system tray, and when the user touches on it, will launch a custom activity. So, before coding it, let's create that activity.

First, create a new Activity by right-clicking on the package name, and then selecting New ➤ Activity ➤ Empty Activity. See Figure 9-8.

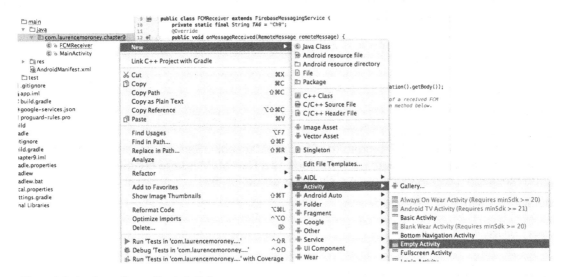

Figure 9-8. Implementing an Empty Activity

You'll be asked to configure the activity. Give it a name like 'IncomingMessage'. See Figure 9-9.

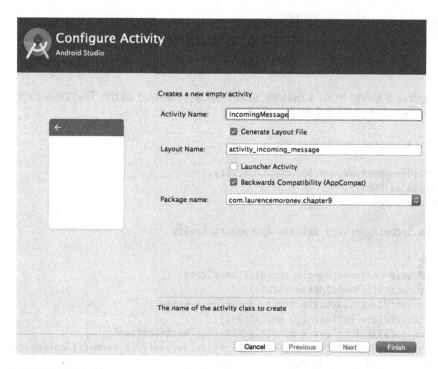

Figure 9-9. Configuring the Activity

Click Finish, and the activity will be created.

Edit the layout file of the activity to add a TextView:

```
<TextView
    android:layout_width="wrap_content"
    android:layout_height="wrap_content"
    android:text="Activated from Notification!"
    android:id="@+id/txtNotification"
    android:layout_alignParentTop="true"
    android:layout_centerHorizontal="true"
    android:layout_marginTop="122dp"
    android:textSize="48dp" />
```

Now take a look at the code for the activity you just created. It should look something like this:

```
package com.laurencemoroney.chapter9;

import android.support.v7.app.AppCompatActivity;
import android.os.Bundle;

public class IncomingMessage extends AppCompatActivity {

    @Override
    protected void onCreate(Bundle savedInstanceState) {
```

```
        super.onCreate(savedInstanceState);
        setContentView(R.layout.activity_incoming_message);
    }
}
```

Edit it to receive a string from a bundle, and then set the text of the TextView to that string. When you're done, it should look like this:

```
package com.laurencemoroney.chapter9;

import android.support.v7.app.AppCompatActivity;
import android.os.Bundle;
import android.widget.TextView;

public class IncomingMessage extends AppCompatActivity {

    @Override
    protected void onCreate(Bundle savedInstanceState) {
        super.onCreate(savedInstanceState);
        setContentView(R.layout.activity_incoming_message);
        Bundle bundle = getIntent().getExtras();
        String notificationText = bundle.getString("Notification");
        TextView txtNotification = (TextView) findViewById(R.id.txtNotification);
        txtNotification.setText(notificationText);
    }
}
```

You now have an activity that can be launched, which will read text from a bundle and render it on the screen. Let's next take a look at the method that will achieve this from the incoming message.

Implementing the sendNotification Method

Earlier you coded the receiver for the message, which extracted a string from it, and passed that to a method called 'sendNotification'. This method should take that string, and turn it into an on-Device notification, which, when touched, will launch an activity containing that string. Let's implement that now.

Start by adding the method to your FCMReceiver class:

```
private void sendNotification(String messageBody){

}
```

In the previous step you created an IncomingMessage class, so within this method, create a PendingIntent that can be used to launch it.

```
Intent intent = new Intent(this, IncomingMessage.class);
intent.addFlags(Intent.FLAG_ACTIVITY_CLEAR_TOP);
intent.putExtra("Notification", messageBody);
PendingIntent pendingIntent = PendingIntent.getActivity(this, 0 /* Request code */, intent,
        PendingIntent.FLAG_ONE_SHOT);
```

Then, using the Android NotificationBuilder you can create an on-device notification, which allows you to configure an icon and sound. You'll specify this pending intent as the content intent:

```
Uri defaultSoundUri= RingtoneManager.getDefaultUri(RingtoneManager.TYPE_NOTIFICATION);
NotificationCompat.Builder notificationBuilder = new NotificationCompat.Builder(this)
        .setSmallIcon(R.drawable.ic_stat_name)
        .setContentTitle("FCM Message")
        .setContentText(messageBody)
        .setAutoCancel(true)
        .setSound(defaultSoundUri)
        .setContentIntent(pendingIntent);

NotificationManager notificationManager =
        (NotificationManager) getSystemService(Context.NOTIFICATION_SERVICE);

notificationManager.notify(0 /* ID of notification */, notificationBuilder.build());
```

> **Note** For this app I used the NotificationCompat from the android.support.v4.app namespace.

If ic_stat_name isn't working for you, it's easy to add. Simply right click on 'drawable' in the project, and select New ➤ Image Asset. See Figure 9-10.

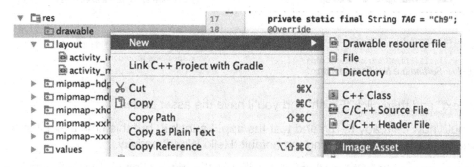

Figure 9-10. Adding an Image Asset

Select 'Notification Icons' in the drop down, and you'll see the android icon as the source asset. See Figure 9-11.

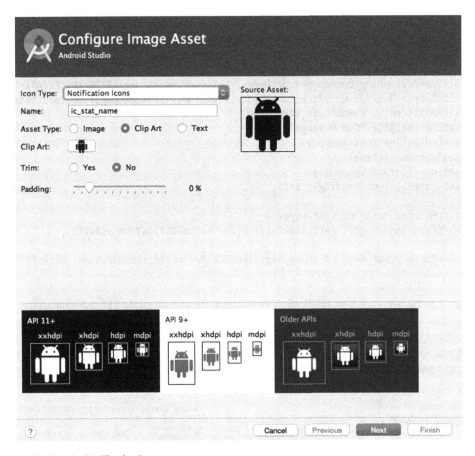

Figure 9-11. Setting the Notification Icon

Click 'Next' and then click 'Finish' and you'll have the asset added.

You should now be ready to run and test the app. Launch it, but this time leave it in the foreground. It will launch, showing the default 'Hello World' activity.

Send a message from FCM, and you'll shortly see the notification appear, with the icon you selected instead of the default circle. You'll also hear a tone. See Figure 9-12.

Figure 9-12. *Receiving the default notification*

In this case, the notification contained the text 'Hello from FCM!' – see Figure 9-13.

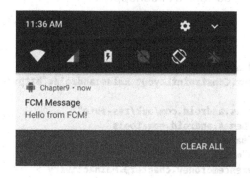

Figure 9-13. *The Notification Text*

Now, if you touch on the notification the IncomingMessage activity you created will launch, and the TextView will be set to 'Hello from FCM!' See Figure 9-14.

Figure 9-14. *Showing the 'Hello from FCM!' message*

Understanding Topics

In the previous example you built an app that can receive notifications, and you saw how to send a notification to all users of your app. This is generally infeasible, particularly if you have a large international audience that speaks multiple languages. For example, users that prefer Japanese don't want notifications in English, and vice versa. Going beyond just language though, users may only want to receive notifications that are relevant to them, and topics are a great way to achieve this. Consider, for example, you're building an app that helps users understand public transport around them. If your user lives in London, then they'll want updates on the London public transport. When they travel to Tokyo, they'll want updates on *that* system while they are there, and the updates should stop when they return home to London.

Using analytics about the device and its owner won't help in that scenario, so having something where there's a publish/subscribe channel that the user can opt into, and they then receive notifications for gives a much more elegant solution.

Note that topic messaging supports *unlimited* topics and subscriptions per app. Message payload is a little smaller than the typical 4Kb – a topic message is limited to 2 Kb.

Let's take a look at how to use Topics in our app.

First, edit the activity_main.xml file to add a couple of buttons – one for London and one for Tokyo.

```xml
<?xml version="1.0" encoding="utf-8"?>
<android.support.constraint.ConstraintLayout xmlns:android="http://schemas.android.com/apk/
res/android"
    xmlns:app="http://schemas.android.com/apk/res-auto"
    xmlns:tools="http://schemas.android.com/tools"
    android:layout_width="match_parent"
    android:layout_height="match_parent"
    tools:context="com.laurencemoroney.chapter9.MainActivity">

    <LinearLayout
        android:layout_width="368dp"
        android:layout_height="495dp"
        android:orientation="vertical"
        tools:layout_editor_absoluteY="8dp"
        tools:layout_editor_absoluteX="8dp">
    <Button
        android:layout_width="wrap_content"
        android:layout_height="wrap_content"
        android:text="Tokyo"
        android:id="@+id/tokyoButton"/>
    <Button
        android:layout_width="wrap_content"
        android:layout_height="wrap_content"
        android:text="London"
        android:id="@+id/londonButton"/>
    </LinearLayout>
</android.support.constraint.ConstraintLayout>
```

Now in the MainActivity, add some code to have onClickListeners active for these buttons:

```
package com.laurencemoroney.chapter9;

import android.support.v7.app.AppCompatActivity;
import android.os.Bundle;
import android.view.View;
import android.widget.Button;

public class MainActivity extends AppCompatActivity {
    Button londonButton, tokyoButton;
    @Override
    protected void onCreate(Bundle savedInstanceState) {
        super.onCreate(savedInstanceState);
        setContentView(R.layout.activity_main);
        londonButton = (Button) findViewById(R.id.londonButton);
        londonButton.setOnClickListener(new View.OnClickListener() {
            @Override
            public void onClick(View v) {


            }
        });
        tokyoButton = (Button) findViewById(R.id.tokyoButton);
        tokyoButton.setOnClickListener(new View.OnClickListener() {
            @Override
            public void onClick(View v) {


            }
        });

    }
}
```

To subscribe to a topic, use the subscribeToTopic method on the Firebase messaging instance. Similarly to unsubscribe, you use unsubscribeFromTopic. So, when we press the 'London' button we want to subscribe to updates on the London topic, and unsubscribe to updates on the Tokyo topic. When we press the Tokyo button, we do the opposite. Here's the code for London:

```
londonButton.setOnClickListener(new View.OnClickListener() {
    @Override
    public void onClick(View v) {
        FirebaseMessaging.getInstance().subscribeToTopic("London");
        FirebaseMessaging.getInstance().unsubscribeFromTopic("Tokyo");
    }
});
```

Implement this code, and the similar one for Tokyo, then run your app. After running, press the 'Tokyo' button.

Then, go to the Notifications link in the Firebase Console, and create a message. Address this to the Tokyo topic as shown in Figure 9-15. Don't worry if you see a message saying the topic was not found. It can take some time for topics to propagate through the system, and as this is your first time running the app, the topic isn't recognized yet. The messaging will still work though!

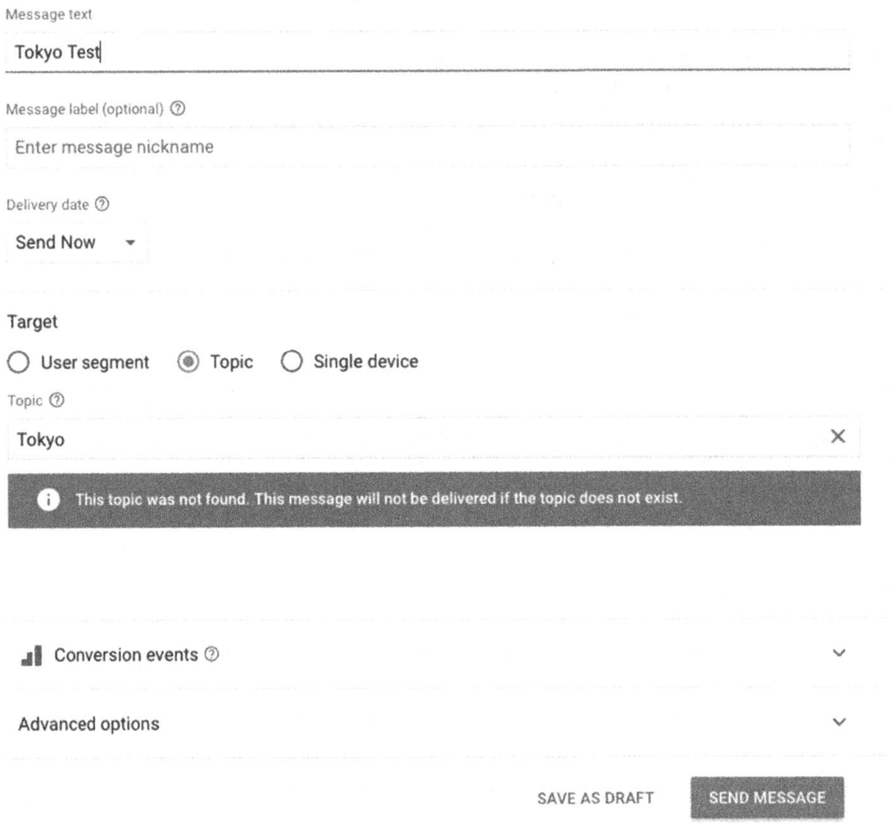

Message text

Tokyo Test

Message label (optional) ⓘ

Enter message nickname

Delivery date ⓘ

Send Now   ▾

Target

◯ User segment   ⦿ Topic   ◯ Single device

Topic ⓘ

Tokyo   ✕

ⓘ This topic was not found. This message will not be delivered if the topic does not exist.

▁▊ Conversion events ⓘ   ⌄

Advanced options   ⌄

SAVE AS DRAFT   SEND MESSAGE

Figure 9-15. *Sending a message to the Tokyo topic*

The message will be received by the device as before. See Figure 9-16.

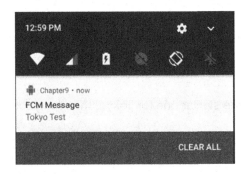

Figure 9-16. *Receiving the topic notification*

Sending Messages Using Analytics

As you build a user base, then you'll begin to see analytics get accumulated. Using these, you can build audiences to help you find the right people to send messages to. So, for example, you might want to reach different nation groups in their own language, so you could pick an audience of all people whose device is in Japan, or who speak Japanese, and define that as your Japanese audience, sending a message to them in Japanese. Audiences can be defined using Google Analytics for Firebase, and you can learn more about them in Chapter 14.

To send a message to an audience, you simply pick them as the user audience. So, for example in Figure 9-15, I previously created a Japanese audience, so if I want to send a notification to them, I can do it by selecting them as a user audience. See Figure 9-17.

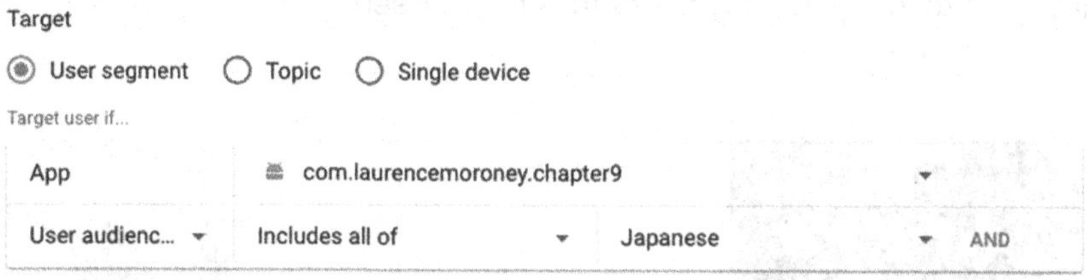

Target

◉ User segment   ◯ Topic   ◯ Single device

Target user if...

| App | | com.laurencemoroney.chapter9 | | | ▾ |
| User audienc... ▾ | Includes all of | | ▾ | Japanese | ▾ | AND |

Figure 9-17. Sending a notification to an audience

If you don't want to create an audience, the tools are also there for you to pick users to send messages to, based on language, version, or user properties. User properties are custom analytic events that you can track and follow, and you'll learn about them in Chapter 14.

Building a Custom App Server for FCM

Another common pattern for Firebase Cloud Messaging development is to create your own app server that uses the FCM server APIs to dispatch messages for you. This is really useful if you want to keep track of your users, and in particular build device groups, where you create logical groups of devices. For example – you could have one set of devices that are testers, and they receive messages not meant for others. In this section you'll see how to build an app server using PHP and MySQL. The code for this server is available at https://github.com/lmoroney/fcm-app-server.

In order for your App server to know the details about each device, so they can address them in messages, the FCM API gives you a registration token that is unique to each device. See Figure 9-18.

Figure 9-18. *Getting the registration token*

Once you have this token, you pass the details to your server. It will need them when it calls the FCM API. See Figure 9-19.

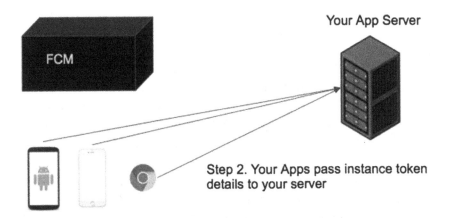

Figure 9-19. *Posting the token to your server*

Then, whenever you want to send a message, code in your app server will call the FCM APIs, using the registration token to address the message. See Figure 9-20.

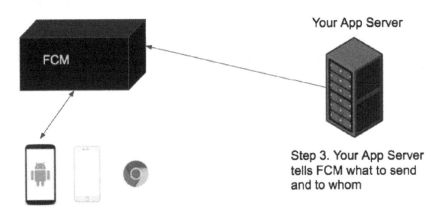

Figure 9-20. *Using the FCM API to send messages*

In this section, you'll learn how to build this server, and update your client to use it.

Creating the Database

On the server you'll create a MySQL database to store the registration tokens and when they were registered with the app server. Using SQL to create this table will look like this:

```
CREATE TABLE IF NOT EXISTS `fcm_users` (
`id` int(11) NOT NULL,
`created_at` timestamp NOT NULL DEFAULT CURRENT_TIMESTAMP,
`fcm_regID` text NOT NULL
)
```

When a user launches their app and gets a registration token from FCM, they will then tell your app server about it. To this end, a registration endpoint on your server is necessary. Here's a simple one that receives a registration token via an HTTP POST and stores it in the MySQL database.

```php
<?php

// response json
$json = array();

/**
 * Registering a user device
 * Store reg id in users table
 */
if (isset($_POST["regid"])) {
    $fcm_regid = $_POST["regid"]; // GCM Registration ID
    // Store user details in db
    include_once 'db_functions.php';
    $db = new DB_Functions();
    $res = $db->storeUser($fcm_regid);
    echo "Done!";
} else {
    // user details missing
    echo "Problem with parameters";
}
?>
```

For this exercise, you'll create a web page on the server that lists all the registered devices. You can then send a message to each one individually, or to all of them as a group. This web page should read the database of registered devices, and create text fields so that you can send a message to each. In addition to that, one text field that is used to send to all devices. You can see an example of a page like this in Figure 9-21.

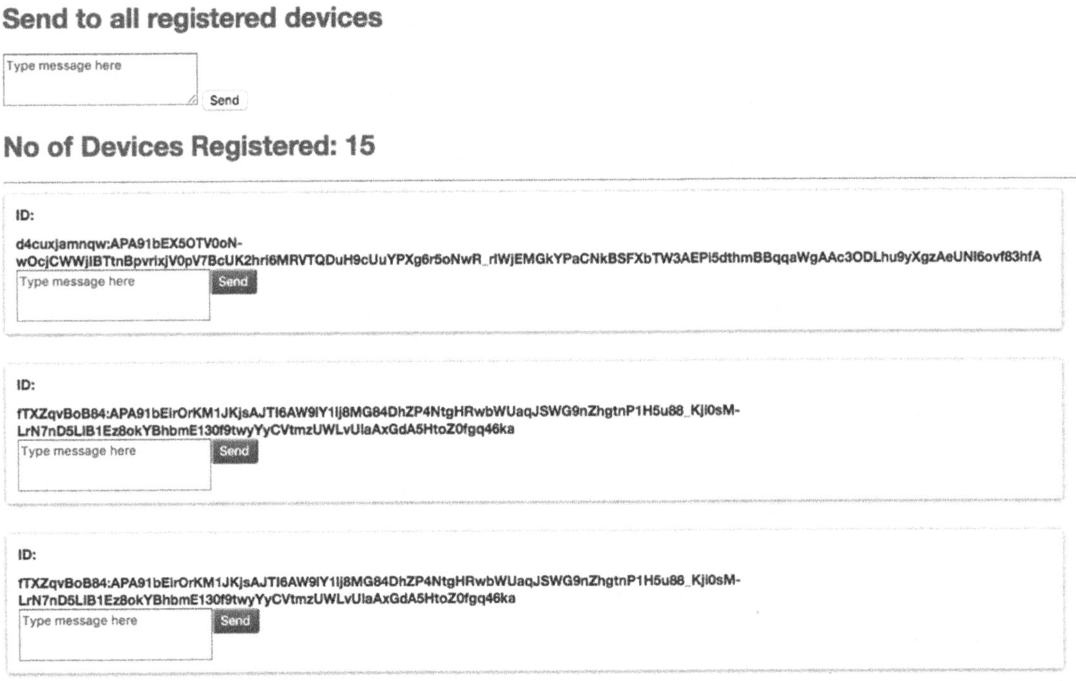

Send to all registered devices

```
Type message here
```
Send

No of Devices Registered: 15

ID:

d4cuxjamnqw:APA91bEX5OTV0oN-
wOcjCWWjIBTtnBpvrixjV0pV7BcUK2hrI6MRVTQDuH9cUuYPXg6r5oNwR_rIWjEMGkYPaCNkBSFXbTW3AEPi5dthmBBqqaWgAAc3ODLhu9yXgzAeUNI6ovf83hfA

```
Type message here
```
Send

ID:

fTXZqvBoB84:APA91bEirOrKM1JKjsAJTI6AW9lY1Ij8MG84DhZP4NtgHRwbWUaqJSWG9nZhgtnP1H5u88_KjI0sM-
LrN7nD5LIB1Ez8okYBhbmE130f9twyYyCVtmzUWLvUlaAxGdA5HtoZ0fgq46ka

```
Type message here
```
Send

ID:

fTXZqvBoB84:APA91bEirOrKM1JKjsAJTI6AW9lY1Ij8MG84DhZP4NtgHRwbWUaqJSWG9nZhgtnP1H5u88_KjI0sM-
LrN7nD5LIB1Ez8okYBhbmE130f9twyYyCVtmzUWLvUlaAxGdA5HtoZ0fgq46ka

```
Type message here
```
Send

Figure 9-21. Example of FCM App Server

The code for this page is here.

```html
<!DOCTYPE html>
<html>
    <head>
        <title>FCM Test Page</title>
        <link rel="stylesheet" type="text/css" href="fcmsite.css">
        <meta http-equiv="Content-Type" content="text/html; charset=UTF-8">
        <script src="http://ajax.googleapis.com/ajax/libs/jquery/1.8.2/jquery.min.js">
        </script>
        <script type="text/javascript">
        function sendPushNotification(id){
                var rid;
                var msg;
                if(id=='all'){
                    rid = 'all';
                    msg = $('#allform textarea[name=message]').val();
                } else {
                    rid = $('#form' + id + ' input[name=regId]').val();
                    msg = $('#form' + id + ' textarea[name=message]').val();
                }
                $.ajax({
                        url: "lm_send.php?message=" + msg + "&regid=" + rid
                });
                return false;
        }
```

```php
        </script>

</head>
<body>
    <?php
    include_once 'db_functions.php';
    $db = new DB_Functions();
    $users = $db->getAllUsers();
    if ($users != false)
        $no_of_users = mysql_num_rows($users);
    else
        $no_of_users = 0;
    ?>
    <div class="container">
            <h1>Send to all registered devices</h1>
        <form id="allform" name="" method="post" onsubmit="return sendPush
        Notification('all')">
            <div class="send_container">
                <textarea rows="3" name="message" id="message" cols="25"
                class="txt_message" placeholder="Type message here"></textarea>
                <input type="submit" class="send_btn" value="Send" onclick=""/>
            </div>
        </form>


        <h1>No of Devices Registered: <?php echo $no_of_users; ?></h1>
        <hr/>
        <ul class="devices">
            <?php
            if ($no_of_users > 0) {
                ?>
                <?php
                while ($row = mysql_fetch_array($users)) {
                    ?>
                    <li>
                        <form id="form<?php echo $row["id"] ?>" name="" method="post"
                        onsubmit="return sendPushNotification('<?php echo $row["id"] ?>')">
                            <label>ID: </label> <span><?php echo $row["fcm_regID"] ?>
                            </span>
                            <div class="clear"></div>
                            <div class="send_container">
                                <textarea rows="3" name="message" id="message" cols="25"
                                class="txt_message" placeholder="Type message here">
                                </textarea>
                                <input type="hidden" name="regId" id="regId"
                                value="<?php echo $row["fcm_regID"] ?>"/>
                                <input type="submit" class="send_btn" value="Send"
                                onclick=""/>
                            </div>
                        </form>
                    </li>
                <?php }
```

```
            } else { ?>
                <li>
                    No Users Registered Yet!
                </li>
            <?php } ?>
        </ul>
    </div>
</body>
</html>
```

The core functionality is in the sendPushNotification() javascript code near the top. As you can see, it gets the message text and calls lm_send.php with it and either the registration token (in the case of addressing a single device) or the word 'all'. Let's take a look at the code for lm_send.php next:

```php
<?php

    if(isset($_GET["message"])){
        $message = $_GET["message"];
    } else {
        $message = "Test Message";
    }
    $data = array("m" => $message);

    if(isset($_GET["regid"])){
        $regid = $_GET["regid"];
    } else {
        $regid = "testid";
    }

    if($regid=='all'){
        include_once 'db_functions.php';
    $db = new DB_Functions();
    $sql = mysql_query("select fcm_regid FROM fcm_users");
        $regdata = array();
        while($row = mysql_fetch_array($sql)){
            $regdata[] = $row[0];
        }

    } else {
        $regdata = array($regid);
    }

    echo($regdata[0]);
```

```php
$url = 'https://fcm.googleapis.com/fcm/send';
$headers = array(
        'Authorization: key=<Your Auth Key>',
        'Content-Type: application/json'
);

$fields = array(
        'registration_ids' => $regdata,
        'data' => $data
);

$ch = curl_init();
curl_setopt($ch, CURLOPT_URL, $url);
curl_setopt($ch, CURLOPT_POST, true);
curl_setopt($ch, CURLOPT_HTTPHEADER, $headers);
curl_setopt($ch, CURLOPT_RETURNTRANSFER, true);
    curl_setopt ($ch, CURLOPT_SSL_VERIFYHOST, 0);
curl_setopt($ch, CURLOPT_SSL_VERIFYPEER, false);
curl_setopt($ch, CURLOPT_POSTFIELDS, json_encode($fields));
$result = curl_exec($ch);
if ($result === FALSE) {
    die('Curl failed: ' . curl_error($ch));
}
curl_close($ch);
echo($result);

?>
```

To use the FCM APIs to send messages, you call the https://fcm.googleapis.com/fcm/ send endpoint, passing it headers containing your authorization info, and posting a JSON message to it containing a list of ids that you want to send to, and the message you want to send. This code achieves that by creating the message as a JSON array with a key/value pair of 'm' (for message) as the key, and the string you want to send as the value. To get the list of registration IDs, you simply read them from the database (in the case of all), or take the one that was passed in. It's really that simple!

To get an authorization key for FCM, navigate to the project settings and the 'Cloud Messaging' tab, and you'll see a Server Key was autopopulated for you when you created the project.

In the next step we'll update the app so it registers itself with this app server, and then we can send messages to it from the home page.

Updating the App

First of all, let's add another button to register the app with the app server. Update the activity_main.xml layout file to this:

```xml
<LinearLayout
    android:layout_width="368dp"
    android:layout_height="495dp"
    android:orientation="vertical"
    tools:layout_editor_absoluteY="8dp"
    tools:layout_editor_absoluteX="8dp">
    <Button
        android:layout_width="wrap_content"
        android:layout_height="wrap_content"
        android:text="Register"
        android:id="@+id/registerButton"/>
    <Button
        android:layout_width="wrap_content"
        android:layout_height="wrap_content"
        android:text="Tokyo"
        android:id="@+id/tokyoButton"/>
    <Button
        android:layout_width="wrap_content"
        android:layout_height="wrap_content"
        android:text="London"
        android:id="@+id/londonButton"/>
</LinearLayout>
```

Now in your main activity, when the user presses the button, the registration id should be attained from Firebase, and passed to the server. As this needs to be asynchronous and not executed on the main thread, a service called 'CallFCM' will be used. You'll see that in the next step.

```java
registerButton = (Button) findViewById(R.id.registerButton);
registerButton.setOnClickListener(new View.OnClickListener() {
    @Override
    public void onClick(View v) {
        HashMap<String, String> params = new HashMap();
        params.put("regid", FirebaseInstanceId.getInstance().getToken());
        new CallFCM().execute(params);
    }
});
```

To create a service to manage the asynchronous communication, add a new Class to your project, and superclass it with android.os.AsyncTask as shown in Figure 9-22.

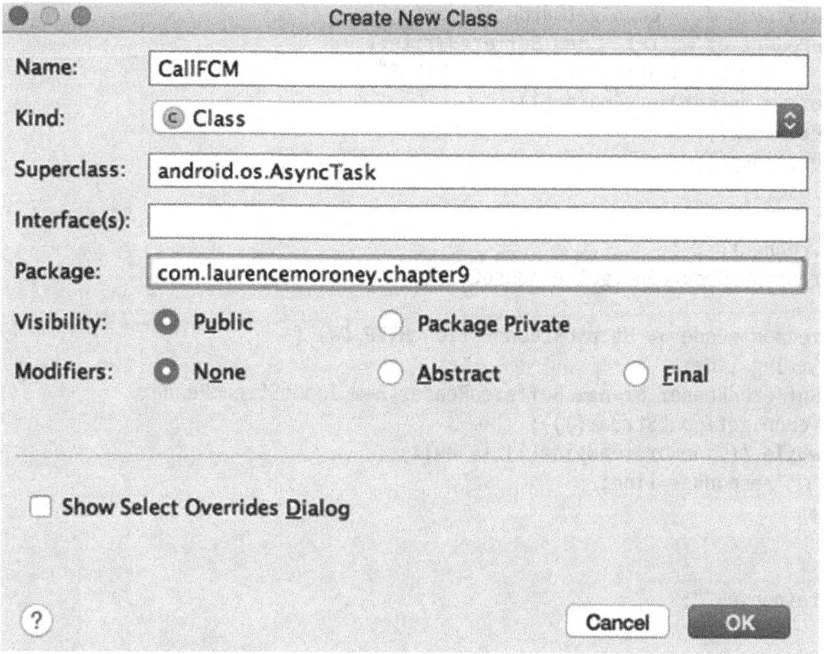

Figure 9-22. Adding an asynchronous class

An asynchronous task needs to overwrite the doInBackground method. In addition to that, as we're passing in a hash map of key/value pairs, the signature needs to be updated, like this:

```
public class CallFCM extends AsyncTask<HashMap<String, String>, String, String> {
    @Override
    protected String doInBackground(HashMap<String, String>... params) {
        return doCall(params[0]);
    }
}
```

This will take in the hashmaps, and pass it to the doCall function. This should post the parameters to your register endpoint.

```
private String doCall(HashMap<String, String> params){

    String response = "";
    try {
        // Replace this URL with your register script.
        URL url = new URL("http://laurencemoroney.com/fcm/register.php");

        HttpURLConnection conn = (HttpURLConnection) url.openConnection();
        conn.setReadTimeout(10000);
        conn.setConnectTimeout(15000);
        conn.setRequestMethod("GET");
        conn.setDoInput(true);
        conn.setDoOutput(true);
```

```
        OutputStream os = conn.getOutputStream();
        BufferedWriter writer = new BufferedWriter(
                new OutputStreamWriter(os, "UTF-8"));
        writer.write(getQuery(params));
        writer.flush();
        writer.close();
        os.close();

        conn.connect();
        int responseCode=conn.getResponseCode();

        if (responseCode == HttpsURLConnection.HTTP_OK) {
            String line;
            BufferedReader br=new BufferedReader(new InputStreamReader
            (conn.getInputStream()));
            while ((line=br.readLine()) != null) {
                response+=line;
            }
        }
        else {
            response="";

        }
    } catch (Exception e) {
        e.printStackTrace();
    }
    return response;
}
```

This function uses a helper method called getQuery that turns the hashmap into a UTF-8 encoded query string:

```
private String getQuery(HashMap<String, String> params) throws UnsupportedEncodingException
{
    StringBuilder result = new StringBuilder();
    boolean first = true;

    for (Map.Entry<String,String> pair : params.entrySet())
    {
        if (first)
            first = false;
        else
            result.append("&");

        result.append(URLEncoder.encode(pair.getKey(), "UTF-8"));
        result.append("=");
        result.append(URLEncoder.encode(pair.getValue(), "UTF-8"));
    }

    return result.toString();
}
```

Now when you launch your app and press the 'Register' button, it will register itself with the app server, and you'll see a new entry for it on the home page. See Figure 9-23.

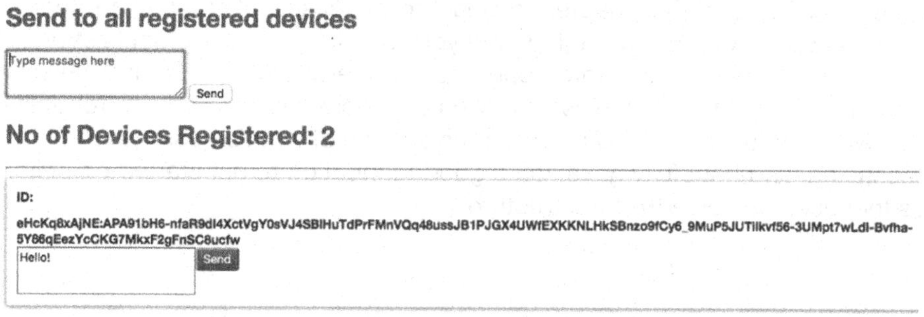

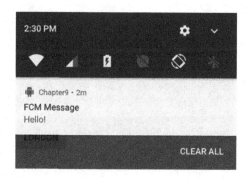

Figure 9-23. *Your device is registered*

Then, when you send from this page, your device will receive the notification as shown in Figure 9-24.

Figure 9-24. *Receiving the Message*

Next Steps

Now that you've built the foundations of your own app server, the possibilities for the next steps are limited only by your imagination. In this case you used the send endpoint on the FCM APIs to tell Firebase to send messages on your behalf. You can learn more about what you can do with the Firebase Cloud Messaging server API at: https://firebase.google.com/docs/cloud-messaging/server.

Summary

Firebase Cloud Messaging offers you a no-cost, reliable messaging platform for sending messages to your users. In this chapter you learned the basics of creating an Android app that uses Firebase Cloud Messaging, and you saw how to receive notifications in the background, or override them in a foreground app. You also saw how to use the server APIs in a PHP/MySQL server application, which gives you more fine-grained control over how to interface with your users. This touched on the surface of what's possible with Firebase Cloud Messaging, and hopefully gave you a good foundation to get started on building your own apps that use this powerful infrastructure.

Chapter 10

Firebase App Indexing

Firebase App Indexing is a technology that helps re-engage your users by leveraging something they do on their devices every day – search.

It works in two ways:

Public Content Indexing lets you connect your site to your app, so when users search for content that Google Search has crawled, this content may then be opened in your app instead of in the browser. The user has invested time and effort in installing your app on their device, so it makes sense that they may want to consume that content in your app too. About one-third of apps are only ever used once. This helps your app not be one of those.

Personal Content Indexing lets your users store their personal content from the app on their device, which creates an on-device index that can appear in the Google App on their device. This personal content index only exists on the user's device, but please refer to the Documentation for more information about privacy: https://firebase.google.com/docs/app-indexing/.

Public Content Indexing

Public Content Indexing works when you have a web site and a corresponding app. When the user searches the Web with Google, links to that content are typically opened with a web browser. Using Public Content Indexing, you can tell the search engine that you'd prefer this content to be opened in an app instead, where the potential for a richer experience is possible. To do this, the site and app need to be connected. On the site, you provide a file called a Digital Asset Links file that specifies which app the site can be opened with. On the app you implement code to accept incoming links from the search engine, and which activities in the app are used to consume them. We'll look at that first.

© Laurence Moroney 2017

L. Moroney, *The Definitive Guide to Firebase*, https://doi.org/10.1007/978-1-4842-2943-9_10

Create an App That Receives Incoming Links

Create a new Android App with an empty activity. Use the Firebase Assistant to connect the app to Firebase and then add the App Indexing Libraries to your app. These are steps 1 and 2 in the assistant.

Once you've done that, add two new empty Activities to your app. In Android Studio you do this by right-clicking on the package name, then selecting New ➤ Activity ➤ Empty Activity.

When you're done, you should have two new activities, and your AndroidManifest.xml file will be updated to look something like this:

```xml
<?xml version="1.0" encoding="utf-8"?>
<manifest xmlns:android="http://schemas.android.com/apk/res/android"
   package="com.laurencemoroney.chapter10">

   <application
       android:allowBackup="true"
       android:icon="@mipmap/ic_launcher"
       android:label="@string/app_name"
       android:roundIcon="@mipmap/ic_launcher_round"
       android:supportsRtl="true"
       android:theme="@style/AppTheme">
       <activity android:name=".MainActivity">
           <intent-filter>
               <action android:name="android.intent.action.MAIN" />

               <category android:name="android.intent.category.LAUNCHER" />
           </intent-filter>
       </activity>
       <activity android:name=".Activity1"></activity>
       <activity android:name=".Activity2"></activity>
   </application>

</manifest>
```

To receive incoming links from the search app, you'll need to specify the intent filters for Activity1 and Activity2. Android uses these to route which URLs are processed by which activity.

So, in this case, I have two pages on my site: laurencemoroney.com/equilibrium/ and everything under it should get routed to Activity1; and laurencemoroney.com/google/ and everything under it should get routed to Activity2.

Here's what your AndroidManifest should look like once you've updated it with these intent filters:

```xml
<?xml version="1.0" encoding="utf-8"?>
<manifest xmlns:android="http://schemas.android.com/apk/res/android"
   package="com.laurencemoroney.chapter10">
```

```
<application
    android:allowBackup="true"
    android:icon="@mipmap/ic_launcher"
    android:label="@string/app_name"
    android:roundIcon="@mipmap/ic_launcher_round"
    android:supportsRtl="true"
    android:theme="@style/AppTheme">
    <activity android:name=".MainActivity">
        <intent-filter>
            <action android:name="android.intent.action.MAIN" />

            <category android:name="android.intent.category.LAUNCHER" />
        </intent-filter>
    </activity>
    <activity android:name=".Activity1">
        <intent-filter android:label="Activity1Filter" android:autoVerify="true">
            <action android:name="android.intent.action.VIEW" />
            <category android:name="android.intent.category.DEFAULT"></category>
            <category android:name="android.intent.category.BROWSABLE"></category>
            <data android:scheme="http" android:host="laurencemoroney.com"
                android:pathPrefix="/equilibrium/"></data>
        </intent-filter>
    </activity>
    <activity android:name=".Activity2">
        <intent-filter android:label="Activity2Filter" android:autoVerify="true">
            <action android:name="android.intent.action.VIEW" />
            <category android:name="android.intent.category.DEFAULT"></category>
            <category android:name="android.intent.category.BROWSABLE"></category>
            <data android:scheme="http" android:host="laurencemoroney.com"
                android:pathPrefix="/google/"></data>
        </intent-filter>
    </activity>
</application>

</manifest>
```

To test to see if this works, add some code to Activity1 where we can take a look at the data that is passed in from the intent. Also add a TextView to its layout file. In this case I simply called that 'textView'.

```
@Override
protected void onCreate(Bundle savedInstanceState) {
    super.onCreate(savedInstanceState);
    setContentView(R.layout.activity_1);
    Intent intent = getIntent();
    String action = intent.getAction();
    String data = intent.getDataString();
    TextView textView = (TextView) findViewById(R.id.textView);
    textView.setText(data);
}
```

Run the app and you should see the main activity. You don't have a site link set up yet, and the app isn't in the play store, but you can still simulate what happens when a user touches a link on the Google Search app.

So, for example, if they were to search for content that is on laurencemoroney.com/equilibrium, and then touch on that link, the Google Search app would launch the app with that link as the context. The intent filters would then kick in, and as the one for Activity1 matches that URL, then that activity will launch.

To simulate this, you use the 'adb' command. If you don't have it already, you can easily install it using brew on a mac. You get brew with:

```
ruby -e "$(curl -fsSL https://raw.githubusercontent.com/Homebrew/install/master/install)"
```

Then install the android platform tools:

```
brew cask install android-platform-tools
```

If you use Windows, or another operating system, you can get the SDK Platform Tools at https://developer.android.com/studio/releases/platform-tools.html.

Now that you have adb installed, you can use it to simulate what the search app does. With adb you shell out to the app by its package name (in this case com.laurencemoroney.chapter10), specifying that you want to view it (android.intent.action.VIEW) passing the parameter of the URL as data with the -d switch. Here's the full command:

```
adb shell am start -a android.intent.action.VIEW -d "http://laurencemoroney.com/equilibrium/" com.laurencemoroney.chapter10
```

If all goes as planned, you should see Activity1 get launched, and its textView will be set to contain the data that was passed in. See Figure 10-1.

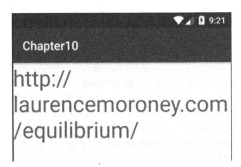

Figure 10-1. Activity 1 launches with the data

To ensure that the routing is working, launch the *other* activity by specifying a different URL, in this case one that matches /google/:

```
adb shell am start -a android.intent.action.VIEW -d "http://laurencemoroney.com/google/" com.laurencemoroney.chapter10
```

You'll see that the routing to Activity2 works as in Figure 10-2 (note that I put a TextView on Activity2 just saying 'This is Activity 2').

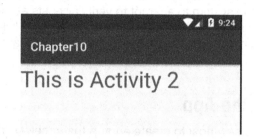

Figure 10-2. Routing to another Activity

Note that we set up the intent filters just to route to specific URLs. If we were to launch another URL, for example, http://laurencemoroney.com/xyzzy, we would get an error. See Figure 10-3.

```
laurences-imac:~ laurencemoroney$ adb shell am start -a android.intent.action.VIEW -d
"http://laurencemoroney.com/xyxxy" com.laurencemoroney.chapter10
Starting: Intent { act=android.intent.action.VIEW dat=http://laurencemoroney.com/... p
kg=com.laurencemoroney.chapter10 }
Error: Activity not started, unable to resolve Intent { act=android.intent.action.VIEW
  dat=http://laurencemoroney.com/... flg=0x10000000 pkg=com.laurencemoroney.chapter10 }
laurences-imac:~ laurencemoroney$
```

Figure 10-3. Error for unsupported Activity

The easiest solution to this is to add another activity, and have that activity be the catch-all for every other URL. So, for example, I created an Activity3, and updated the Android Manifest with these details:

```
<activity android:name=".Activity3">
    <intent-filter
        android:autoVerify="true"
        android:label="Activity3Filter">
        <action android:name="android.intent.action.VIEW" />

        <category android:name="android.intent.category.DEFAULT" />
        <category android:name="android.intent.category.BROWSABLE" />

        <data
            android:host="laurencemoroney.com"
            android:pathPrefix="/"
            android:scheme="http" />
    </intent-filter>
</activity>
```

Now, when I launch the app with a URL that isn't directly supported by any other activity this one can launch. You could use this to provide a generic error message to your end users.

Understanding Auto Verification

Note when you created the intent filters you set android:autoVerify to 'true'. This, on Android 6.0 or higher devices, causes the system to attempt to verify all hosts associated with the URLs. Should this pass, the app will then become the default way to open links at the associated URLs. In order to pass you need a digital asset links file on the site, and you'll explore that in the next section.

Connect a Site to the App

In the previous section you saw how to create an app that receives incoming links from the Google Search App. You tested it using the adb tool. In a real scenario, a user has installed your app from the Play Store, and is searching the Web using the Google Search App. They find content and launch your app that way. In order to do this, your web site needs to tell the Google Search engine what the associated app is. This is done with a Digital Asset Links (DAL) file. You can learn more about how DAL files are structured at: https://developers. google.com/digital-asset-links/v1/getting-started.

For Firebase App Indexing you need a DAL file containing a *relation* that specifies that you'll open all URLS, and a *target* that specifies the app that you'll open. The app is identified using its package name and its sha256 cert fingerprint. Getting this fingerprint is beyond the scope of this book. You get it as part of the process of signing your app to deploy it to the Play Store. When the user gets your app from the store, it can be verified based on that signature, which is secure as well as unique. You can learn more about the App publishing process, and getting the fingerprint at: https://developer.android.com/studio/publish/app-signing.html.

Here's an example of a DAL file:

```
[{
  "relation": ["delegate_permission/common.handle_all_urls"],
  "target" : { "namespace": "android_app",
      "package_name": "com.laurencemoroney.chapter10",
      "sha256_cert_fingerprints": ["hash_of_app_certificate"] }
}]
```

The file must be hosted at https://<hostname>/.well-known/assetlinks.json or it won't be found or auto verified.

Thus, when you've published your app to the Play Store, and if you have a web site containing content that you want people to view in your app, the process of doing so is as easy as following these steps. In the next section, we'll take that further by giving them the ability to have their own user-generated content saved on-device, and available for search.

Personal Content Indexing

With Personal Content Indexing, the Google Search App can find user-generated content in your app. The user's personal content is never uploaded to Google's servers, and is just kept on-device, so when the Search App is working it looks in an on-device index for it.

To see this in Action, edit the MainActivity in the app you've been working on in this chapter. First, edit the layout file so that you can enter a note, giving it a title and some text. Here's a rough implementation:

```xml
<?xml version="1.0" encoding="utf-8"?>
<android.support.constraint.ConstraintLayout xmlns:android="http://schemas.android.com/apk/
res/android"
    xmlns:app="http://schemas.android.com/apk/res-auto"
    xmlns:tools="http://schemas.android.com/tools"
    android:layout_width="match_parent"
    android:layout_height="match_parent"
    tools:context="com.laurencemoroney.chapter10.MainActivity">

<LinearLayout
    android:layout_width="368dp"
    android:layout_height="495dp"
    android:orientation="vertical"
    tools:layout_editor_absoluteY="8dp"
    tools:layout_editor_absoluteX="8dp">
    <LinearLayout
    android:layout_width="wrap_content"
    android:layout_height="wrap_content"
    android:orientation="horizontal">
        <TextView
            android:layout_width="wrap_content"
            android:layout_height="wrap_content"
            android:text="Title:"/>

        <EditText
            android:id="@+id/titleText"
            android:layout_width="wrap_content"
            android:layout_height="wrap_content"
            android:width="180dp" />
    </LinearLayout>
    <LinearLayout
        android:layout_width="wrap_content"
        android:layout_height="wrap_content"
        android:orientation="horizontal">
        <TextView
            android:layout_width="wrap_content"
            android:layout_height="wrap_content"
            android:text="Note:"/>

        <EditText
            android:id="@+id/noteText"
            android:layout_width="wrap_content"
            android:layout_height="wrap_content"
            android:width="180dp" />
```

```
    </LinearLayout>
    <Button
        android:layout_width="wrap_content"
        android:layout_height="wrap_content"
        android:text="Save"
        android:id="@+id/saveButton"/>
</LinearLayout>

</android.support.constraint.ConstraintLayout>
```

Now, in your Main Activity, you'll need to implement code on the Save Button to save the note to the index.

To do this you create an **Indexable** object. This is done using a builder on the **Indexables** abstract class. There are a number of document types that this supports, and note is one of them. To save a note you need three pieces of data – the name of the note, its text, and a URL. The user has entered the name and text for the note, so we need to generate a unique URL for each one. To do this I simply use a hard-coded URL and add a unique value on the end of it using System.currentTimeMillis().

Here's the code:

```
Indexable noteToIndex = Indexables.noteDigitalDocumentBuilder()
      .setName(titleText.getText().toString())
      .setText(noteText.getText().toString())
      .setUrl("http://laurencemoroney.com/notes/" + System.currentTimeMillis())
      .build();
```

The FirebaseAppindex abstract class gives you a number of methods that you can use for managing personal content indexing. In this case, you have an Indexable note; you simply save that to the on-device index using its update method. This gives you a task, so that it operates asynchronously, and gives you a callback when it succeeds and when it fails.

Here's the code:

```
Task<Void> task = FirebaseAppIndex.getInstance().update(noteToIndex);
task.addOnSuccessListener(new OnSuccessListener<Void>() {
   @Override
   public void onSuccess(Void aVoid) {
      Log.d("Ch10", "Successfully added note to index");
   }
});
task.addOnFailureListener(new OnFailureListener() {
   @Override
   public void onFailure(@NonNull Exception e) {
      Log.d("Ch10", "Failed to add note. Reason: " + e.getMessage());
   }
});
```

This gives you everything you need to save the note to the index. Run the app and give it a try. See Figure 10-4 to see it in action where I am creating a note.

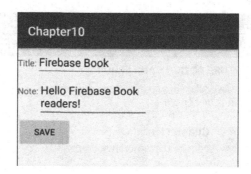

Figure 10-4. Creating an Indexable note

Then, when I search with the Google Search App, and go to the In Apps tab on the right-hand side, I can see that this content is available in an App called Chapter10! See Figure 10-5.

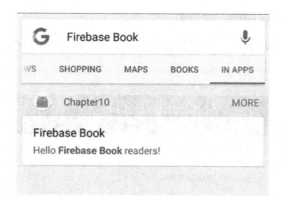

Figure 10-5. Finding your Indexed content

You can see what you've indexed using the Settings app on Android. Make sure your phone is in Developer Mode before continuing. To get into Developer Mode, go to Settings ➤ About. Scroll to the bottom, and find the Build Number setting. Tap it a number of times until you see a message about Developer Mode being enabled.

Once you're in Developer Mode, you can go to Settings ➤ Google. Scroll to the bottom, and you'll see Developer Mode settings, including Firebase App Indexing. Select it, and you'll see all apps that are using Firebase App Indexing to store personal content. See Figure 10-6.

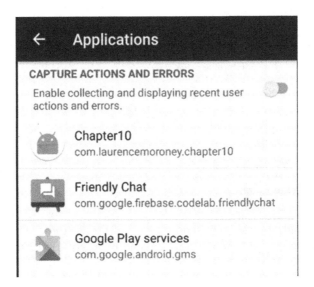

Figure 10-6. *Apps using Personal Content Indexing*

Select your app, in this case Chapter 10, and you'll see details on what it has indexed. See Figure 10-7.

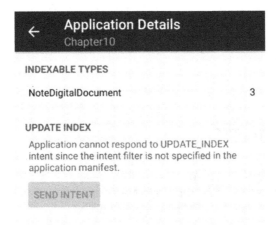

Figure 10-7. *Application Details*

You can't update the index yet because you haven't specified an intent filter for doing so. We'll discuss that shortly. You can see that there are three NoteDigitalDocument objects available, and you can select that entry to see them. See Figure 10-8.

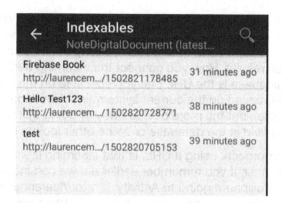

Figure 10-8. *Browsing the saved Indexables*

You can also select each Indexable to see details on it. See Figure 10-9 for an example.

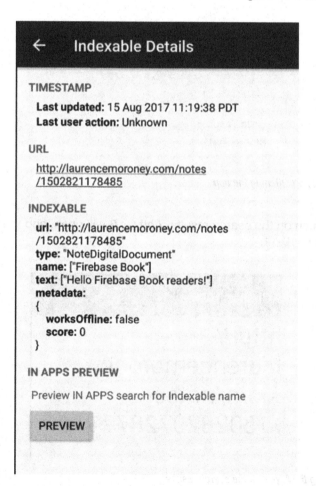

Figure 10-9. *Details of an Indexable*

In this case we only save the contents of the notes to the index, and don't save the notes locally. A typical note-taking app would, of course, save details on the notes so you can retrieve and view them at a later date. This would typically be done when the user touches on the note in the search results. How you connect the incoming details from the search results with your own database is the URL that you specified on the note. In this case, I used a unique identifier, based on the current system time (see /notes/1502821178485 in Figure 10-9 as an example), but the more obvious way of doing this would be the primary key index number of the field in the database or some other lookup identifier.

What's nice about this approach, using a URL, is that incoming links can then be directed to activities using an intent filter. If you remember earlier on, we had incoming links from http://laurencemoroney.com/equilibrium going to Activity 1, http://laurencemoroney.com/google going to Activity 2, and everything else going to Activity 3. The same mechanism is used, so when you touch on the search results, you'll open Activity 3. See Figure 10-10 for the search results.

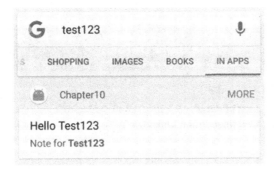

Figure 10-10. *Searching for content in the app*

And then when I touch on the search results, Activity 3 will open, and the URL will be displayed. See Figure 10-11.

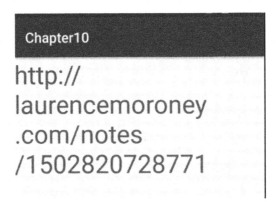

Figure 10-11. *Launching the App from the search results*

(To render the URL you'll need to edit Activity 3. See earlier for how I did Activity 1, and just follow the same process.)

Going Further

This just gave you a simple taste for what's possible with Personal Content Indexing. To go further, there are lots of other things you can do to build a better user experience.

Regular Indexing

In this example, the content was indexed at the moment of creation. As you saw, there was an asynchronous callback that was performed. If you create a lot of content, this may not be the most efficient way of doing it. Instead, you should consider implementing an intent filter for UPDATE_INDEX and using that to trigger an IntentService to batch save new content to the index. The recipe app codelab for App Indexing has a great example of this: https://codelabs.developers.google.com/codelabs/app-indexing.

Other Content Types

In this scenario you saved a simple note, but there are many different types of custom content that are built in and savable, including things like PersonBuilder for contact details, MessageBuilder for messages, and many more. You can see the full list at: https://firebase.google.com/docs/reference/android/com/google/firebase/appindexing/builders/package-summary.

User-Defined Content Types

The Indexable.Builder class allows you to create your own indexable types, so if you have some data types that are unique to your app, or not covered in the builders, you can create your own and have them indexed.

Summary

In this chapter you looked at Firebase App Indexing, a technology that helps you re-engage your users and maintain the growth of your app as a result. You saw how it works by integrating with search in two ways: **Public Content Indexing** by connecting your public indexable content (on a web site) with your app, so users searching the web for this content can be directed to your app to consume it; and **Personal Content Indexing**, which can create an on-device personal index of user-generated content that is available to the Search App so that users can re-engage with your app once they find it. Using these technologies, you can plug your app into the regular, daily, search workflow that your users follow.

Chapter **11**

Remote Configuration

Firebase Remote Configuration (aka Remote Config) is a technology that allows you to change the behavior and appearance of your app without publishing an app update. It's a cloud service that can store variables on your behalf. The magic is when these variables can be set using Analytics. So, for example, consider the scenario in which you have an e-commerce application where you provide a standard discount to your end users. You have a lot of customers in the USA, but very few in the UK. So you decide to offer a 10% discount to people in the UK, while keeping it at 0% in the USA. While you're at it, you also want to grow in Ireland, so you offer them a 10% discount, too. Think about how you would do this in an app – you'd likely have code that says something like the following:

```
if(user_in_uk || user_in_ie){
    discount=10;
} else {
    discount=0;
}
```

Then you suddenly get lots of users in the UK, but not enough in Ireland. What do you do? Continue losing money in the UK because your introductory discount is too big? Or change your code so that only users in the UK get a discount? This would mean you'd have to push out an app update with new code.

You can get this flexibility using Remote Configuration. In this case you set a variable for the discount on the Firebase Console, and set its value using Analytics. Then, in the console you say the default value, and the amount for each audience. At runtime you read the value, so, in the above scenario, you would just make the changes on the Firebase Console, the app would get the new discount, and you haven't forced an update on your users.

© Laurence Moroney 2017
L. Moroney, *The Definitive Guide to Firebase*, https://doi.org/10.1007/978-1-4842-2943-9_11

Building an App for Remote Config

Create a new app and connect it to Firebase using the Firebase Assistant. Once you've done this, make sure you add the Remote Config libraries in the appropriate step.

As part of this process you would have created a Firebase project. Open it and find the Remote Configuration tab. On there you can add a parameter. Give it the key 'GREETINGS_TEXT' and a value something like 'Hi from Remote Config!' Once you've entered it, hit the ADD PARAMETER button. See Figure 11-1.

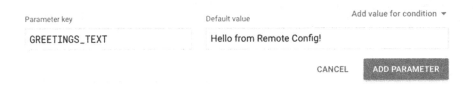

Figure 11-1. Adding a Remote Config Variable

Be sure to also press the PUBLISH CHANGES button at the top of the screen to commit the new values. It's a common mistake to miss this! See Figure 11-2.

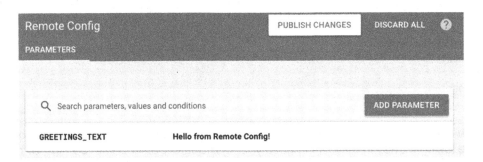

Figure 11-2. Publish Changes

Back in Android Studio, edit the layout file to give the TextView an ID. In this example I called it 'greetingsText'. Once you're done, edit the MainActivity code as follows.

First, you'll initialize the TextView and greetings strings:

```
greetingsTextView = (TextView) findViewById(R.id.greetingsText);
greeting = "Hello, World!";
```

Then you'll need an instance of the Firebase Remote Config class. You can do this by calling getInstance() on the FirebaseRemoteConfig abstract class:

```
final FirebaseRemoteConfig mFirebaseRemoteConfig = FirebaseRemoteConfig.getInstance();
```

Before calling remote config, you should set the configuration settings. There are a number of settings you can use, but the important one when learning and developing is to use Developer Mode. Firebase Remote Config reads are strongly throttled so as to avoid denial-of-service attacks, but when you are building and testing an app these throttles can cause your app to misbehave, so use developer mode, where there are no throttles; but a limited number of devices can be turned on using configuration settings. Here's the code:

```
FirebaseRemoteConfigSettings configSettings = new FirebaseRemoteConfigSettings.Builder()
        .setDeveloperModeEnabled(BuildConfig.DEBUG)
        .build();
mFirebaseRemoteConfig.setConfigSettings(configSettings);
```

Now it's time to fetch remote config variables. Instead of an API to fetch each one individually, Firebase provides the facility to fetch all at once in an asynchronous manner. Once you have them all you can then grab each individual one. The values will be fetched from either your local cache (aka the Default config) or the Remote Configuration Server. When you aren't running in developer mode, the values will be cached for 12 hours after a successful read. In developer mode (as we are here), you can set the cache expiration.

By passing a value to the fetch() method you can specify how long the local cache expires in. For development, if you always want to fetch from the server, use a very low value here – like 0. If you use greater than 0, you'll cache the values for that number of seconds.

```
mFirebaseRemoteConfig.fetch(0)
        .addOnCompleteListener(this, new OnCompleteListener<Void>() {
            @Override
            public void onComplete(@NonNull Task<Void> task) {
                if(task.isSuccessful()){
                    mFirebaseRemoteConfig.activateFetched();
                    greeting = mFirebaseRemoteConfig.getString("GREETINGS_TEXT");
                    greetingsTextView.setText(greeting);
                } else {
                    // Task Failed, handle it
                }
            }
        });
```

It's an asynchronous task, so when it completes, the onComplete method will fire. In this you can check if the task is successful or not. If it retrieves configuration data, you can then activate it, and read it piece by piece. In this case I have a remote config variable called GREETINGS_TEXT that I read into a local string and then use to set the caption of the TextView.

For convenience, here's the full code for the Activity:

```
package com.laurencemoroney.firebasech11;

import android.support.annotation.NonNull;
import android.support.v7.app.AppCompatActivity;
import android.os.Bundle;
import android.widget.TextView;
```

```java
import com.google.android.gms.tasks.OnCompleteListener;
import com.google.android.gms.tasks.Task;
import com.google.firebase.remoteconfig.FirebaseRemoteConfig;
import com.google.firebase.remoteconfig.FirebaseRemoteConfigSettings;

public class MainActivity extends AppCompatActivity {

    TextView greetingsTextView;
    String greeting;
    @Override
    protected void onCreate(Bundle savedInstanceState) {
        super.onCreate(savedInstanceState);
        setContentView(R.layout.activity_main);
        greetingsTextView = (TextView) findViewById(R.id.greetingsText);
        greeting = "Hello, World!";
        final FirebaseRemoteConfig mFirebaseRemoteConfig = FirebaseRemoteConfig.getInstance();
        FirebaseRemoteConfigSettings configSettings = new FirebaseRemoteConfig
        Settings.Builder()
                .setDeveloperModeEnabled(BuildConfig.DEBUG)
                .build();
    mFirebaseRemoteConfig.setConfigSettings(configSettings);
    mFirebaseRemoteConfig.fetch(0)
            .addOnCompleteListener(this, new OnCompleteListener<Void>() {
                @Override
                public void onComplete(@NonNull Task<Void> task) {
                    if(task.isSuccessful()){
                        mFirebaseRemoteConfig.activateFetched();
                        greeting = mFirebaseRemoteConfig.getString("GREETINGS_TEXT");
                        greetingsTextView.setText(greeting);
                    } else {
                        // Task Failed, handle it
                    }
                }
            });
    }
}
```

When you run the app, if everything works, you'll see that instead of the default 'Hello World' label on the screen, you'll get whatever value you entered into Remote Config. See Figure 11-3.

Figure 11-3. Getting the Remote Config Value in the App

Using Default Values

In this example, we had a very simple case of reading a string from Remote Config and then rendering it in a TextView. The string was already set to 'Hello World!' prior to this, giving it a default value in case Remote Configuration failed. Should the absence of a value cause an issue in your app, it makes sense to have default values set. There are a number of ways you could do this – for example, doing it in code or as part of a layout file, but not all of these are consistent (you can't set the value of a variable as part of a layout, for example), so using an XML resource file for the default values makes sense. Remote Config can load a specially structured XML file with the setDefaults() method. Let's check it out.

In your Android Studio project, right-click the 'res' folder and select New ➤ Android resource file. See Figure 11-4.

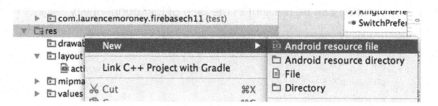

Figure 11-4. Adding a new Resource File

In the New Resource File dialog, give the file the name 'defaults' and ensure that the Resource Type is set to XML and the Root element to 'defaultsMap'. See Figure 11-5.

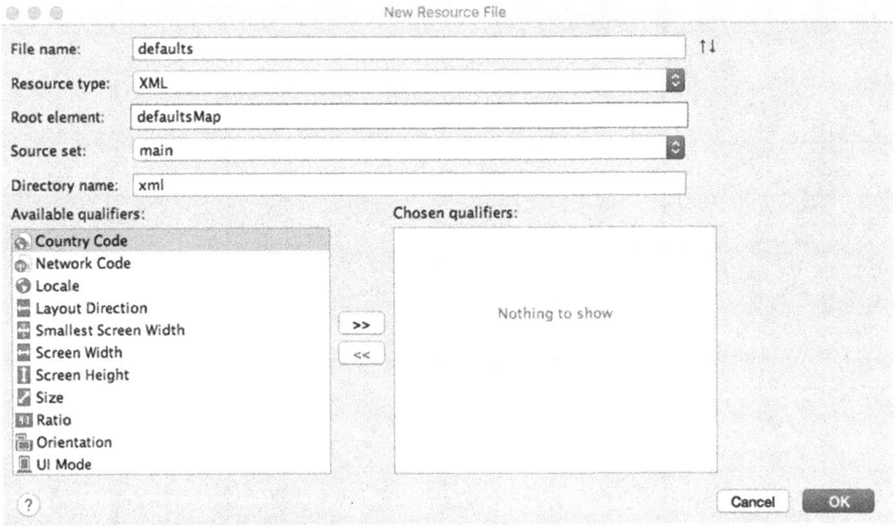

Figure 11-5. *Creating the XML Defaults File*

Now that you have the file, it's easy to update it to contain keys and values. If the remote configuration values aren't available due to connectivity or other issues, you'll get the defaults.

Here's the XML file:

```
<?xml version="1.0" encoding="utf-8"?>
<defaultsMap>
    <entry>
        <key>GREETINGS_TEXT</key>
        <value>Well howdy there, how are you?</value>
    </entry>
</defaultsMap>
```

And here's the code to read it:

```
mFirebaseRemoteConfig.setDefaults(R.xml.defaults);
```

This way your application can be resilient in the face of lost connectivity.

Supported Data Types

In this example you retrieved a String value from Remote Config. In addition to this you also have the following methods, each retrieving their named data type:

- getBoolean()
- getByteArray()
- getDouble()
- getLong()

Each one will use a String key, and if Remote Config stores that type, make sure that you use the correct method in order to ensure that the returned value is of the right data type.

Using Conditions with Remote Config

Where Remote Configuration gets really powerful is when you use Conditions. These set the value of the variable based on details about the user or app derived from Google Analytics for Firebase. So, for example, in our 'Hello World' app, we could change the greeting based on the country the user is coming from.

You create a condition in the Firebase Console. If you have conditions, you'll see a tab at the top of the Remote Config screen; otherwise you can add one from within editing a parameter. If you've been following this chapter, you'll see the GREETINGS_TEXT parameter. Click the pencil icon beside it to enter the editor. At the top of the screen you'll see 'Add value for condition'. See Figure 11-6.

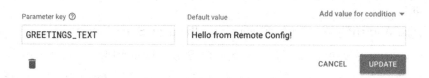

Figure 11-6. Adding a value for a Condition

Click it and you'll see an option to 'Define a new condition'. This will give you a popup that allows you to name a condition, give it a color, and then specify when that condition applies. See Figure 11-7.

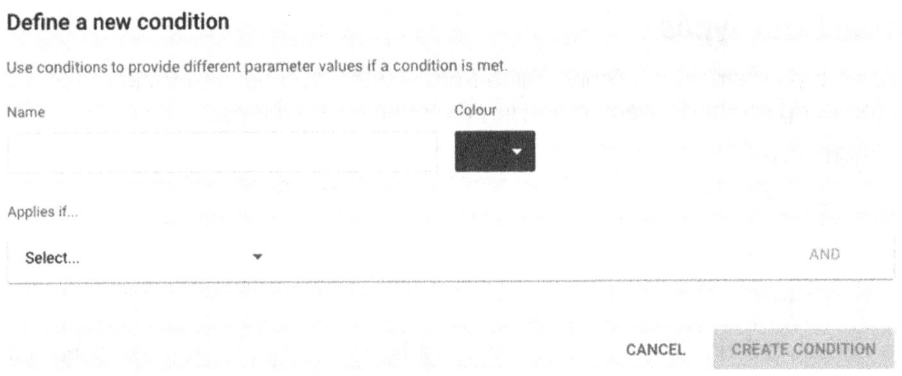

Define a new condition

Use conditions to provide different parameter values if a condition is met.

Name   Colour

Applies if...

Select...   ▼   AND

                                                          CANCEL   CREATE CONDITION

Figure 11-7. Defining a new Condition

The 'Applies If...' section allow you to pick when you want that condition to apply based on the following:

- ■ App Version: You can have multiple versions of the app or multiple apps in the Firebase project, and can set a condition for that.

- ■ OS Type: Android or iOS.

- ■ User in random percentile: Each user will have a persistent percentile that is randomly assigned on a per-project basis. You can use this to set a condition for users that are in a given percentile.

- ■ Device Language: Including locale.

- ■ Country or Region: As inferred from the device. You can set multiple ones.

- ■ User Audience: Analytics audience for the user. See Chapter 14.

- ■ User Property: Analytics user property. See Chapter 14.

By combining these you have a very powerful and flexible way to determine a condition, and you can then set the Remote Config variable for that. So, for example, Figure 11-8 shows where I set a condition called 'EnglishSpeaking' for four countries (USA, UK, Canada, Ireland).

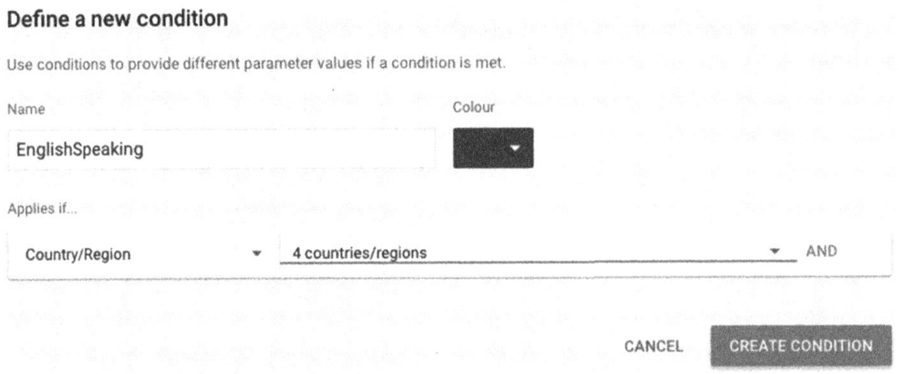

Define a new condition

Use conditions to provide different parameter values if a condition is met.

Name   Colour

EnglishSpeaking

Applies if...

Country/Region   ▼   4 countries/regions   ▼   AND

                                                          CANCEL   CREATE CONDITION

Figure 11-8. Creating a new condition

When done, click 'Create Condition' and you'll be returned to the value editor. You can now set the value for that parameter. See Figure 11-9.

Parameter key ⑦   Value for **EnglishSpeaking**   Add value for condition ▾

GREETINGS_TEXT   Good day to you, sir!   DELETE

                                         Default value

                                         Hello from Remote Config!

🗑   CANCEL   UPDATE

Figure 11-9. Updating the value

Don't forget to click UPDATE and then Publish to get Remote Config to read from this value going forward.

You'll also notice that the Conditions tab has now appeared at the top of the screen, and you can use this to manage the Conditions directly. See Figure 11-10.

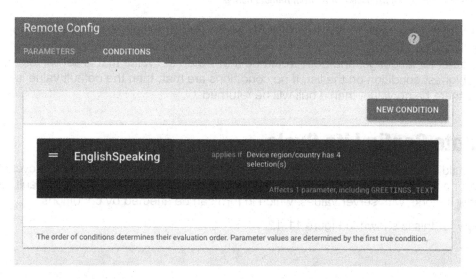

Figure 11-10. Managing Conditions

Now when you run the app, the value will be read from Remote Config using the condition. See Figure 11-11.

Figure 11-11. Condition-based Value read from Remote Config

You can, of course, have multiple conditions, each setting multiple values. When it comes to conflicting conditions being met – for example you could perhaps set one for country and another for language, and both would be met – then the value that is set will be the one for the highest condition on the list. If no conditions are met, then the default value is set. Should there be no value, then a null will be returned.

Remote Config Life Cycle

When building apps that use Remote Config, it's important to understand the life cycle for how your app interfaces with Remote Config with regard to how it works with default values, and how it works with server values, which in turn can be affected by conditions.

The flow for this is shown in Figure 11-12.

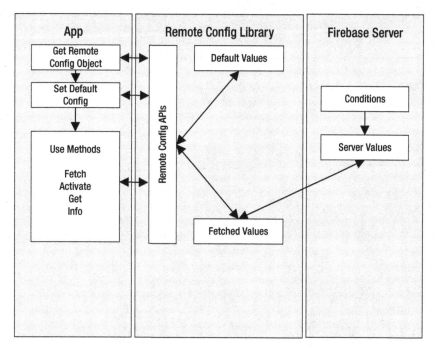

Figure 11-12. How Remote Config gets values

First your app will create a Remote Config object using the API. When it has this, it can set its configuration, including where it will get default values from. At this point the object is initialized with default values, so if you can go no further, you'll have a functional data set for your app. Once you've done this, you can then fetch data from Remote Config via the APIs. If the cache hasn't expired, then the API will get fetched values for you. Fetched values are attained from the server. At the time of fetching, the conditions will be applied, and the correct values for the condition will be downloaded, and made available to the app via the API.

Remote Config will typically cache the values after the first successful fetching. By default, the cache will expire after 12 hours but you can override this as shown earlier. It keeps track of the values in the cache, and if they are older than the expiration, then fresh values will be retrieved and re-cached.

Summary

In this chapter you saw how Remote Configuration works in Firebase, and how it can be used to store variable values, set by conditions and analytics, on the server. With this you can implement functionality that changes the behavior of your app without requiring you to redeploy your app. This can be used to provide customized onboarding experiences, apps with dynamic discounts, A/B testing, and much more. You saw how to use conditions and analytics to set the value of the variable, giving it great flexibility, and also how to access Remote Config variables from inside your Android App!

Chapter **12**

Dynamic Links and Invites

Firebase Dynamic Links are links to an app that contain context about what you want the end user to see in the app, which will be maintained whether the app is installed or not – the context is maintained through the install process.

In this chapter we'll first look at Dynamic Links, and how you can create and process them. We'll then go into how you can expand on these using Firebase Invites, which give you an intelligent way to share your app with the contacts in your user's address book over either email or SMS. When the user opts to share your app, Google will give them a set of intelligently sorted contacts – suggestions for who to share with based on the contacts that the user communicates with frequently.

Dynamic Links

To use Dynamic Links, first create a new project called FirebaseCh12-DL, and use the assistant to connect it to a project and add Dynamic Links to it. Once you've done this and created a project on the Firebase Console, you can use it to create Dynamic Links for you. There are a number of methods to create links, including a REST API, and a builder in Android Studio, but we'll look at the console first.

In the console, select the Dynamic Links tab on the left. Then click the 'New Dynamic Link' button, and you'll be presented with the steps to create a link. Start by defining a URL for the deep link, and giving it a name. I'm going to go with <context>.website.com as the format. Then, if I am using the dynamic link on the desktop, instead of mobile, there's a web site it can go to. So, for example I created a subdomain on my website as http://link-activity. laurencemoroney.com/. So if I set up a deep link to that URL, when the desktop user clicks on it, they'll go to the web site. When the mobile user clicks on it, they'll get the mobile app with a custom activity that can read the context from the link.

So, in step 1, fill out the URL and the name you want to give to the Dynamic Link. See Figure 12-1.

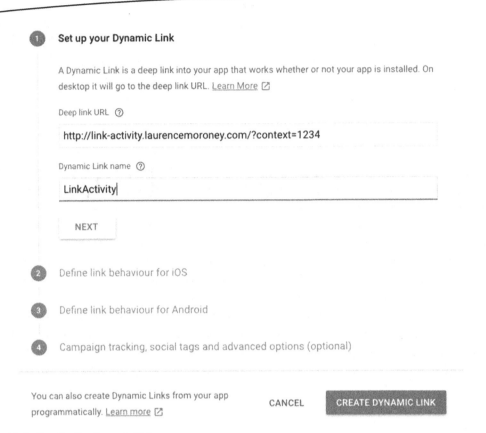

Figure 12-1. Creating the Dynamic Link

Step 2 defines the link behavior for iOS. As we're just covering Android in this book, you can keep the defaults and move to step 3.

In step 3, you specify the behavior for Android. Select 'Open the deep link in your Android App', and specify the app to use. If you created the project via the Android Studio Assistant, your app should be here. If not you'll need to connect and app to the project first. See Figure 12-2 for the settings. Make sure you pick 'Google Play page for your app' for when the app isn't installed. Nothing will happen now, but later, if you deploy the app to the Play Store, users without the app installed will be able to install the app directly and keep the context.

Figure 12-2 shows the settings.

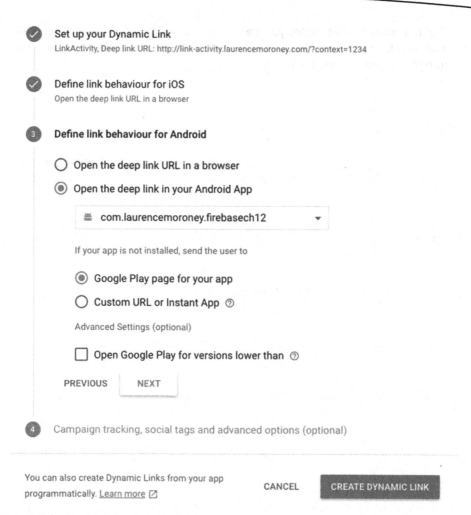

Figure 12-2. Defining the link behavior for Android

You can skip step 3, and just click 'Create Dynamic Link'. You'll be returned to the list of links, and it may take a moment before you see your new link. When you have it, you'll see its URL, as well as the name, created date, and in time data about its usage. See Figure 12-3.

Figure 12-3. Your dynamic links

To the right of the list is a caret where you can select the following options: Link Details, Link Analytics, and Link Preview. Select 'Link Preview' and you'll get a visual for how it is expected to behave. See Figure 12-4.

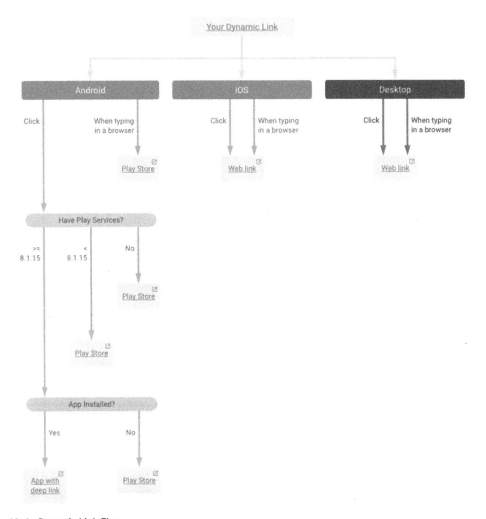

Figure 12-4. Dynamic Link Flow

From here you can see how it will behave on iOS and the Desktop – because we didn't specify behavior for iOS, both will lead to a web link. In the case of Android, you can also see the behavior of the app – if it is installed, it will be launched, otherwise, or if it doesn't support the requisite Google Play services, the user will get a play store link.

If you select 'LinkActivity', you'll see the full details on the link. See Figure 12-5.

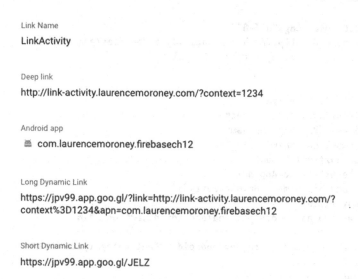

Link Name

LinkActivity

Deep link

http://link-activity.laurencemoroney.com/?context=1234

Android app

com.laurencemoroney.firebasech12

Long Dynamic Link

https://jpv99.app.goo.gl/?link=http://link-activity.laurencemoroney.com/?
context%3D1234&apn=com.laurencemoroney.firebasech12

Short Dynamic Link

https://jpv99.app.goo.gl/JELZ

Figure 12-5. *Dynamic Link details*

As you can see, the deep link is what we specified, and this was converted into a long dynamic link containing it and the app as parameters. In addition to this Firebase has an auto-link shortening service that provides the short version of the Dynamic Link.

Indeed, if you are on a desktop, you can try it – typing https://jpv99.app.goo.gl/JELZ will take you to the deep link as a website. See Figure 12-6.

Chapter 12 link activity

Figure 12-6. *Visiting the deep link site*

So now let's take a look at opening an activity from the app, and getting details about the context.

Editing the App

First of all, in the app, you'll need to edit the AndroidManifest.xml to include an intent filter that handles URLs matching those from the incoming link. This is very similar to what you did for App Indexing in Chapter 10. The main activity has an existing intent filter for launching it, so be sure to add a second one containing the details of the incoming URL that you want to be browsable. Here's the complete AndroidManifest.xml file with both intent filters.

```xml
<?xml version="1.0" encoding="utf-8"?>
<manifest xmlns:android="http://schemas.android.com/apk/res/android"
    package="com.laurencemoroney.firebasech12_dl">

    <application
        android:allowBackup="true"
        android:icon="@mipmap/ic_launcher"
        android:label="@string/app_name"
        android:roundIcon="@mipmap/ic_launcher_round"
        android:supportsRtl="true"
        android:theme="@style/AppTheme">
        <activity android:name=".MainActivity">
            <intent-filter>
                <action android:name="android.intent.action.MAIN" />

                <category android:name="android.intent.category.LAUNCHER" />
            </intent-filter>
            <intent-filter>
                <action android:name="android.intent.action.VIEW"/>
                <category android:name="android.intent.category.DEFAULT"/>
                <category android:name="android.intent.category.BROWSABLE"/>
                <data
                    android:host="laurencemoroney.com"
                    android:scheme="https"/>
                <data
                    android:host="laurencemoroney.com"
                    android:scheme="http"/>
            </intent-filter>
        </activity>
    </application>

</manifest>
```

When you created the app it had a basic layout on the activity containing a TextView. This TextView control didn't have an id attribute set, so be sure to edit activity_main.xml to contain one. Here's the code:

```xml
<?xml version="1.0" encoding="utf-8"?>
<android.support.constraint.ConstraintLayout xmlns:android="http://schemas.android.com/apk/res/android"
    xmlns:app="http://schemas.android.com/apk/res-auto"
    xmlns:tools="http://schemas.android.com/tools"
    android:layout_width="match_parent"
    android:layout_height="match_parent"
    tools:context="com.laurencemoroney.firebasech12_dl.MainActivity">

    <TextView
        android:layout_width="wrap_content"
        android:layout_height="wrap_content"
        android:text="Hello World!"
        android:id="@+id/contentText"
        app:layout_constraintBottom_toBottomOf="parent"
```

```
        app:layout_constraintLeft_toLeftOf="parent"
        app:layout_constraintRight_toRightOf="parent"
        app:layout_constraintTop_toTopOf="parent" />

</android.support.constraint.ConstraintLayout>
```

Now in MainActivity in your onCreate you can set up your activity to parse the incoming Dynamic Link in the scenario where the app is launched using one.

This is achieved using FirebaseDynamicLinks.getInstance(). On this you can add a success listener and failure listener. The success listener takes PendingDynamicLinkData as a parameter, and when this is not null, your link details are available in its getLink() method. The onFailure listener will catch failures, passing exception details that you can log. So, for example, here's how to catch the dynamic link details and render them in the Main Activity.

```
contentText = (TextView) findViewById(R.id.contentText);
FirebaseDynamicLinks.getInstance()
        .getDynamicLink(getIntent())
        .addOnSuccessListener(this, new OnSuccessListener<PendingDynamicLinkData>() {
            @Override
            public void onSuccess(PendingDynamicLinkData pendingDynamicLinkData) {
                // Get deep link from result (may be null if no link is found)
                Uri deepLink = null;
                if (pendingDynamicLinkData != null) {
                    deepLink = pendingDynamicLinkData.getLink();
                }

                if (deepLink != null) {
                    contentText.setText(deepLink.toString());
                } else {
                    Log.d("CH12-DL", "getDynamicLink: no link found");
                }
                // [END_EXCLUDE]
            }
        })
        .addOnFailureListener(this, new OnFailureListener() {
            @Override
            public void onFailure(@NonNull Exception e) {
                Log.w("CH12-DL", "getDynamicLink:onFailure", e);
            }
        });
```

Run the app, and you should see the familiar 'Hello World' in the empty activity. See Figure 12-7.

Figure 12-7. *Launching without Dynamic Link*

Now email the dynamic link to an account that is on the device, so that it can be launched from there, something like you see in Figure 12-8.

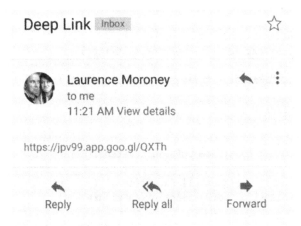

Figure 12-8. *Receiving a Dynamic Link in an email*

Now touch on the link, and your app will open. You may be asked how to open the app and be given a number of options. If so, select 'Google Play services' as the method to open it. When it opens the details of the Dynamic Link will be shown in the TextView. See Figure 12-9.

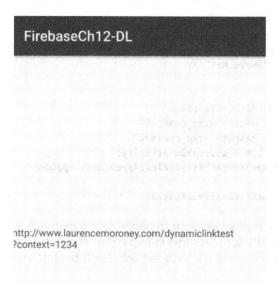

Figure 12-9. Opening the Dynamic Link

In this case we caught all URLs in the Main Activity by specifying it in the intent filter. Should we decide to, we could set up separate activities for different URLs, but in the case where you could have very many dynamic links (for example, if the users create their own as you'll see shortly), it's best to have a single activity to handle them all, and then based on the parameters passed into it, you could pick different activities to load.

Creating a Dynamic Link Within the App

The most useful context for sharing Dynamic Links, with context, is when a user with your app can pick content or an activity and then share that with other users. In order to do this they should be able to create Dynamic Links on-the-fly, and Firebase offers an API to do that. Let's explore that next.

In your app, add a new Activity called ShareableActivity. Give this activity a simple UI with a button and a TextView. Here's an example:

```xml
<?xml version="1.0" encoding="utf-8"?>
<android.support.constraint.ConstraintLayout xmlns:android="http://schemas.android.com/apk/
res/android"
    xmlns:app="http://schemas.android.com/apk/res-auto"
    xmlns:tools="http://schemas.android.com/tools"
    android:layout_width="match_parent"
    android:layout_height="match_parent"
    tools:context="com.laurencemoroney.firebasech12_dl.ShareableActivity">
    <LinearLayout
        android:layout_width="match_parent"
        android:layout_height="match_parent"
        android:orientation="vertical">
        <Button
```

```
        android:id="@+id/shareButton"
        android:layout_width="wrap_content"
        android:layout_height="wrap_content"
        android:text="Share Me!" />

    <TextView
        android:id="@+id/shareTextView"
        android:layout_width="wrap_content"
        android:layout_height="wrap_content"
        android:text="I'm a shareable activity!"
        android:textAppearance="@style/TextAppearance.AppCompat.Headline" />
    </LinearLayout>
</android.support.constraint.ConstraintLayout>
```

When the user clicks the button we want to generate a dynamic link that can then be shared with others. The API supports this in two different steps. The first is to create the link itself, and the second is to create a shortened link. Look back to Figure 12-5 and you'll see examples of these.

To create a dynamic link, you first need the Uri that you want to link to. In this case, I'm just hard-coding a simple one, but if this activity was rendering data from a database, you'd probably want to parameterize an identifier on that database. You'll also need the *link domain*. This is visible in the Firebase Console when you look in the dynamic links section. So, for example, take a look at Figure 12-10, and you can see that my link domain is jpv99. app.goo.gl. Make sure you know what yours is before proceeding.

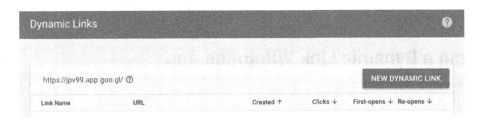

Figure 12-10. Finding the link domain

Now that you have the destination link and the link domain, you can use a FirebaseDynamicLinks.getInstance() to create a dynamic link like this:

```
DynamicLink.Builder builder = FirebaseDynamicLinks.getInstance()
        .createDynamicLink()
        .setDynamicLinkDomain(linkdomain)
        .setAndroidParameters(new DynamicLink.AndroidParameters.Builder()
            .setMinimumVersion(minVersion)
            .build())
        .setLink(destinationLink);
DynamicLink link = builder.buildDynamicLink();
```

The DynamicLink object that is created supports a getUri() method that you can use to determine the Uri of the returned Dynamic Link.

Now that you have this, you can then create a shortened link using the same API. This works asynchronously so you have to use it within a Task<> to create a ShortDynamicLink object. You simply pass it the Uri of the long link and ask it to build a short link from it. Here's the code:

```
Task<ShortDynamicLink> task = FirebaseDynamicLinks.getInstance()
      .createDynamicLink()
      .setLongLink(uri)
      .buildShortDynamicLink()
      .addOnCompleteListener(new OnCompleteListener<ShortDynamicLink>() {
          @Override
          public void onComplete(@NonNull Task<ShortDynamicLink> task) {
              if (task.isSuccessful()) {
                  Uri shortLink = task.getResult().getShortLink();
                  shareTextView.setText(shortLink.toString());
              } else {
                  shareTextView.setText("Error retrieving link");
              }
          }
      });
```

For convenience, here's the full code for the Share Activity showing how this is triggered on a button press:

```
package com.laurencemoroney.firebasech12_dl;

import android.net.Uri;
import android.support.annotation.NonNull;
import android.support.v7.app.AppCompatActivity;
import android.os.Bundle;
import android.view.View;
import android.widget.Button;
import android.widget.TextView;

import com.google.android.gms.tasks.OnCompleteListener;
import com.google.android.gms.tasks.Task;
import com.google.firebase.dynamiclinks.DynamicLink;
import com.google.firebase.dynamiclinks.FirebaseDynamicLinks;
import com.google.firebase.dynamiclinks.ShortDynamicLink;

public class ShareableActivity extends AppCompatActivity {

    TextView shareTextView;
    @Override
    protected void onCreate(Bundle savedInstanceState) {
        super.onCreate(savedInstanceState);
        setContentView(R.layout.activity_shareable);
        shareTextView = (TextView) findViewById(R.id.shareTextView);
        Button shareButton = (Button) findViewById(R.id.shareButton);
        shareButton.setOnClickListener(new View.OnClickListener() {
            @Override
            public void onClick(View view) {
```

```java
                    Uri uri = getDynamicLink(Uri.parse("http://www.laurencemoroney.
                    com/?shareactivity=1234"),0);
                    Task<ShortDynamicLink> task = FirebaseDynamicLinks.getInstance()
                            .createDynamicLink()
                            .setLongLink(uri)
                            .buildShortDynamicLink()
                            .addOnCompleteListener(new OnCompleteListener<ShortDynamicLink>() {
                                @Override
                                public void onComplete(@NonNull Task<ShortDynamicLink> task) {
                                    if (task.isSuccessful()) {
                                        Uri shortLink = task.getResult().getShortLink();
                                        shareTextView.setText(shortLink.toString());
                                    } else {
                                        shareTextView.setText("Error retrieving link");
                                    }
                                }
                            });
                }
        });
    }

    private Uri getDynamicLink(@NonNull Uri destinationLink, int minVersion){
        String linkdomain = "jpv99.app.goo.gl";
        DynamicLink.Builder builder = FirebaseDynamicLinks.getInstance()
                .createDynamicLink()
                .setDynamicLinkDomain(linkdomain)
                .setAndroidParameters(new DynamicLink.AndroidParameters.Builder()
                    .setMinimumVersion(minVersion)
                    .build())
                .setLink(destinationLink);
        DynamicLink link = builder.buildDynamicLink();

        return link.getUri();
    }
}
```

To test this, add a button to the Main Activity that opens the share activity when pressed. Here's the code for that:

```java
Button gotoShareButton = findViewById(R.id.gotoShareButton);
gotoShareButton.setOnClickListener(new View.OnClickListener() {
    @Override
    public void onClick(View view) {
        Intent intent = new Intent(view.getContext(), ShareableActivity.class);
        startActivity(intent);
    }
});
```

Now when you run the application and press the button in the main activity, you'll be taken to the share activity. Press the button on that, and you should see something like Figure 12-11.

Figure 12-11. *Generating a Dynamic Link within the app*

Of course if you now try to open this link, you'll be taken to the main activity. We don't want that because we shared from *this* activity, so let's take a look at parsing the link in the main activity, and if it detects this set of parameters it would open the share activity instead.

Fortunately this is made easy by the getQueryParameterNames() method on a Uri. In the MainActivity when we get the deeplink, we can get a set of its parameters, and then check if a parameter exists. If it does, we can then trigger launching an activity based on its existence, or based on its value. Here's a simple piece of code in the MainActivity showing that in action:

```
if (deepLink != null) {
    Set<String> params = deepLink.getQueryParameterNames();
    if(params.contains("shareactivity")){
        Intent intent = new Intent(getApplicationContext() , ShareableActivity.class);
        startActivity(intent);
    }
    contentText.setText(deepLink.toString());
} else {
    Log.d("CH12-DL", "getDynamicLink: no link found");
}
```

So now, whenever a link containing the parameter 'shareactivity' is found, that Activity will load, and can parse the parameter. Otherwise the MainActivity will handle the parameter. This technique allows you to pick the right activity for the right Dynamic link, and activate the activity accordingly.

Dynamic Links and Analytics

As you may have noticed in the Firebase Console, you can also check the efficacy of Dynamic Links that you create using Analytics. See Figure 12-12.

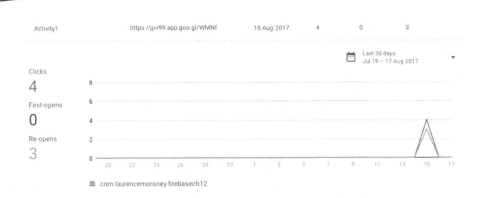

Figure 12-12. Dynamic Links Analytics

This chart lets you look at how your links have been working, including the number of clicks on the link, and how that led to 'first open' events (where the link caused someone to install and open the app for the first time) and 're-open' events (where the link caused someone who already had the app to open it). This is useful when you create a dynamic link to support a campaign – maybe sometimes you want to optimize for new users, and the first open measurement would be your success metric.

Sometimes you want to re-engage users of your app – so you could, for example, send an FCM message containing a Dynamic Link. On these the re-opens would be higher, as people already with your app would receive it.

Of course you also want your users to share with their contacts, and Firebase Invites has been built to use Dynamic Links to make that easy. Let's look at that in the next section. You aren't limited to using Invites, of course – technologies like Firebase Cloud Messaging make for easy and powerful avenues for sharing!

Using Firebase Invites

One of the best ways to learn about apps is through the referrals of people you trust. When they like an app, they generally tell you about it. The goal of Firebase Invites is to make the process of sharing an app in this way as friction free as possible. It's an out-of-the-box solution that lets app details to be shared, via a dynamic link, using email or SMS. The API has been designed to make it not only easy to share, but also to plug into Google's machine learning behind the scenes in provided suggested people with whom to share the app. This suggestions list is based on the contacts that the user communicates with frequently. And because it's built on Dynamic Links, any context of the share (like a referral bonus, for example) will be maintained through an installation of the app.

Let's take a look at what it takes to add Firebase Invites to an app, so you can see how straightforward it is to do so.

You create an invite dialog using the AppInviteInvitation intent builder. This takes a number of parameters such as the Message that you're sending to a user, the title for the dialog, the deep link URL to the application and a call to action. You use this to create an intent and start a new activity for that. Android will then present the user with a dialog containing suggested contacts as well as an alphabetically sorted list of email and SMS contacts. In the Activity result, the data returned contains an array of invitation IDs that you can use for tracking successful invites if you like – but using a Dynamic Link would be more effective because you have the built-in analytics.

Add a button to the share activity, and use this code to define its onClickListener:

```
Button inviteFriendsButton = (Button) findViewById(R.id.inviteButton);
inviteFriendsButton.setOnClickListener(new View.OnClickListener() {
    @Override
    public void onClick(View view) {
        Intent intent = new AppInviteInvitation.IntentBuilder("Try out my cool app!")
                .setMessage("Hey, this app is really cool. I thought you might like it!")
                .setDeepLink(Uri.parse("http://laurencemoroney.com/?shareactivity=1234"))
                .setCallToActionText("Let's do this!")
                .build();
        startActivityForResult(intent, REQUEST_INVITE);
    }
});
```

This creates an intent using the AppInviteInvitation intent builder, and starts an activity for it. Then, when the user clicks the button in your app, they'll get the invite dialog, which you can see in Figure 12-13.

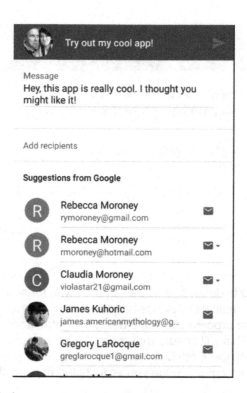

Figure 12-13. Sharing with contacts

As you can see the messages that were specified in the intent builder are shown, and a suggested list of people who might enjoy the app is given. Beneath them is an alphabetically sorted list of email and SMS contacts, or you can tap on where it says 'Add recipients' and enter recipients with auto-completion as a handy shortcut. See Figure 12-14, where I typed 'lm' and received a contact matching that – myself!

Figure 12-14. Sharing with auto-complete

When you send the invite it will be distributed based on the contact type – so email contacts will receive an email, and SMS contacts will receive an SMS. It's all automated to the end user, so they don't have to do any further action.

You can see the received email with the dynamic link behind the text so as to make it more attractive in Figure 12-15.

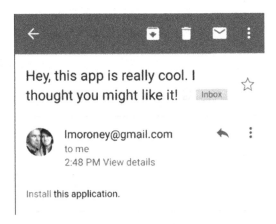

Figure 12-15. Receiving an Invite

In every activity that could be launched as part of the invite (based on parameters in the invite, you could have multiple activities handling it as we saw in the Dynamic Links section earlier), you should process the invite using the getInvitation(data) method on the FirebaseAppInvite class. This will ensure that the invite gets cleared in the Firebase system as having happened so you get First-Open credit in Analytics, preventing the invite from being treated in subsequent times – once you've installed the app the invite cycle should be complete.

To do this, simply use this code:

```
FirebaseAppInvite invite = FirebaseAppInvite.getInvitation(pendingDynamicLinkData);
if (invite != null) {
    String invitationId = invite.getInvitationId();
}
```

And that's how easy and quick it is to add the ability to have friends refer friends to your app!

Summary

In this chapter you saw how Dynamic Links work in Firebase, and how you can create them in the console. You then saw how to build an app that catches the link, and launches in response to it, or gets installed if not already present on the device. You also learned how to create Dynamic Links on-the-fly within your app, sharing context about where you are in the app at a particular time. Building on this technology you saw, Firebase Invites is a simple intent-based API that gives you the User Interface and back end for sharing with friends via SMS or Email, and how this uses dynamic links to track context about shares!

Chapter 13

Using AdMob

AdMob provides APIs that allow you to monetize mobile apps with in-app advertising that can be targeted to users. If you're an existing AdMob user, Firebase integrates with it without requiring changes to your existing configuration. When using AdMob, you have a number of methods of rendering ads including banner ads – where a small banner is shown on your activity; video ads, where a short video will run; interstitial ads where an advert will run while migrating between activities; and *native* ads where they are added to platform native user interface components. When using Android, you also have the option to allow users to do in-app purchases directly from ads. Note that if you want to use AdMob, you don't have to use it as a part of Firebase; it is available as a full stand-alone also. Details at: https://goo.gl/CvXQUQ.

Getting Started

Before going further, create a new Android app using Android Studio, and in the usual manner use the Firebase Assistant to connect it to Firebase and add the AdMob APIs to your build.gradle. Once you're done with this, edit your layout file to add an **AdView** component.

You'll need to declare the ads schema in the root element of the layout file (which will be a ConstraintLayout if you built from the empty activity template) using this code:

```
xmlns:ads="http://schemas.android.com/apk/res-auto"
```

Then you can add the AdView to your activity with this:

```
<com.google.android.gms.ads.AdView
    android:id="@+id/adView"
    android:layout_width="wrap_content"
    android:layout_height="wrap_content"
    android:layout_centerHorizontal="true"
    android:layout_alignParentBottom="true"
    ads:adSize="BANNER"
    ads:adUnitId="@string/banner_ad_unit_id">
</com.google.android.gms.ads.AdView>
```

© Laurence Moroney 2017

L. Moroney, *The Definitive Guide to Firebase,* https://doi.org/10.1007/978-1-4842-2943-9_13

Don't worry if the adUnitId setting highlights as red; that's because you haven't defined the string resource yet.

Remove the 'Hello World' TextView that was created by the template. Here's what your layout file should look like when you're done:

```xml
<?xml version="1.0" encoding="utf-8"?>
<android.support.constraint.ConstraintLayout xmlns:android="http://schemas.android.com/apk/
res/android"
    xmlns:app="http://schemas.android.com/apk/res-auto"
    xmlns:tools="http://schemas.android.com/tools"
    xmlns:ads="http://schemas.android.com/apk/res-auto"
    android:layout_width="match_parent"
    android:layout_height="match_parent"
    tools:context="com.laurencemoroney.firebasech13.MainActivity">

    <com.google.android.gms.ads.AdView
        android:id="@+id/adView"
        android:layout_width="wrap_content"
        android:layout_height="wrap_content"
        android:layout_centerHorizontal="true"
        android:layout_alignParentBottom="true"
        ads:adSize="BANNER"
        ads:adUnitId="@string/ad_id">
    </com.google.android.gms.ads.AdView>
</android.support.constraint.ConstraintLayout>
```

Now you'll need to edit your activity to load the ad.

The ad is rendered in the AdView control that you just added to the layout, and is loaded using an AdRequest, which you can build using the AdRequest.Builder() API like this:

```java
public class MainActivity extends AppCompatActivity {

    private AdView myAd;

    @Override
    protected void onCreate(Bundle savedInstanceState) {
        super.onCreate(savedInstanceState);
        setContentView(R.layout.activity_main);
        myAd = (AdView) findViewById(R.id.adView);
        AdRequest adRequest = new AdRequest.Builder().build();
        myAd.loadAd(adRequest);
    }
}
```

You'll notice that myAd.loadAd gives a warning because you don't have Internet permissions in the app. To get these, add this line to your AndroidManifest.xml file – put it outside the <application> tag, but inside the <manifest> tag:

```xml
<uses-permission android:name="android.permission.INTERNET"></uses-permission>
```

The final thing you'll need is to specify the missing ad_id parameter that caused the layout setting to fail. You can do this as a string in your res/values/strings.xml file. There's already an entry for 'app_name' in that file, so just add another, like this:

```
<resources>
    <string name="app_name">FirebaseCh13</string>
    <string name="ad_id">Value Goes here</string>
</resources>
```

You don't have this value yet, but you can get it from AdMob, so let's do that next.

Signing Up for AdMob

The first task is to sign up for Google AdMob, which you can do at https://www.google.com/admob. Once you've signed up and signed in, you will see the AdMob screen with a 'GET STARTED' button. See Figure 13-1.

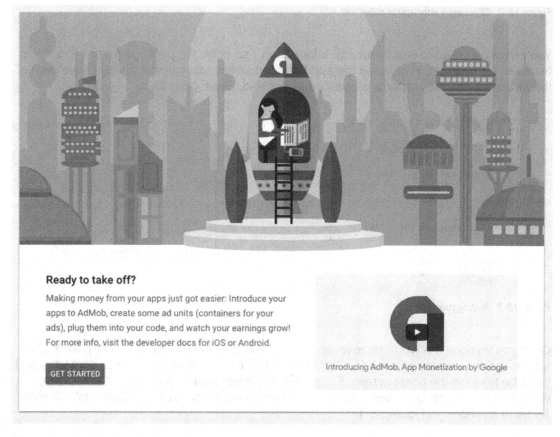

Figure 13-1. Getting Started with AdMob

When you click the button, you'll be asked if your app has been published on the Google Play or App Store. I'm going to follow the 'no' flow in this chapter assuming you haven't. See Figure 13-2.

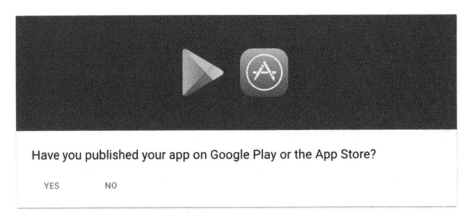

Figure 13-2. Checking if your app is published

You'll then be asked to enter your app information – so enter the package name of your app here. So, for example, in my case the app I created earlier was called com.laurencemoroney. firebasech13, and the platform is selected as Android. See Figure 13-3.

Enter your app information

com.laurencemoroney.firebasech13

32 / 80

Platform

◉ Android   ◯ iOS

ADD   GO BACK

Figure 13-3. Adding your app

Once you've done that you'll have an app on AdMob, and it will be given an App ID. You'll see an option to create a new ad unit or another for "I'll do it later'. Choose to do it later, and you'll be taken to the home screen. From here, you'll see your app on the left-hand side, with options for 'App Overview', 'Ad units', 'Blocking controls', and 'App Settings'. Choose Ad Units as shown in Figure 13-4.

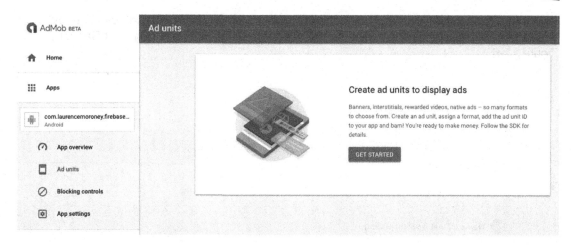

Figure 13-4. Working with Ad Units

Press the 'Get Started' button and you'll be given the option of building Banner, Interstitial, Rewarded video, or Native ads. See Figure 13-5.

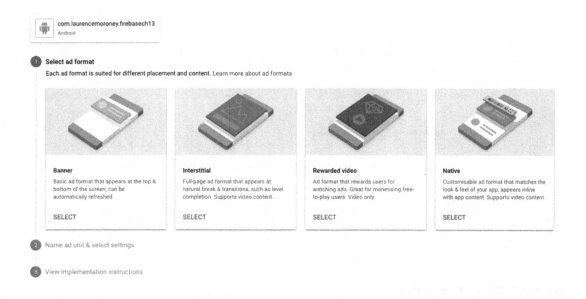

Figure 13-5. Choosing the Ad Type

Select the Banner Ad type. You'll be asked to fill out some details, with defaults already created for you. Make sure you give the ad unit a name, for example, 'My First Banner', in Figure 13-6.

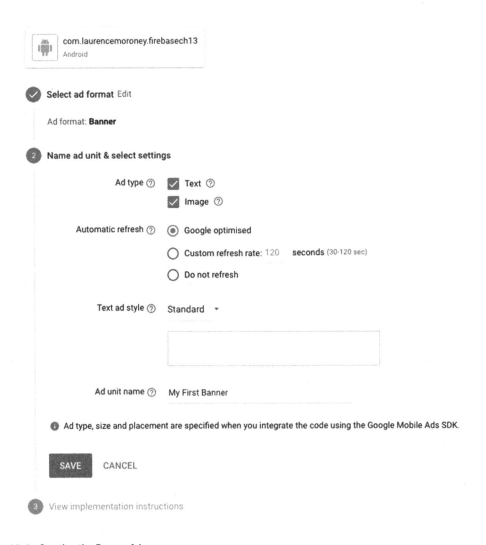

Figure 13-6. Creating the Banner Ad

Save this and you'll see the details for the ad including the App ID and the Ad unit ID. See Figure 13-7.

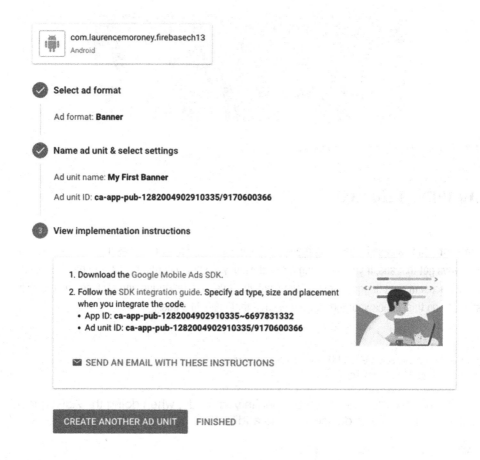

Figure 13-7. *Getting your Ad details*

Use the latter of these – the Ad unit ID, and paste it into strings.xml as the value for ad_id. The App ID is a unique number for your app within AdMob, but as each App can have multiple ads, you distinguish the ad based on the Ad unit ID.

Now you can run the app, and you'll see the ad banner rendering test content. See Figure 13-8.

Figure 13-8. *Rendering the banner ad in your app*

Testing with a Device

> **Important**   In this case I was using the emulator, which is *always* treated as a test device, so you will always get test ads. If you are using a real device, you should configure 13-it to be a test device lest your account gets flagged for suspicious activity if you are rendering and clicking on ads while testing. To do this, check your logs for a message that looks like this:

```
I/Ads: Use AdRequest.Builder.addTestDevice("[Device ID]")
to get test ads on this device.
```

Take note of the device ID that is listed. Then in your code, when doing the AdRequest.build, you would add this as a test device with the addTestDevice() method, like this:

```
myAd = (AdView) findViewById(R.id.adView);
AdRequest adRequest = new AdRequest.Builder()
        .addTestDevice("[Put Device ID Here]")
        .build();
myAd.loadAd(adRequest);
```

Of course be sure to remove this code before your release your app. Also note that while testing you won't see real ads, but the banners shown in these screenshots. That's perfectly normal behavior!

Using Interstitial Ads

Interstitial Ads, as their name suggests, are used in natural breaks in the app. For example, if you are building a game, it makes sense for an interstitial to be shown between game levels, or if you have an app, you might show it between activities. It's always good to be careful about *how* you use these ads, as too many of them can not only degrade your user's experience, it can impact your click-through rates anyway.

To learn how to use them, add a new Activity to your app, called 'DestinationActivity'. Then add a button to the MainActivity like this:

```xml
<?xml version="1.0" encoding="utf-8"?>
<android.support.constraint.ConstraintLayout xmlns:android="http://schemas.android.com/apk/
res/android"
    xmlns:app="http://schemas.android.com/apk/res-auto"
    xmlns:tools="http://schemas.android.com/tools"
    xmlns:ads="http://schemas.android.com/apk/res-auto"
    android:layout_width="match_parent"
    android:layout_height="match_parent"
    tools:context="com.laurencemoroney.firebasech13.MainActivity">
    <LinearLayout
        android:layout_width="match_parent"
        android:layout_height="match_parent"
        android:orientation="vertical"
        android:gravity="center">
        <com.google.android.gms.ads.AdView
            android:id="@+id/adView"
            android:layout_width="wrap_content"
            android:layout_height="wrap_content"
            android:layout_centerHorizontal="true"
            android:layout_alignParentBottom="true"
            ads:adSize="BANNER"
            ads:adUnitId="@string/ad_id">
        </com.google.android.gms.ads.AdView>
        <Button
            android:layout_width="wrap_content"
            android:layout_height="wrap_content"
            android:id="@+id/destinationButton"
            android:text="Push Me"/>
    </LinearLayout>
</android.support.constraint.ConstraintLayout>
```

Now edit the code in the MainActivity to load the DestinationActivity. This will simply load the activity.

```java
destinationButton = findViewById(R.id.destinationButton);
destinationButton.setOnClickListener(new View.OnClickListener() {
    @Override
    public void onClick(View view) {
        Intent intent = new Intent(view.getContext(), DestinationActivity.class);
        startActivity(intent);
    }
});
```

But we want to show an interstitial before it loads, so we'll update the code for that. Before going further, define an interstitial on the AdMob site, so you can get its ID.

Now in your code, in the onCreate() event of the main Activity, set up the Interstitial:

```
private InterstitialAd myInterstitial;
myInterstitial = new InterstitialAd(this);
myInterstitial.setAdUnitId("[[(Ad ID)]]");
myInterstitial.loadAd(new AdRequest.Builder().build());
```

Earlier, in the destinationButton you launched the DestinationActivity, but now you want to show the ad instead, so let's replace the code in the destinationButton's onClickListener to do that:

```
destinationButton.setOnClickListener(new View.OnClickListener() {
    @Override
    public void onClick(View view) {
        if (myInterstitial.isLoaded()) {
            myInterstitial.show();
        } else {
            Log.d("Ch13", "The interstitial wasn't loaded yet.");
        }

    }
});
```

So now, when the Ad is complete we can load the destination activity by setting an Ad Listener on the interstitial, and waiting for the onAdClosed() event to fire. Here's the code:

```
myInterstitial.setAdListener(new AdListener(){
    @Override
    public void onAdClosed() {
        loadDestination();
    }
});

private void loadDestination(){
    Intent intent = new Intent(getBaseContext(), DestinationActivity.class);
    startActivity(intent);
}
```

Now when you run your app and press the button, you'll see the interstitial. When you press on the 'X' to close the ad, the new activity will display. See Figure 13-9.

Figure 13-9. Rendering the Interstitial Ad

In this case you handled the onAdClosed() event to migrate to the new activity upon the user exiting the ad. In addition to this you have the following events:

- onAdLoaded() - When the ad finishes loading

- onAdFailedToLoad() - When the ad request fails. Includes an error code for you to check against

- onAdOpened() - When the ad is displayed

- onAdLeftApplication - When the user leaves your app in response to the ad

Using a Rewarded Video Ad

A rewarded video ad is a full-screen video that users can watch in exchange for in-app rewards. You, as an app developer, are rewarded by AdMob for getting users to watch it, and in turn, to incentivize users you can give them in-app rewards such as extra lives or other credit.

On your AdMob console, create a new 'Rewarded Video' ad, and get its Ad ID.

To implement, add a new button to your MainActivity and call it 'VideoButton'

```
<Button
    android:layout_width="wrap_content"
    android:layout_height="wrap_content"
    android:id="@+id/videoButton"
    android:text="Push Me For Video"/>
```

Then, in your Main Activity's onCreate function, set up the RewardedVideo ad, replacing [[(Ad ID)]] with the one you got earlier:

```
private RewardedVideoAd myVideoAd;
myVideoAd = MobileAds.getRewardedVideoAdInstance(this);
myVideoAd.loadAd("[[(Ad ID)]]", new AdRequest.Builder().build());
```

Now you can show the ad when the user clicks the button:

```
videoAdButton = (Button) findViewById(R.id.videoButton);
videoAdButton.setOnClickListener(new View.OnClickListener() {
    @Override
    public void onClick(View view) {
        if (myVideoAd.isLoaded()) {
            myVideoAd.show();
        }
    }
});
```

If you want to reward your user for watching the Video ad, you need to implement the RewardedAdListener() interface on the class. Edit the MainActivity declaration to do this:

```
public class MainActivity extends AppCompatActivity implements RewardedVideoAdListener
```

Don't worry if you see a warning at this point – it just means you haven't yet implemented the required interfaces. To do this, you'll need to add overrides for the following methods:

- OnRewardedVideoAdLoaded - when the ad loads
- OnRewardedVideoAdFailedToLoad - failure to load, contains an error code
- onRewardedVideoAdStarted - when the video starts to play back
- onRewardedVideoAdOpened - when the video ad opens

- onRewardedVideoAdClosed - when the ad is closed by the user

- onRewardedVideoAdLeftApplication - when the user interacts with the ad, leaving your app to go somewhere else

- onRewarded - contains a Reward item, and fires when the user receives the reward

Here's the code to implement them:

```java
@Override
public void onRewardedVideoAdLoaded() {
    Log.d("Ch13", "Video Ad Loaded");
}

@Override
public void onRewardedVideoAdFailedToLoad(int errorCode) {
    Log.d("Ch13", "Video Ad Failed to Load");
}

@Override
public void onRewardedVideoStarted() {
    Log.d("Ch13", "Video Started");
}

@Override
public void onRewardedVideoAdOpened() {
    Log.d("Ch13", "Video Ad Opened");
}

@Override
public void onRewardedVideoAdClosed() {
    Log.d("Ch13", "Video Closed");
}

@Override
public void onRewardedVideoAdLeftApplication() {
    Log.d("Ch13", "You left the app");
}

@Override
public void onRewarded(RewardItem reward) {
    Log.d("CH13", "On Rewarded: Type:" + reward.getType() + " Amount: " + reward.getAmount());
}
```

Now when you launch the app and press the video button, a video ad will play back. On the video player you can see controls for silencing the video, a countdown for how long is remaining in the video, and an 'install' button for the app that is represented in the video. See Figure 13-10.

Figure 13-10. *Rewarded Video playback*

When the video stops playing (indicated by the end of the countdown), the onRewarded event will fire, and you can see the RewardItem. This defaults to a type of 'coins' and a value of '10', but you can override it easily, or simply ignore it and write your own reward code in the onRewarded callback.

The video will also be replaced by a full-screen static ad upon completion, as seen in Figure 13-11. This is the sample ad – when running on a real device with test mode off, you would, of course see a real one, related to the video that you just watched.

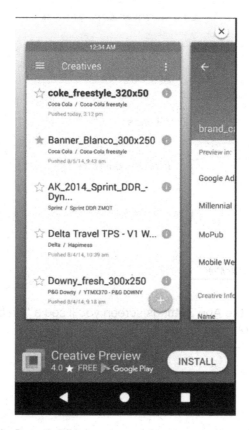

Figure 13-11. Ad at the end of the Rewarded Video

Connecting AdMob with Firebase

A final step you should take is to ensure that your app is connected with Firebase within the AdMob portal. This lets you use your Google Analytics for Firebase data (see Chapter 14) with AdMob allowing you to understand how people are interacting with your ads, so you can optimize the ad types or content to use.

To do this, go to the AdMob portal, and for your app, select 'App Settings'. See Figure 13-12.

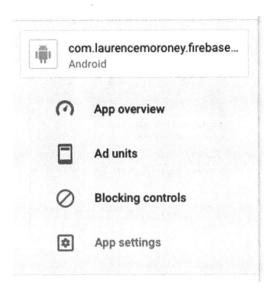

Figure 13-12. *Pick App Settings in AdMob*

Once you've done that, in the App Settings screen you'll see a 'Firebase Link' area with a 'LINK TO FIREBASE' button. See Figure 13-13.

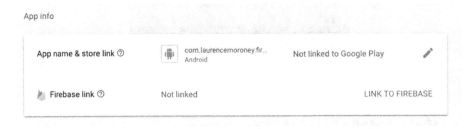

Figure 13-13. *App Settings for Firebase*

Select this, and you'll be given a policy confirmation dialog. If you agree with the policy, click
CONFIRM; otherwise, click CANCEL. See Figure 13-14.

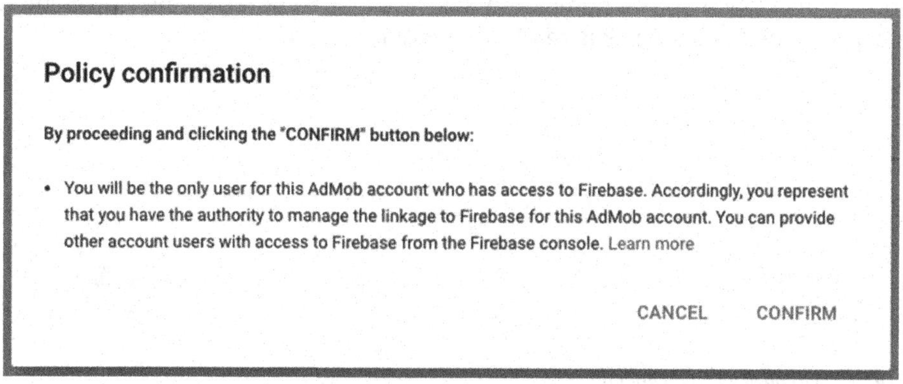

Policy confirmation

By proceeding and clicking the "CONFIRM" button below:

- You will be the only user for this AdMob account who has access to Firebase. Accordingly, you represent
  that you have the authority to manage the linkage to Firebase for this AdMob account. You can provide
  other account users with access to Firebase from the Firebase console. Learn more

CANCEL   CONFIRM

Figure 13-14. Link to Firebase Policy Confirmation

You'll need to specify the package name for your app. Be sure to get it right, because you
cannot change it later! Once you've entered it, you'll be asked how you want to connect it.
As you have an existing Android App and a Firebase Project, you can select that option, as
shown in Figure 13-15. If you don't, there are other options to follow.

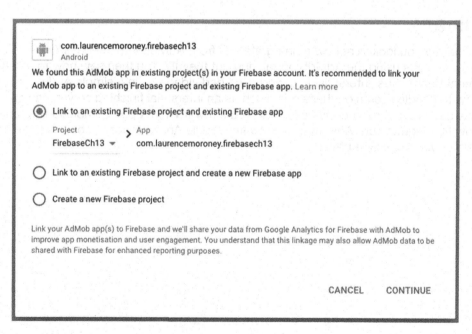

Figure 13-15. Linking to a Firebase Project

Clicking Continue will give you a verification screen, asking if you want to download configuration information. If you've followed the steps in this chapter – most notably linking to Firebase using the Assistant in Android studio, you have all of this already, so you don't need to do it again. Once you've completed this, you'll be returned to the App Settings and now you can see the Firebase link is ready. See Figure 13-16.

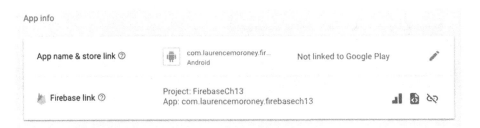

Figure 13-16. *The Firebase Link is complete*

The three icons, from left to right give you a direct link to the Google Analytics for Firebase console (Chapter 14), give you instructions on how to integrate, and unlink from Firebase.

With this done, analytics from your Firebase users will flow into AdMob so you can manage your ads with that intelligence in mind.

Summary

In this chapter you looked at how to integrate ads from AdMob into Firebase Apps. You saw how to create ads using the AdMob portal, and get their ID. You then saw how to use that to implement banner ads, interstitial ads, and rewarded video ads in a simple Android app. You saw how to handle events on these ads, such as an interstitial finishing so you can continue your navigation, or a RewardedVideo giving you a reward item upon completion. You also saw how to integrate your AdMob account with Google Analytics for Firebase so you can understand your ad usage better!

Chapter 14

Google Analytics for Firebase

Many of the technologies that you've seen in this book are driven or enhanced by Google Analytics for Firebase. This is a free solution to provide insights on how people are using and engaging with your app. There are many app events that are captured *automatically* for you – you don't need to write any code – and there's an API that allows you to define your own *custom* events to capture, so you can finely tune the data that your app captures, and have a set of visual tools that helps you understand how your users behave. It also gives you the ability to define user groupings, called *audiences*, which you can then use to define functionality for that particular group. So, for example, you define an audience of people in Japan who have made an in-app purchase, and send them a message using Firebase Cloud Messaging, or people who have experienced a crash while using your app.

In this chapter you'll get an introduction to how you can implement Google Analytics for Firebase into your app and a tour of what's available in the console. The number of things you can do with analytics is so broad it could span several books in its own right, but when you're done you should have a good grasp of what's possible, and how you can get started using it.

Automatically Gathered Analytics

Let's start by building a new app based on the empty activity template in Android Studio. Connect it to a Firebase project and add the analytics dependencies using the Firebase Assistant. You now have everything you need to collect lots of common events and user properties without writing a single line of code. Some of the events that are gathered are the following:

- `first_open`: As the name suggests, when the user first opens your app after installing or re-installing it.

- `in_app_purchase`: When the user completed an in-app purchase using either the App Store for iOS or Google Play for Android. It receives details such as the product ID, name, currency, and amount spent.

- `user_engagement`: This is sent periodically while the app is in the foreground, so you know the user is interacting with your app.

- `session_start`: This is gathered when the user interacts with your app for more than a certain period of time. It defaults to 10 seconds, but you can override this value in code. It's only gathered after a session timeout (defaults to 30 minutes) so as to avoid multiple session starts in a single session.

- `app_update`: Gathered when the user updates your app to a new version and re-launches.

- `app_remove`: Gathered when the app is uninstalled from an Android device (not available on iOS).

- `os_update`: When the operating system on the device is upgraded.

- `app_exception`: When the app crashes or throws an exception.

- `app_clear_data`: When the user clears the app data using Android settings.

There are others gathered when notifications are used, such as `notification_foreground`, gathered when an app receives a notification while it is in the foreground; `notification_received` when the app is in the background; `notification_open` when the user opens the notification; and `notification_dismiss` (Android only) that is gathered when the user dismisses the notification.

Similarly there's a set of analytics gathered for dynamic links: `dynamic_link_first_open`, when a user opens an app for the first time because of a dynamic link; `dynamic_link_app_open`, when a user reopens an app because of a dynamic link; and `dymanic_link_app_update`, when the app is updated to a new version and opened via a dynamic_link.

Beyond events, your app also gathers a number of user properties. These are attributes about the user or their device, as opposed to things that they do in your app, and they include the following:

- Age: Defined in a category such as 18–24, 25–34 etc.

- App Store: Where they got the app

- App Version: The version name on Android or the Bundle version on iOS

- Country: Where they reside

- Device Brand: Details on the type of device they use (e.g., Google Pixel XL)

- Device Category: The type of device (e.g., Tablet or Phone)

- Device Model: The model name/number of the device (e.g., iPhone 5s)

- First Open Time: The time at which they first opened the app, rounded up to the next hour

- Gender: Identified as either male or female

- Interests: Things they are interested in such as Sports

- Language: The language setting on their device

- New: The user has first opened the app in the last 7 days

- Established: The user first opened the app more than 7 days ago

- OS Version: The version of the OS (i.e., iOS 9.2.1)

Exploring the Analytics Console

Now that you've built an app that can gather all of the above analytics, let's take a look at the analytics console so you can see what you can do with that data. In Firebase Console, select the analytics tab, and you should see something like Figure 14-1.

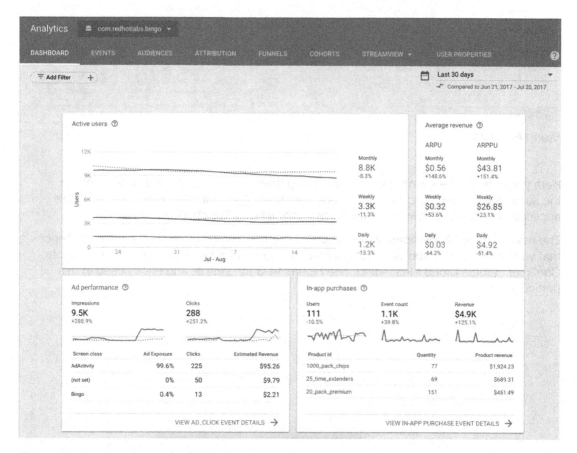

Figure 14-1. The Firebase Analytics Console

Here you can see an app that has been gathering analytics for some time, and the default dashboard is showing details like Active users, average revenue, the performance of ads that were implemented in the app, and feedback from in-app purchases. These are all filtered by time, which you can see at the top right-hand side of the screen, so in this case, this is the data from the last 30 days.

Across the top of the screen are entries for other data that has been gathered. Click **Events** to see this data. See Figure 14-2.

Event name ↑	Count		Value		Users		Mark as conversion
achievements_page_viewed	1,238	-19.7%	.		706	-1.1%	
ad_click	288	+251.2%	.		215	+330%	
ad_impression	9,461	+288.9%	.		1,831	+308.7%	
app_clear_data	140	-33.6%	.		67	+24.1%	
app_exception	3,243	-2.5%	.		1,118	-10.6%	
app_installed	5,171	-12.5%	.		5,031	-10.7%	
app_remove	4,815	-11.1%	.		4,806	-11.1%	
app_update	865	-62.9%	.		850	-63.1%	
app_updated_dialog_popped	2,103	+2.9%	.		1,989	+1.3%	
bingo_button_highlighted	4,388	-13.6%	.		4,163	-11.5%	

Rows per page: 10 ▼   1-10 of 70 < >

Figure 14-2. *Events*

Here you can see the events that the app has gathered analytics on. Many of them are the automatically collected events we saw a moment ago, but others are custom to this application. You'll see how to create those a little later in this chapter.

The next tab is for **Audiences**, where you can see how many people you have in audiences that you define. These audiences can then also be used for functionality such as Remote Config or Google Cloud Messaging. See Figure 14-3 for a list of audiences used in this particular app.

Audience name ↑	Description	Users ⓘ		Created on	
All Users	All app users	8,813	-8.3%	Jan 25, 2016	⋮
Crashing Users	.	2,397	-10%	Aug 15, 2016	⋮
Highly Engaged Users	Users who are leveling up	7,268	-9%	Aug 16, 2016	⋮
New Users	Users who are new to the app	7,823	-7.7%	Aug 18, 2016	⋮
Purchasers	Users who have made a purchase	255	-6.6%	Jan 25, 2016	⋮
test		5,180	-9.6%	Sep 30, 2016	⋮
Test Audience	Short description	< 10 Users	.	Nov 11, 2016	⋮
Test2	User ID	8,277	-8.8%	Nov 11, 2016	⋮

Figure 14-3. *Audiences*

We'll discuss how to create new audiences later in this chapter.

The next tab is **Attribution**, which shows you where your conversion events came from. Conversion events are things such as when the user first opens your app or when they make an in-app purchase. To track your marketing events it's good to know where your conversions are coming from, and attribution gives you that.

In Figure 14-4 you can see the conversion events for this app. When the event has a monetary value associated with it (in this case in_app_purchase), you can also see the value of that.

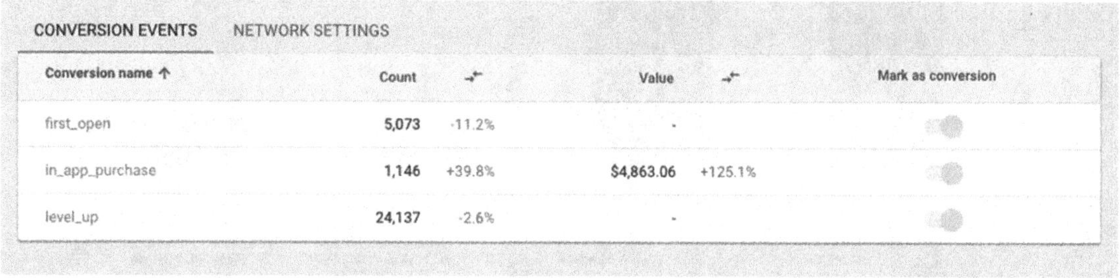

CONVERSION EVENTS	NETWORK SETTINGS			
Conversion name ↑	Count		Value		Mark as conversion
first_open	5,073	-11.2%	·		
in_app_purchase	1,146	+39.8%	$4,863.06	+125.1%	
level_up	24,137	-2.6%	·		

Figure 14-4. Conversion Events in Attribution

The Network Settings tab beside this lists the different networks that you may be using and allows you to inspect them.

The **Funnels** tab allows you to take a look at the completion rate of a series of steps, each marked by an event, in your app. So, for example, if you define a tutorial on how to use your app, and that tutorial has a number of steps, you can turn it into a funnel. Viewing these analytics helps you understand users' behavior going through this funnel, and if you have a large dropoff of users at a particular step, you can then refine it and test again. See Figure 14-5 for an example of a tutorial funnel.

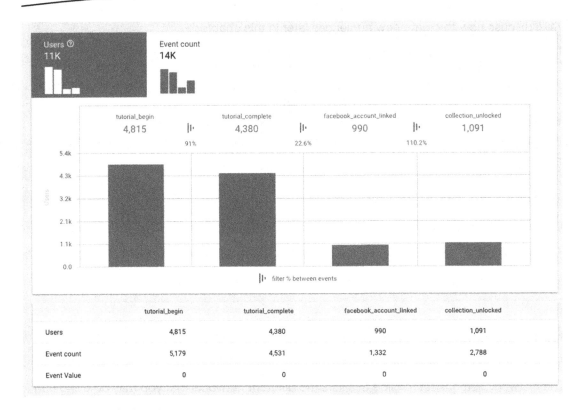

Figure 14-5. A Tutorial Funnel

The **Cohorts** tab lets you look at groups of users who started using your app at the same time. So for example in Figure 14-6 you can see rows beneath the graph showing cohorts for weekly users.

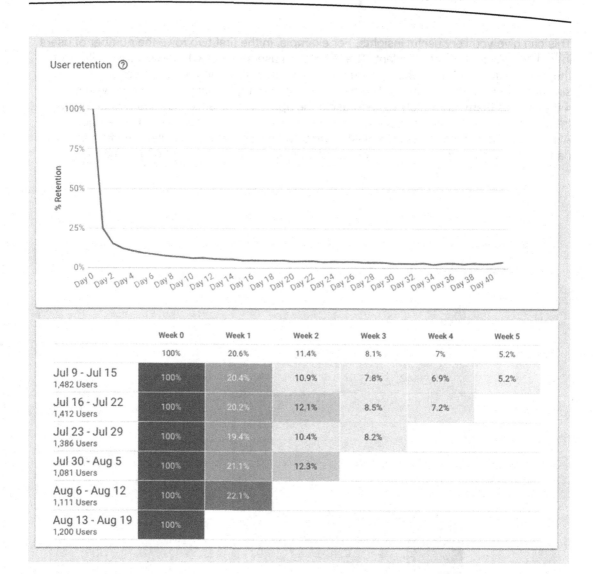

Figure 14-6. Exploring cohorts

This can give you very useful insights. For example, in the first two rows the number of users in that cohort is roughly equivalent. The drop-off in users to week 1 is also very similar, but the users in the first row drops off far more sharply than those in the second row. You can see similarity between rows 3 and 4. There's something about the users gathered in weeks 2 and 4 that makes them more likely to keep using the app 2 weeks after they first got it. You can trace this perhaps to campaigns that you've run to see why this behavior may be happening. Also, in this case the cohorts are weekly over 6 weeks. By setting the filter time frame, you can make this more granular. So, for example, Figure 14-7 shows a set of *daily* cohorts.

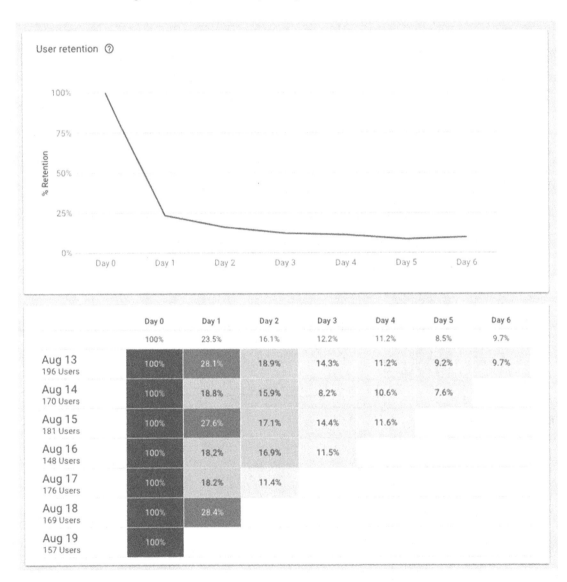

	Day 0	Day 1	Day 2	Day 3	Day 4	Day 5	Day 6
	100%	23.5%	16.1%	12.2%	11.2%	8.5%	9.7%
Aug 13 196 Users	100%	28.1%	18.9%	14.3%	11.2%	9.2%	9.7%
Aug 14 170 Users	100%	18.8%	15.9%	8.2%	10.6%	7.6%	
Aug 15 181 Users	100%	27.6%	17.1%	14.4%	11.6%		
Aug 16 148 Users	100%	18.2%	16.9%	11.5%			
Aug 17 176 Users	100%	18.2%	11.4%				
Aug 18 169 Users	100%	28.4%					
Aug 19 157 Users	100%						

Figure 14-7. Daily Cohorts

The **StreamView** tab gives you a powerful look at users in your app over the last 30 minutes. It's a live look-in on the health of your app around the globe. See Figure 14-8.

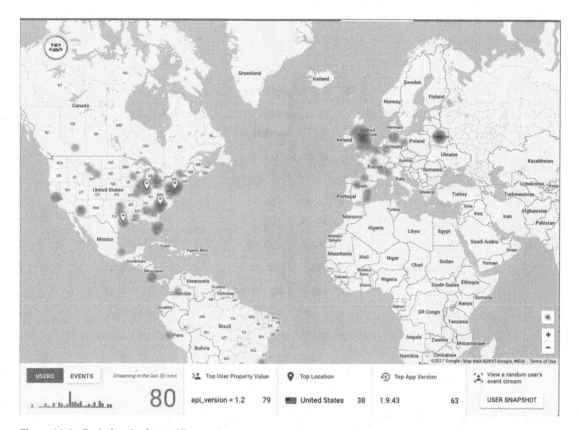

Figure 14-8. *Exploring the StreamView analytics*

In addition to an animated map showing people coming online as a heat map, you can also inspect what's going on in your app. So, for example, if you click the Users button on the bottom left, and then select 'Trending', you can get a live look at user properties that are trending at the moment. See Figure 14-9.

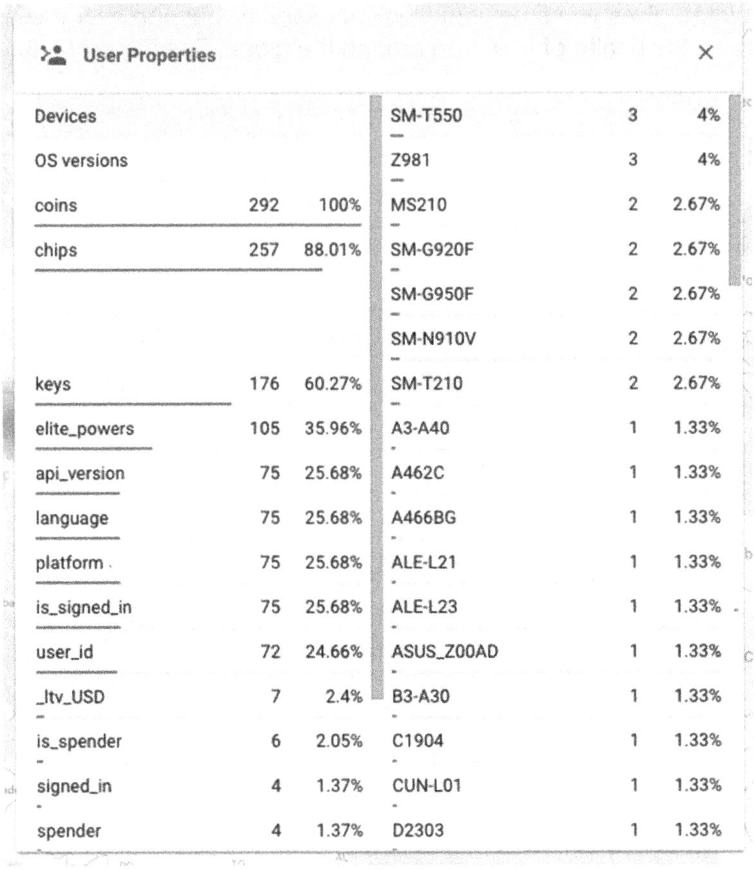

User Properties					
Devices			SM-T550	3	4%
OS versions			Z981	3	4%
coins	292	100%	MS210	2	2.67%
chips	257	88.01%	SM-G920F	2	2.67%
			SM-G950F	2	2.67%
			SM-N910V	2	2.67%
keys	176	60.27%	SM-T210	2	2.67%
elite_powers	105	35.96%	A3-A40	1	1.33%
api_version	75	25.68%	A462C	1	1.33%
language	75	25.68%	A466BG	1	1.33%
platform	75	25.68%	ALE-L21	1	1.33%
is_signed_in	75	25.68%	ALE-L23	1	1.33%
user_id	72	24.66%	ASUS_Z00AD	1	1.33%
_ltv_USD	7	2.4%	B3-A30	1	1.33%
is_spender	6	2.05%	C1904	1	1.33%
signed_in	4	1.37%	CUN-L01	1	1.33%
spender	4	1.37%	D2303	1	1.33%

Figure 14-9. Exploring trending properties

There are lots of other things you can explore, such as trending events, how many users are in which location, etc. A particularly powerful and useful tool here is the 'User Snapshot' button on the lower right-hand side. This picks a random user who uploaded their details in the last 30 minutes, and lets you see their analytics time line. User properties, such as device type, location, etc., are displayed. So, for example in Figure 14-10, I can see a user in England who received some in-app keys, and then was able to level up just a few moments later. By exploring their time line I can begin to understand how they're using the app.

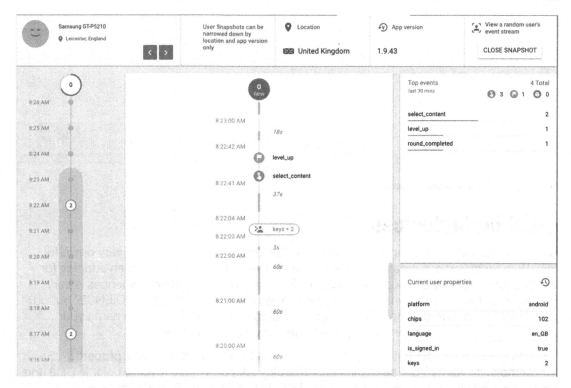

Figure 14-10. User Snapshot

It's a little like those test labs where you bring people in to use your app and watch them doing it to learn how they like to interact with it!

In addition to StreamView, you can also do a **Debug View,** where if you have enabled debug mode on devices and log events, you can see them in a similar manner to streamview. As a result if you run a beta of your app, for example, with contributors all over the world, you can look into debug events that they may have encountered.

Finally the **User Properties** tab allows you to create and keep track of user properties. We saw earlier how user properties show up in analytics, such as the stream view, but if you want to track something more granular, where the user provides you this data, such as their favorite color, you can do so with a user property. To create a user property simply click the 'NEW USER PROPERTY' button, and fill out the details. Figure 14-11 shows me creating a favorite_color property.

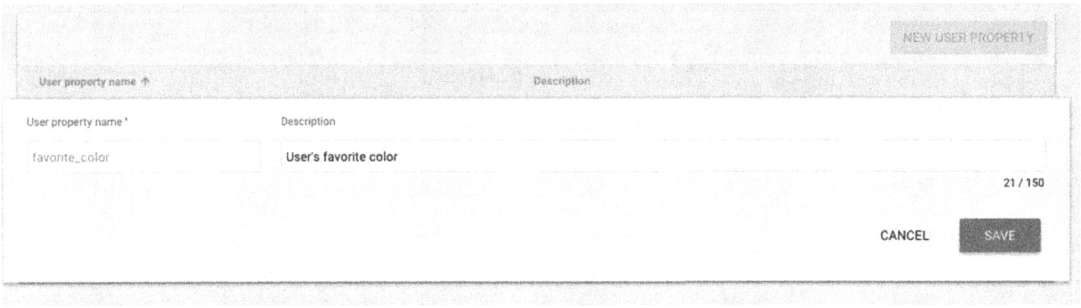

Figure 14-11. Creating a user property

Creating Audiences

As you've seen in many chapters in this book, Audiences in analytics are a very powerful tool. With them you can create segments of your user base that you can then address for things such as Firebase Cloud Messaging or Remote Config. Creating Audiences is very simple using the console. On the Audiences tab, simply click the 'NEW AUDIENCE' button, and you'll be taken to the tool for creating an Audience. From here you can name your audience and provide a short description to help you remember them.

You can then define your audience using a combination of events and user properties. So, for example, if I want to get as granular as 'People in Japan whose favorite color is Blue and who have made an in-app purchase', I can do so with a combination of events and user properties. See Figure 14-12. In this case the 'favorite_color' is a custom user property I defined on the user properties tab in the previous section.

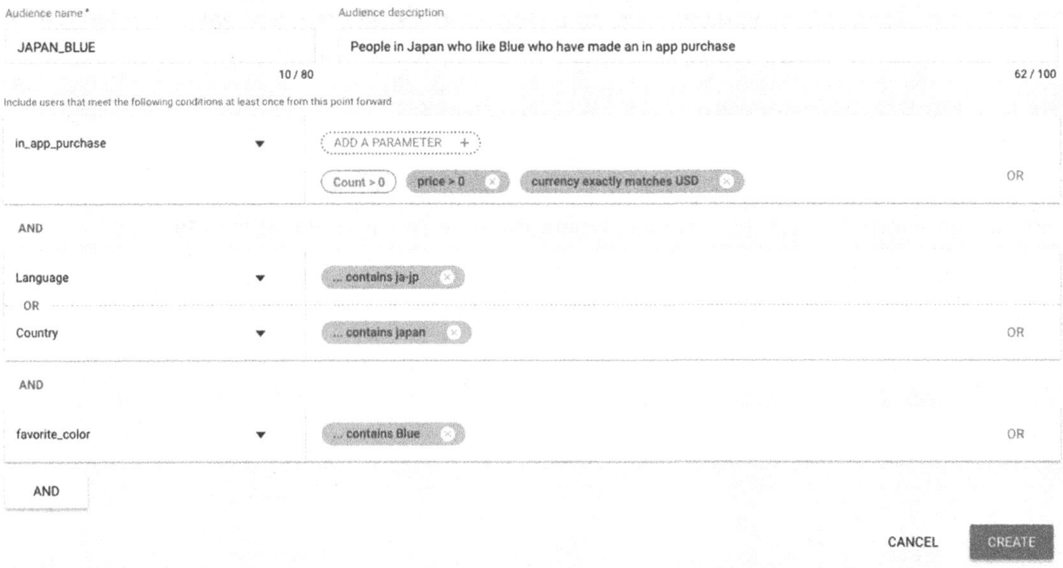

Figure 14-12. Creating an Audience

Now that I've created that audience, I can track how many users are in it, and use it for things such as Firebase Cloud Messaging, where I can send messages just to people in Japan whose favorite color is blue!

Coding for Analytics

In addition to the events and user properties that are gathered automatically, you may want to gather your own events or user properties. Say you're building a game, and you want to define that beating the boss on level 3 is an event, you can do so. Or, as we saw in the previous section, we want to track the user's favorite color, so we can define audiences based on that, and then that's a user property that you want to track. To do that you'll use the analytics SDK and we'll explore some examples in this section.

Logging Events

Let's take a look at an example of logging events. Edit the app you created earlier to add two buttons to the activity. We'll call these the red button and the blue button. Here's the code:

```xml
<?xml version="1.0" encoding="utf-8"?>
<android.support.constraint.ConstraintLayout xmlns:android="http://schemas.android.com/apk/
res/android"
    xmlns:app="http://schemas.android.com/apk/res-auto"
    xmlns:tools="http://schemas.android.com/tools"
    android:layout_width="match_parent"
    android:layout_height="match_parent"
    tools:context="com.laurencemoroney.firebasech14.MainActivity">
    <LinearLayout
        android:layout_width="match_parent"
        android:layout_height="match_parent"
        android:orientation="vertical">

        <Button
            android:id="@+id/redButton"
            android:layout_width="match_parent"
            android:layout_height="wrap_content"
            android:background="@android:color/holo_red_light"
            android:text="Red" />

        <Button
            android:id="@+id/blueButton"
            android:layout_width="match_parent"
            android:layout_height="wrap_content"
            android:background="@android:color/holo_blue_light"
            android:text="Blue" />
    </LinearLayout>
</android.support.constraint.ConstraintLayout>
```

In your AndroidManifest.xml file you need to set a number of permissions in order for Analytics to log custom events. These are to allow access to the Internet, access network state, and wake the device if it's asleep to perform processing. Here's the AndroidManifest. xml file with these permissions added:

```xml
<?xml version="1.0" encoding="utf-8"?>
<manifest xmlns:android="http://schemas.android.com/apk/res/android"
    package="com.laurencemoroney.firebasech14">

    <application
        android:allowBackup="true"
        android:icon="@mipmap/ic_launcher"
        android:label="@string/app_name"
        android:roundIcon="@mipmap/ic_launcher_round"
        android:supportsRtl="true"
        android:theme="@style/AppTheme">
        <activity android:name=".MainActivity">
            <intent-filter>
                <action android:name="android.intent.action.MAIN" />

                <category android:name="android.intent.category.LAUNCHER" />
            </intent-filter>
        </activity>
    </application>
    <uses-permission android:name="android.permission.INTERNET"></uses-permission>
    <uses-permission android:name="android.permission.WAKE_LOCK"></uses-permission>
    <uses-permission android:name="android.permission.ACCESS_NETWORK_STATE"></uses-
permission>
</manifest>
```

Once you've done this, logging events is possible using the FirebaseAnalytics.logEvent method. This takes two parameters – a string defining the event and a bundle containing parameters about the event. As we have a red button and a blue button, let's create an event called 'color_ pressed', and set the 'color' parameter to be either red or blue, logging that in Analytics.

Here's the code:

```java
redButton.setOnClickListener(new View.OnClickListener() {
    @Override
    public void onClick(View view) {
        Bundle params = new Bundle();
        params.putString("color", "red");
        mAnalytics.logEvent("color_pressed", params);
    }
});
```

```
blueButton.setOnClickListener(new View.OnClickListener() {
    @Override
    public void onClick(View view) {
        Bundle params = new Bundle();
        params.putString("color", "blue");
        mAnalytics.logEvent("color_pressed", params);
    }
});
```

Note that in addition to being able to use custom parameters like these, Firebase also has a number of standard analytics that may be referred to using constants. For example, if you're writing a travel application that requires the 'Destination' to be logged in analytics, instead of using your own, you can use Param.DESTINATION like this:

```
params.putString(FirebaseAnalytics.Param.DESTINATION,
        "Mountain View, CA");
```

A full list of these parameters is available in the documentation at: https://goo.gl/nGBM2G.

Now run the application, and you should see a simple app like that in Figure 14-13.

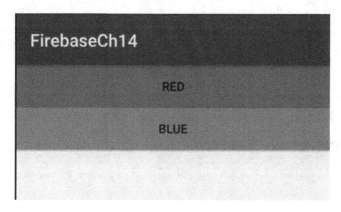

Figure 14-13. Running the App

Press the buttons a few times. Do a little of each. After a few minutes, go to the Analytics dashboard and take a look at the streamview. You should see one user pop up. I live in the Pacific North West, and you can see what happened on mine in Figure 14-14.

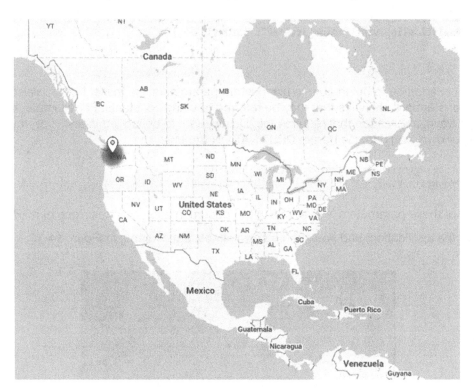

Figure 14-14. *A single user shows up in StreamView*

Despite only one user of your app, and that's in an emulator, you are still collecting data. So, for example you can click on Events to see them – and you'll see the 'color_pressed' event having fired a few times. See Figure 14-15. You'll also notice automatically gathered events like 'first_open' and 'user_engagement' on the list.

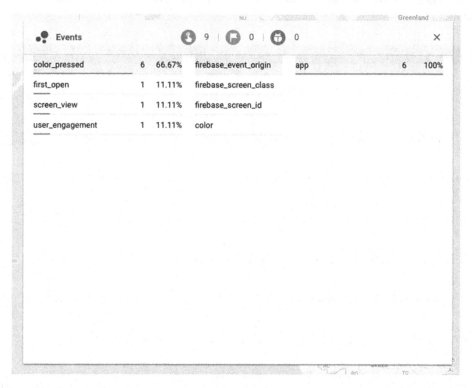

Figure 14-15. Showing your Event

Indeed, you can also look at how the user interacted with the app. I pressed the buttons a number of times to generate 'color_pressed' events, and put a string containing the color in the parameters bundle. In Figure 14-16 you can see these on the time line, including the contents of the bundle – with the color, and the name of the Activity that led to the event being fired. Note that the only data I sent was 'red'. The rest was gathered for me automatically.

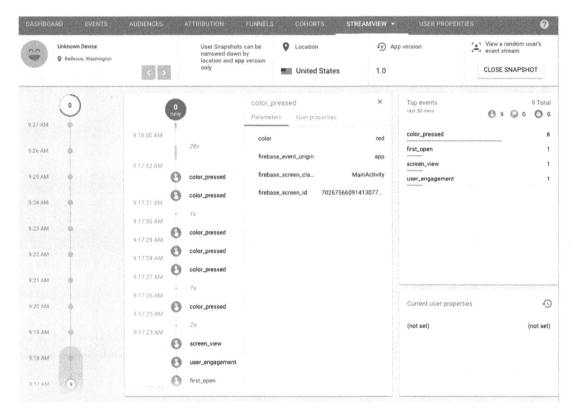

Figure 14-16. Inspecting the Event Details

In addition to this, within 24 hours you'll see the events tab on analytics get populated. This will contain the count of times the event was hit, the delta of that against the previous period, and other data. As you're running this for the first time, you won't see much, but refer back to Figure 14-2 for details of what this can look like in time.

In addition to creating your own custom event that you did here ('color_pressed'), there's also a suite of standard events that you can leverage that can help you maintain consistency across apps. The full list of these can be found in the documentation under the FirebaseAnalytics.Event class. Using them is very straightforward; simply use the FirebaseAnalytics.Event.<NAME> in place of your custom string when logging the event. So, for example to log a LEVEL_UP in a game, you would use:

```
mAnalytics.logEvent(FirebaseAnalytics.Event.LEVEL_UP, params);
```

Now that you have a grasp of logging user events, let's take a look next at logging user properties.

Logging User Properties

Logging a user property is very similar to logging an event. In this case you'll use the setUserProperty method, passing it the name of the property, and the value you want to set.

So, if you've been building the app in this chapter, it's an easy modification. Here's the layout code to add a simple Spinner with a list of colors:

```
<LinearLayout
    android:layout_width="match_parent"
    android:layout_height="120px"
    android:orientation="horizontal">
    <TextView
        android:layout_width="wrap_content"
        android:layout_height="match_parent"
        android:text="Tell me your favorite color:"/>
    <Spinner
        android:id="@+id/colorSpinner"
        android:layout_width="wrap_content"
        android:layout_height="wrap_content"
        android:entries="@array/colorlist" />
    <Button
        android:layout_width="wrap_content"
        android:layout_height="match_parent"
        android:text="Send"
        android:id="@+id/favoriteButton"/>
</LinearLayout>
```

The colors are in strings.xml like this:

```
<resources>
    <string name="app_name">FirebaseCh14</string>
    <string-array name="colorlist">
        <item>Red</item>
        <item>Orange</item>
        <item>Yellow</item>
        <item>Green</item>
        <item>Blue</item>
        <item>Indigo</item>
        <item>Violet</item>
    </string-array>
</resources>
```

And then in code, for the 'Send' button, you can read the value from the spinner and set it to the user property.

```
favoriteButton.setOnClickListener(new View.OnClickListener() {
    @Override
    public void onClick(View view) {
        mAnalytics.setUserProperty("favorite_color", colorSpinner.getSelectedItem().toString());
    }
});
```

It can take a little while before the property is collected on the console, but to test if it's working, you can always check logcat. See Figure 14-17 for an example.

```
08-20 15:31:08.750 5990-6008/com.laurencemoroney.firebasech14 D/FA: Setting user property (FE): favorite_color, Green
08-20 15:31:08.760 5990-6008/com.laurencemoroney.firebasech14 V/FA: Using measurement service
08-20 15:31:08.760 5990-6008/com.laurencemoroney.firebasech14 V/FA: Connecting to remote service
08-20 15:31:08.770 5990-6008/com.laurencemoroney.firebasech14 D/FA: Connected to remote service
08-20 15:31:08.771 5990-6008/com.laurencemoroney.firebasech14 V/FA: Processing queued up service tasks: 1
```

Figure 14-17. Logcat output when setting user property

It's really as simple as that! But as you can see with the console tool you get some very powerful dashboards to understanding the data that your app produces. This data should hopefully be very valuable in helping you understand how people are using your app, and any opportunities you may have to grow it.

Summary

In this chapter you learned how to use Google Analytics for Firebase. You saw the powerful analytics dashboard and its multiple tools for understanding your audience, before delving into programming: seeing events and user properties that are automatically captured for you, before then creating and storing your own events and user properties, and exploring how they work in the console. With this, you're now equipped to go out and do great things with Firebase! Do be sure to tell us all about them! :)

Index

■ S

sendNotification method, 168, 170–173
    default notification, 172–173
    FCMReceiver class, 170
    Image Asset, 171
    IncomingMessage class, 170
    Notification Icon, 172
    TextView, 173
setImageBitmap method, 87

StorageMetadata object, 92
System.currentTimeMillis(), 196

■ T

takePictureAndUpload() method, 78

U, V, W, X, Y, Z

User Security flow, 27

Get the eBook for only $5!

Why limit yourself?

With most of our titles available in both PDF and ePUB format, you can access your content wherever and however you wish—on your PC, phone, tablet, or reader.

Since you've purchased this print book, we are happy to offer you the eBook for just $5.

To learn more, go to http://www.apress.com/companion or contact support@apress.com.

Apress®

Printed in the United States
By Bookmasters